A Human Relations Approach to the Practice of Educational Leadership

Ronald W. Rebore

Saint Louis University

Boston   New York   San Francisco
Mexico City   Montreal   Toronto   London   Madrid   Munich   Paris
Hong Kong   Singapore   Tokyo   Cape Town   Sydney

Vice President: *Paul A. Smith*
Senior Editor: *Arnis E. Burvikovs*
Editorial Assistant: *Matthew Forster*
Marketing Manager: *Tara Whorf*
Editorial-Production Service: *Whitney Acres Editorial*
Manufacturing Buyer: *JoAnne Sweeney*
Cover Administrator: *Kristina Mose-Libon*
Electronic Composition: *Omegatype Typography, Inc.*

For related titles and support materials, visit our online catalogue at www.ablongman.com.

Between the time Website information is gathered and published, some sites may have closed. Also, the transcription of URLs can result in unintended typographical errors. The publisher would appreciate notification where these occur so that they may be corrected in subsequent editions.

CIP data not available at the time of publication.

ISBN 0-205-30631-4

Printed in the United States of America

10   9   8   7   6   5   4   3   2   1   07   06   05   04   03   02

To my brother, Dr. William Rebore, and my sister, Debra Happel, both of whom are also educators. They have been constant sources of support and encouragement throughout my life.

CONTENTS

Preface xi

PART ONE **Psychological Foundations of Human Relations** 1

1 **Psychological Approaches to Human Relations** 3

Psychodynamic Approach to Human Relations 3
Freudian Psychoanalytic Psychology 3 ■ Jungian Psychology 5
■ Adlerian Psychology 6 ■ Human Relations Principles 7

Humanistic Approach to Human Relations 7
Existential Psychology 8 ■ Client-Centered Psychology 9
■ Human Relations Principles 10

Cognitive-Behavioral Approaches to Human Relations 10
Behavioral Psychology 10 ■ Rational-Emotive Behavior Psychology 11
■ Cognitive Psychology 12 ■ Reality Psychology 13 ■ Human
Relations Principles 13

Discussion Questions and Statements 14
EXERCISE 1.1   Assessment of Human
Relations Orientation 14

Summary 16

Endnotes 18

Selected Bibliography 18

2 **Use of Power and Its Impact on Human Relations** 19

Nature of Power 19

Power Tactics 21

Defensive Tactics 22

Servant Leadership 24

Discussion Questions and Statements 25

Assessing Leadership Style   25

EXERCISE 2.1   Overt Administrator Power
Tactics Assessment   26

EXERCISE 2.2   Defensive Power Tactics Assessment   26

EXERCISE 2.3   Servant Leadership Assessment   27

Case Study: The Newly Appointed Superintendent of Schools   28

Summary   30

Endnotes   31

Selected Bibliography   31

3 The Empathetic Administrator   32

Nature of Empathy   32

Discussion Questions and Statement   36

Assessing Empathy   36

EXERCISE 3.1   Empathetic Relationships Assessment   36

Summary   38

Endnotes   39

Selected Bibliography   39

4 The Genuine Administrator   40

Congruency   41

EXERCISE 4.1   Congruency Assessment   41

Positive Regard   42

EXERCISE 4.2   Positive Regard Assessment   43

Warmth and Trust   44

Empowerment   45

Process of Empowerment   46

EXERCISE 4.3   Empowerment Process Assessment   47

Assessment of Empowerment   48

EXERCISE 4.4   Empowerment Assessment   48

Discussion Questions and Statements   49

Summary   49

Endnotes   50

Selected Bibliography   51

P A R T   T W O **Ethical and Philosophical Foundations of Human Relations** **53**

5 **Human Relations in an Ethical Context** **55**

Approaching Ethics **56**
Norms   56   ■   Social Ethics   59   ■   Human Consequences   60
■   The Virtues   61   ■   Ethical Decisions   65   ■   Meaning
in Life   66

Ethical Principles of Human Relations **69**

Discussion Questions and Statements **70**
EXERCISE 5.1   Ethics of Human Relations Assessment   70

Summary **71**

Endnotes **73**

Selected Bibliography **74**

6 **Transcendental Leadership and Human Relations** **75**

Nature of Transcendental Leadership **76**
Transcendental Leadership Premise   78   ■   Elements of
Transcendental Leadership   79

Discussion Questions and Statements **83**
EXERCISE 6.1   Political Tensions Assessment   83

Summary **84**

Endnotes **85**

Selected Bibliography **85**

Appendix A: Monitoring Reports **86**

7 **Administrator Responsibility and Effective Human Relations** **90**

Categorical Imperative **90**

Philosophy of Right **93**

Duty of Citizens **94**

Meditations **and The Stoics' Approach** **93**

Pragmatism **97**

Human Relations Implications   100

Discussion Questions and Statements   100
EXERCISE 7.1   Assessment of Duty in Human Relations   100

Summary   101

Endnotes   103

Selected Bibliography   104

8   Conflict, Pluralism, and Human Relations   105

Aspects of Pluralism   106

Discussion Questions and Statements   109
EXERCISE 8.1   Assessment of Conflict
Resolution Awareness   110

Summary   111

Endnotes   112

Selected Bibliography   112

9   Social Justice in a Human Relations Context   113

A Theory of Justice   115

Discussion Questions and Statements   118
EXERCISE 9.1   Assessment of Social Justice Awareness   118

Summary   119

Endnotes   120

Selected Bibliography   120

10   Public Discourse in a Human Relations Context   121

Nature of Public Discourse   122

Discussion Questions and Statement   124
EXERCISE 10.1   Assessment of Public
Discourse Awareness   125

Summary   125

Endnotes   126

Selected Bibliography   127

**PART THREE   Human Communication and
Human Relations   129**

**11   Basic Principles of Communication
in Human Relations   131**

Aspects of Human Communication   131
Assumptions about the Communication's Message   131   ■   Personal
Development and Communication Skills   132   ■   Communication's
Consequences   133   ■   Communication's Content   134
■   Communication's Cultural Context   136

Communicative Praxis   137

The Social Covenant and Communication   138

Definition of Communication   139

Principles of Communication   139

Discussion Questions and Statement   140

Summary   140

Endnotes   142

Selected Bibliography   142

12   Cultural Communication and Human Relations   144

Organizational Culture and Communication   144
Definition of Culture   145   ■   Components of Culture   145   ■   Expressions
of Culture   147   ■   Analysis of Culture   148

Discussion Questions and Statements   155
EXERCISE 12.1   Observation Analysis Assessment   155

Summary   156

Endnotes   158

Selected Bibliography   158

13   Written Communication and Human Relations   159

Power of the Written Word   160

Function of Writing in Educational Leadership   161

Interpretation of the Written Word   162

Discussion Questions and Statements   164
E X E R C I S E   1 3 . 1   Written Communications Assessment   164

Summary   165

Endnotes   166

Selected Bibliography   167

14   **Nonverbal Communication and Human Relations**   168

Premises of Nonverbal Communication   168

Aspects of Nonverbal Communication   170

Types of Nonverbal Communication   171
Physical Expressions   171   ■   Environmental Expressions   173
■   Vocalizations   174

Discussion Questions and Statements   174
E X E R C I S E   1 4 . 1   Nonverbal Awareness Assessment   175

Summary   176

Endnotes   177

Selected Bibliography   177

15   **Verbal Communication and Human Relations**   179

Premises of Verbal Communication   179

Ramifications of Verbal Communication   181

Discussion Questions and Statements   184
E X E R C I S E   1 5 . 1   Verbal Awareness Assessment   184

Summary   185

Endnotes   186

Selected Bibliography   186

Epilogue   187
Index   188

PREFACE

There is no secret that the numbers of applicants for administrator positions in general, and for the superintendency and principalship in particular, continue to decline. Furthermore the stress level in all administrator positions continues to rise. The turnover in many schools and school districts is problematic. In addition, the burnout rate in the administrative ranks also continues to increase, with the effect of losing some very talented administrators to private business and industry.

Some of those who stay are eventually asked to leave by either the superintendent of schools or the board of education. One reason why these situations are troublesome is because they possibly could have been avoided. The commonly observed fact is that many professional difficulties arise because a given administrator does not know how to relate effectively to other administrators, teachers, staff members, students, parents, and members of the community. Some administrators are in desperate need of developing human relations skills; others could significantly enhance their professional lives if they could improve their human relations skills. In other words, they lack effective human relations skills in a milieu that demands such skills to a higher degree than in past generations.

The purpose of this book is to help those preparing to become administrators and those who are already administrators to enhance their human relations skills. This is especially important for those preparing to become administrators because such skills have been incorporated into the Interstate School Leaders Licensure Consortium (ISLLC) standards. ISLLC is a program of the Council of Chief State School Officers, which crafted a set of model standards for school leaders. These standards were drafted by personnel from twenty-four state education agencies and representatives from various professional associations. The standards are being used by many states in assessing candidates for administrator licensure.

The content and methods of this book are rooted in the first four ISLLC standards. Each standard is operationalized through three dimensions: knowledge, dispositions, and performances. All the dimensions of these standards are not addressed in this book. However, what follows is a designation as to the chapters in which the standards and certain dimensions of each standard are addressed.[1]

Standard 1

A school administrator is an educational leader who promotes the success of all students by facilitating the development, articulation, implementation, and stewardship of a vision of learning that is shared and supported by the school community.

Knowledge

The administrator has knowledge and understanding of

- Effective communication
- Effective consensus-building and negotiation skills.

Dispositions

The administrator believes in, values, and is committed to

- Inclusion of all members of the school community
- Willingness to continuously examine one's own assumptions, beliefs, and practices.

Performances

The administrator facilitates processes and engages in activities to ensure that

- The vision and mission of the school are effectively communicated to staff, parents, students, and community members;
- The vision is developed with and among stakeholders;
- The contributions of school community members to the realization of the vision are recognized and celebrated.

This standard and its accompanying knowledge, dispositions, and performances are treated in Chapters 1, 2, 3, 4, 5, 6, 7, 8, 9, 10, 11, 13, and 15.

Standard 2

A school administrator is an educational leader who promotes the success of all students by advocating, nurturing, and sustaining a school culture and instructional program conducive to student learning and staff professional growth.

Knowledge

The administrator has knowledge and understanding of

- Diversity and its meaning for educational programs.

Performances

The administrator facilitates processes and engages in activities to ensure that

- All individuals are treated with fairness, dignity, and respect;
- Students and staff feel valued and important;
- The responsibilities and contributions of each individual are acknowledged.

This standard and its accompanying knowledge and performances are treated in Chapters 2, 3, 4, 5, and 8.

Standard 3

A school administrator is an educational leader who promotes the success of all students by ensuring management of the organization, operations, and resources for a safe, efficient, and effective learning environment.

Dispositions

The administrator believes in, values, and is committed to

- Trusting people and their judgments
- Accepting responsibility.

Performances

The administrator facilitates processes and engages in activities to ensure that

- Effective problem-framing and problem-solving skills are used;
- Effective conflict resolution skills are used;
- Effective consensus-building and group process skills are used.

This standard and its accompanying dimensions of dispositions and performances are treated in Chapters 4, 6, 7, 8, and 10.

Standard 4

A school administrator is an educational leader who promotes the success of all students by collaborating with families and community members, responding to diverse community interests and needs, and mobilizing community resources.

Knowledge

The administrator has knowledge and understanding of

- Conditions and dynamics of the diverse school community.

Dispositions

The administrator believes in, values, and is committed to

- Collaboration and communication with families
- Involvement of families and other stakeholders in school decision-making processes
- The proposition that diversity enriches the school.

Performances

The administrator facilitates processes and engages in activities to ensure that

- High visibility, active involvement, and communication with the larger community are priorities;
- Credence is given to individuals and groups whose values and opinions may conflict;
- Community stakeholders are treated equitably;
- Diversity is recognized and valued.

This standard and its accompanying dimensions of knowledge, dispositions, and performances are treated in Chapters 3, 4, 8, 9, 10, 11, 12, 13, 14, and 15.

Thus this book is appropriate for a numbers of readers; for example, graduate students who will be required to take an assessment based on ISLLC standards and practicing administrators who wish to enhance their human relations skills will find this book valuable. Furthermore professors in educational leadership programs might find this book useful as a primary textbook in courses on human relations or as a secondary source in other school administration courses.

The book is organized into three parts. Part One, "Psychological Foundations of Human Relations," consists of Chapters 1 through 4 and is concerned with establishing the fundamental psychological principles necessary for developing and improving human relations skills. Part Two, "Ethical and Philosophical Foundations of Human Relations," consists of Chapters 5 through 10 and is concerned with establishing the fundamental theoretical principles upon which effective human relations skills are based. Part Three, "Human Communication and Human Relations," sets forth in Chapters 11 through 15 the most important facility for developing effective human relations through a thorough discussion of the various forms of human communication.

The book contains several pedagogical features that will help the reader understand the material. Each chapter contains a summary section as well as a selected bibliography; every chapter contains discussion questions and statements. Further, extensive use has been made of self-administered assessment instruments that will help readers determine the level at which they adhere to the tenets presented in each chapter. There are also other types of exercises, exhibits, figures, tables, and a case study that explicate the nuances of the chapters.

I want to thank Arnis Burvikovs, my editor at Allyn & Bacon, for his patience and encouragement during the writing of this book. I sincerely appreciate his assistance. I also want to thank the following reviewers for their helpful suggestions: Michael L. Cunningham, Marshall University; Roxanna M. DellaVecchia, Towson University; and Teresa Eagle, Marshall University.

Ronald W. Rebore
Saint Louis University

ENDNOTE

1. Council of Chief State School Officers, *Interstate School Leaders Licensure Consortium: Standards for School Leaders.* Washington, D.C.: The Council, 1996. pp. 10–21.

PART ONE

Psychological Foundations of Human Relations

The effective administrator will recognize that the human dimension of educational leadership is just as important as the technical dimension. In fact, accomplishing the technical responsibilities of administration is dependent on the cooperation of people, which is affected by the manner in which they are engaged by any given administrator.

Developing a school budget, ordering supplies and materials, managing pupil transportation, and managing facility maintenance and custodial services will be effective only to the degree that administrators can elicit the cooperation of other staff members. That cooperation is dependent on the quality of the working relationship between the people involved in these and similar tasks and responsibilities. A business manager of a school district can have exceptional knowledge of accounting principles and practices, but if he or she has ineffective human relations skills, the level of performance by the people whom he or she supervises will be significantly impeded by his or her lack of such skills.

Obviously this is just as true for a superintendent of schools, principal of a school, or central office coordinator. But having good human relations skills is not the only requirement for effective leadership in an educational administrative position. The overall perspective that an administrator has about his or her responsibilities to colleagues and those whom he or she supervises can enhance or mitigate the quality of not only his or her performance but also the performance of others. The perspective that is presented here is that superintendents, principals, and other educational administrators exercise their leadership in a more effective manner if they view themselves as having a unique opportunity to be of great personal assistance to those with whom they interact. While it is virtually impossible to work with people on a regular basis and not form some type of relationship with them, the quality of that relationship will determine the extent to which someone can be of assistance.

Of course human relations is predicated on the personal attitudes people bring into relationships. This is critical in educational leadership because superintendents, principals, and other administrators are continually interacting with teachers, staff members, students, parents, and community members. Human psychological nourishment is important to the development of personal attitudes. Thus, attitudes will be explored in relation to the effects they have on people encountering administrators who either possess or do not possess these attitudes.

1 Psychological Approaches to Human Relations

There are three major approaches to human relations. The first is the psychodynamic approach, which focuses on the structure of personality and how personality affects the perceptions, actions, and decisions of educational leaders and other people with whom they interact. The second approach to human relations is the humanistic approach. The orientation of the individual as he or she understands himself or herself has a significant effect on the development of relationships with others. Such relationships will be beneficial or detrimental to the psychological health of the person.

The third approach to human relations is the cognitive-behavioral approach. The behavior of educational leaders will change over time. Behavior is buffeted by an entire range of positive and negative experiences; the reactions of educational leaders to their experiences are molded by their past reactions and by their processing of such reactions in order to modify future behavior.

Psychodynamic Approach to Human Relations

The ideas and concepts of the psychoanalytic theory as first proclaimed by Sigmund Freud have had a tremendous impact on professional approaches to human interaction. Most theories are either extensions of, modifications to, or reactions against what Freud and his disciples first set forth as the dynamics of human personality. For educational administrators, the importance of psychodynamic concepts lies in the understanding of human behavior, which can facilitate the establishment of more effective relationships with others. This understanding pertains to understanding not only the psychodynamics of other people but also the psychodynamics of the administrator's behavior. While there are numerous theoreticians of the psychodynamic approach, only three will be highlighted: Sigmund Freud, Carl Jung, and Alfred Adler.

Freudian Psychoanalytic Psychology

There are six concepts that are essential to an understanding of the psychoanalytic approach to human relations. The first is the influence of the past on the present. The first six years of life are viewed as the breeding ground for the troubles and problems that afflict people in their adult lives. Problems such as aggression, inability to direct one's life, dependency, fear of intimacy, and lack of self-respect have their origin in early childhood development.

The second concept is the importance of the unconscious on human behavior. The unconscious is a reservoir of memories, feelings, desires, and impulses; these elements in the unconscious are prevented from emerging by the conscious ego. The content of the unconscious comes from disturbing early childhood experiences and the feelings that were associated with them. Daily behavior is motivated by the unconscious, and the way to eradicate the consequences of these unconscious factors is by becoming conscious of them so that an individual can recognize that the trauma that was problematic in childhood pales in the light of adulthood.

Third is the phenomenon of anxiety. The repressed feelings, memories, desires, and impulses sometimes try to break through to a person's consciousness, creating a sense of dread and impending doom. This occurs because of factors beyond the control of an individual. Problems with students, teachers, or parents can cause a principal to experience anxiety that is the result of a fear that unconscious material may bubble up into consciousness. Anxiety is often free-floating in the sense that it is a vague general feeling.

The fourth concept deals with ego-defense mechanisms, which are ways people protect themselves from threatening thoughts and feelings. The ego performs conscious functions, which include keeping a person in contact with reality. Anxiety is produced when there is a threat to the ego; defense mechanisms help people to cope with emotional trauma. Repression is a defense mechanism whereby a person excludes from consciousness threatening thoughts and fears. The principal who is afraid of her students because of gang activity in the school may repress her fears of becoming a victim of violence. Similarly denial involves consciously choosing not to attend to a situation. The principal who is concerned about violence might try to just keep the thought of becoming a victim out of her mind. Regression involves reverting to inappropriate behaviors. The principal in question might return to drinking alcohol or using drugs to prevent herself from attending to the potential for physical violence. Projection is the defense mechanism by which a person attributes to others his or her inappropriate feelings, motives, and behaviors. The principal may feel resentment toward the gang members but project that sentiment toward the superintendent, whom she sees as the guilty person for not providing the proper level of security for the school building. Eventually the real culprit becomes the superintendent. Displacement is the redirection of some emotion from the originating source to a substitute. The principal who resents the superintendent is also redirecting her feelings from the real source of the problem, the gang. Reaction formation is behaving in a manner that is opposite of a person's true feelings. Thus the principal may act brazen and unafraid in her relations with gang members. Finally, rationalization is the defense mechanism by which a person tries to justify his or her behavior by attributing it to logical and laudable motives. The principal who is concerned about becoming a victim of violence might justify her fear because of the effect getting injured would have on her family.

Transference is the fifth concept and refers to a person's shifting feelings toward an individual with whom he or she has some form of relationship; such feelings originated as a reaction to other persons in the individual's past life. Transference either can occur on the part of an educational administrator toward others with whom he works or can occur on the part of others toward an administrator. The way in which the person who is the recipient of the transferred feelings reacts to the imposing person can have a beneficial or a negative effect. If a principal is the recipient of the transferred feelings from a teacher, an unthreatening response by the principal may help the teacher to work through her unresolved conflicts. The teacher may be dealing with an emotional reaction that originated in her relationship with a parent, spouse, friend, or even former boss.

The sixth concept is countertransference, which is the projecting of feelings onto another person whom one is trying to help. This is the relationship that sometimes exists in the employee/supervisor milieu. A superintendent may project onto a principal certain traits that he despises in himself. This usually arises from unresolved conflicts and repressed needs. It can be difficult for people in authority to recognize that they are the real problem in a professional relationship.[1]

Jungian Psychology

Wholeness is the essential idea in the psychology of Carl Jung, which is represented by the psyche. The psyche includes all conscious and unconscious feelings and thoughts. Throughout life, people strive to develop this wholeness through the self, which is the center and totality of an individual's entire personality.

There are three levels of consciousness in Jung's theory: conscious, personal unconscious, and collective unconscious. The conscious level has as its focus the ego and is the only level that the person can directly know. The conscious life begins at birth and grows throughout life. This process is called individuation, and it is that which makes people different from each other. The degree to which a person develops her consciousness determines her degree of individuation. The ego is the organizer of the conscious level; it selects the feelings, perceptions, memories, and thoughts that will become conscious. In this way the ego provides the person with a sense of identity and continuity.

The personal unconscious contains those feelings, perceptions, memories, and thoughts that are not allowed into consciousness by the ego. Repressed emotionally charged thoughts and unresolved conflicts that are stored in the unconscious may emerge in dreams.

The collective unconscious contains images and concepts that are independent of consciousness. These images and concepts are called "collective" because they are common and have significance for all humans. Humans inherit a predisposition for certain thoughts and ideas; because all humans have similar physiology and similar environments, they have the capability to view the world in universally common ways.

Included within the collective unconscious are instincts and archetypes. Instincts are impulses to act, such as defending oneself when threatened. Archetypes do not have content but have form; they represent the possibilities of certain types of perceptions. They have emotional strength and have endured from the very beginning of the human species. Common archetypes are birth, death, the wise old man, the child, the persona, the anima and animus, the shadow, and the self. The three that are most important for an understanding of human relations are the persona, the shadow, and the self.

The persona, which means mask in Latin, is the manner in which people present themselves in public. Thus a principal will project how she wants others to perceive her in certain situations. With a parent, she may want to appear in an official way, knowing that she must convince the parent that his or her child should modify disrespectful behavior in order to remain in school. The principal may want to appear benevolent to teachers and project the caring parent image to students.

The shadow is a powerful and potentially dangerous archetype because it contains unacceptable impulses. Aggressiveness, unfriendliness, and defensiveness are certainly not acceptable traits in an administrator; yet these are common manifestations of the shadow archetype.

The self is the central archetype: It is the center of the personality at both the conscious and unconscious levels, and it contains the personality. The goal of human life is to grow in knowledge about the self. Mature people are in touch with the self archetype and are able to bring into consciousness much of what lies in the unconscious.

Archetypes are expressed only through symbols. These symbols are manifested in dreams, fantasies, art, myths, and so forth. As such, these symbols are also a manifestation of the collective wisdom of the human race.

Jung also identified dimensions of personality, which he called types, that have both conscious and unconscious aspects. Jung's research led to his development of personality types, which he categorized according to attitudes and functions. The two attitudes are introversion and extroversion. Introverted people tend to be more concerned about their personal thoughts and ideas while extraverted people tend to be more occupied with other people and things. These attitudes are polarities and are properly considered as existing on a continuum. People can move on this continuum throughout their entire lives and on some occasions may exhibit more introverted than extraverted tendencies, and vice versa at other times. Certain occasions may produce an introverted attitude at one time and an extraverted attitude at a different time.

The four functions are thinking, feeling, sensing, and intuition. Thinking and feeling are polarity functions and are usually tied to decision making. In using the thinking function, people are trying to make connections in order to understand their life-world; when people use their feelings, they are trying to ascertain the values they have in relation to their positive and negative feelings. Sensing and intuition are also polarity functions and are irrational because they are reactions to stimuli. Sensing includes such activities as seeing, hearing, tasting, smelling, and touching. Intuition is usually considered in terms of having a hunch about something that is difficult to articulate.

Eight psychological types can be described by combining each of the two attitudes with each of the four functions. It is important not to think of these types as absolutes in the sense that people are pigeonholed. Rather, they are approximations that allow an individual to analyze personal behaviors or the behaviors of others.[2]

Adlerian Psychology

Alfred Adler was an associate of Sigmund Freud but eventually developed his own theories of human development, which emphasize social rather than biological determinants. People are motivated by social forces and strive to achieve certain goals, of which the goal of significance is the most important. Adler viewed this striving for significance in the context of achieving a unique identity and belonging. People are working to attain power, superiority, and perfection as a way of compensating for inferiority feelings that mitigate a satisfactory identity and sense of belonging.

Each person has a unique personality or lifestyle that began to develop in early childhood in order to compensate for perceived inferiority. An individual's lifestyle consists of views he has about himself and about the world and the behaviors he uses to attain goals. People are self-determining, creative, and dynamic; every action has purpose. Adler's approach is usually termed *individual psychology* because it emphasizes the view that a person is a unified whole. Thus thoughts, feelings, and attitudes emanate from the uniqueness of every person. Furthermore individuals are always considered in light of their social integration. People have a strong need to be united with others; in order to maintain a healthy outlook on life, they must successfully develop friendships, establish intimacy with a person, and contribute to the welfare of society.

As such, individual psychology is subjective in approach; people's worldview is the precipitator that generates their reaction to other people and events. Thus their worldview is of paramount importance. A person's style is learned primarily during the first six years of life. However, it is the person's interpretation of early events that is significant, and it is this interpretation that leads to development of a lifestyle. The lifestyle can be altered and changed through reflection, and faulty notions can be corrected.[3]

Human Relations Principles

There are nine principles emanating from the psychodynamic approaches:

1. The behavior of most people is influenced by their early childhood experiences.
2. People are influenced by their psyche's unconscious dimension, which is a reservoir of memories, feelings, desires, and impulses.
3. The generalized phenomenon of anxiety is a result of unconscious material breaking into a person's consciousness.
4. People's psyches have defense mechanisms that help to protect them from threatening thoughts and feelings.
5. People tend to transfer or shift to other people unconscious feelings, thoughts, desires, and impulses.
6. People inherit a predisposition for certain thoughts and ideas that are universal and are commonly referred to as "the collective unconscious."
7. Most people continually strive during their lives to achieve a sense of significance, which is predicated on a positive self-identity and a feeling of belonging.
8. Because people are self-determining, creative, and dynamic, every action has purpose.
9. A person's worldview is the source of reactions to other people and events that can be changed through reflection.

Humanistic Approach to Human Relations

All approaches to human relations are humanistic in the broad sense of the term, but in detecting the nuances of human relations, it is clear that there are some approaches that call upon the relationships that exist between people as a key factor in understanding human relations. Furthermore the humanistic approach views the individual as empowered to such an extent that she can determine her own destiny. Thus a person's past history and environment do not play as large a part in decision making as do personal capabilities. A person's psychological well-being, and therefore his ability to form good human relationships, is dependent on how he relates to objective reality, to other people, and to his own sense of self. The contributions of two humanistic schools of thought will be highlighted in this section: existential psychology and client-centered psychology.

Existential Psychology

This is probably the most philosophical of all the human relations approaches. It is rooted in the philosophies of Martin Heidegger, Edmund Husserl, Karl Jaspers, Søren Kierkegaard, Rollo May, Friedrich Nietzsche, and Jean-Paul Sartre, as well as a number of well-known theologians, novelists, and playwrights. Thus the preponderance of material is varied and interesting. However, for purposes of this treatment, only the insights of Rollo May will be considered.

May's notion of a person responsible for his own existence as the choosing subject best describes the orientation of existentialism. The individual is thus capable of reflecting on events and attributing meaning to them.[4] He is acutely conscious of his own existence and the potential that such an existence offers for affecting life's direction.

There are three ways of being in the world. The first is being in the biological and environmental world, which is composed of drives, instincts, and natural laws. The person is faced with basic uncontrollable forces such as diseases, storms, and aging. The second is being in relation to other humans and the significance of that relationship. Each relationship has meaning to the degree that a person gives of herself to the other. Significant relationships are those in which the giving of self changes the other person; a mutual supportive awareness of each other exists. The third way of being in the world is the self knowing itself. The person views all other ways of being from the perspective of his self-awareness; thus, all ways of being are interrelated.[5]

The notion of time, particularly future time, is always an issue in existentialism. While the past is important, the present is critical because through it the person is in the process of self-actualization, which will take him into the immediate future. This orientation toward the immediate future confronted in the present creates a sense of anxiety in people because they must find their place in the world. Anxiety is usually played out in particular situations. A principal who has a serious illness or who must make a decision about the employment of a teacher is an example of a situation that usually creates anxiety.

From an existential perspective, these types of situations give people the opportunity to find creative and meaningful ways of being. The seriously ill principal may find ways of coping with her illness through volunteering to work with seriously ill children or by spending more time with her family. People have the freedom to make choices in their lives that are value-laden. However, the real issue is that people are individually responsible for making these choices and cannot relegate blame to others. Each person usually experiences a sense of isolation in the face of personally defining or major life decisions such as how to cope with a serious illness or how to terminate the employment of another person.

Loving relationships can help a person face the isolation that is inevitable in everyone's life. Such relationships must be active and reciprocal; they cannot be predicated on the needs of just one of the two people. These types of relationships also facilitate the search for meaning that each person strives to obtain in life. Meaning is always a transcendental phenomenon in the sense that it deals with values that are beyond a person's immediate needs and experiences. Finding spiritual meaning in life is transcendental under this rubric, as are loving another person and fulfilling responsibilities to others.

Client-Centered Psychology

The originator of client-centered psychology is Carl Ranson Rogers, who had a significant effect on the practice of counseling and psychotherapy. The most fundamental orientation of client-centered psychology is that people are rational, socialized, forward-moving, and realistic.[6] Jealousy, aggression, and other negative reactions are symptomatic of frustrations encountered in satisfying basic human needs such as love and security. Human beings are basically cooperative, constructive, and trustworthy. As such, people are self-regulating and will balance their negative impulses with positive ways of meeting their needs. This tendency toward adjustment is a manifestation of the human tendency of self-actualization. The responsibility of principals, superintendents, and other administrators is to help activate the capacity of each person to be self-creative, which in this context means to be able to guide and regulate oneself. Providing an environment that nurtures human growth and development is the most important responsibility of the educational administrator.

The attitude of the administrator becomes paramount in this approach. He must be a person who recognizes and respects the ability of others to be self-directive.[7] There are a number of concepts that Rogers developed that can help an administrator understand how he can help others become more self-actualized. First, the self develops throughout life because of a differentiation process whereby interaction with significant others in the person's environment leads to the recognition that he is a separate being in objective reality. Second, because of this awareness of self, there arises a need for positive regard from others. This phenomenon is reciprocal in the sense that a person's positive regard is satisfied only when he views himself as satisfying another person's positive regard. The positive regard of another person is the most powerful force in a person's psychological well-being. Third, in relation to the need for positive regard, he develops the need for self-regard, which is influenced by the way others perceive him as being worthy or unworthy of positive regard. Fourth, this evaluation of worthiness sets up a conditionality. It is only through unconditional positive regard, freely given by another person, that an individual can develop unconditional self-regard, which will lead to a state of congruence so necessary for human relations.[8]

The goal of life is to become a fully functioning person. When a person reaches a state of congruence, he becomes a fully functioning person, and all his experiences are symbolized into awareness. He will be open to new experiences and will be able to properly respond to them.

Human Relations Principles

There are eleven principles emanating from the humanistic approaches:

1. People are first and foremost decision makers who are capable of changing their lives through the choices they make.
2. The freedom to make defining decisions gives people the opportunity to make value-laden choices.
3. Because everyone is ultimately and personally responsible for the choices they make, they are alone in their decision making.
4. Human relationships constitute the source from which people draw meaning and purpose in their lives.
5. Positive human relationships must be active and reciprocal.
6. Positive human relationships facilitate the individual's search for meaning.
7. Positive human relationships tend to be transcendental in the sense that they entail values that are beyond a person's immediate needs and experiences.
8. Because most people are self-actualizing, they are rational, socialized, forward-moving, and realistic.
9. People are self-regulating and, as such, are usually cooperative, constructive, and trustworthy.
10. Everyone's ultimate goal is to become a fully functioning person.
11. Becoming a fully functioning person is predicated on being recognized by others with positive regard, which in turn helps a person to develop a sense of positive self-regard.

Cognitive-Behavioral Approaches to Human Relations

Endemic to all cognitive-behavioral approaches is the idea that understanding the causes of human phenomena does not necessarily create change. The goal of cognitive-behavioral approaches is empowerment—to give people control over their actions and ultimately over their life-world. Thought, decision making, and action are the three components necessary for taking control. One without the other two components or two without the third component is ineffective. Behavioral, rational-emotive, cognitive, and reality theories will be presented as the bases for the cognitive-behavioral approaches.

Behavioral Psychology

Of course the forerunner of all behavioral theories is Ivan Pavlov, but major contributions have been made by Albert Bandura, B. F. Skinner, and Joseph Wolpe, in addition to many others. The basic principle of behavior is reinforcement: The consequences of behavior increase the possibility that a given behavior will be performed again; without the consequences, the behavior could be extinguished. All motivation theory is predicated on this principle. To be more specific, when an event follows a behavior and as a consequence the behavior is increased, there is positive reinforcement. A principal who tries to warmly greet the teachers when they arrive at school in the morning is using positive reinforcement in the sense that she is expressing appreciation for the presence of the teachers. Positive reinforcement can emanate from receiving an object, experiencing a pleasurable activity, or receiving social approval: A certificate of perfect attendance given to students is an example of object reinforcement; a student field trip can be a reinforcement activity; and receiving recognition for doing something kind for another person is social reinforcement.

Not attending to certain behaviors is a way of extinguishing unwanted behaviors. This is a common practice with students who are disruptive. When a teacher or principal chooses not to attend to disruptive student behavior, sometimes the student discontinues the behavior. Generalization of behavior occurs when people perform in a certain way because of the reinforcement they received in a prior situation. A teacher who is praised in a faculty meeting by her principal for her work on a curriculum committee may volunteer to serve on other committees because of that recognition. Intentionally shaping the behavior of another occurs when a person calculates how certain reinforcements produce desired behaviors. The principal who tries to extinguish the unwanted behavior of a student may utilize positive reinforcement of appropriate behavior, which is not forthcoming when the student's behavior is unacceptable.

Positive reinforcement is not the only concept in the behavioral approach; an equally important principle involves observational learning. Observing and modeling the actions of others are important ways to modify or change behavior. The observer must accurately perceive what is taking place and must be able to associate the observed behavior with her own behavior in order to properly model the observed behavior. Further, the person wishing to model a certain type of behavior will need to develop some form of retention. This is usually accomplished through imagination and subverbal self-talk. If it is a complex behavior, practice is necessary to effectively model that behavior. When someone is modeling behavior, reinforcement must accompany the behavior in order for it to become a continual event. Self-motivation is a very effective type of reinforcement, but vicarious reinforcement is also important. Vicarious reinforcement occurs when a person observes that someone else is receiving reinforcement for performing an action and concludes that he will also receive reinforcement for performing similar actions.

There are four types of reinforcement that, taken together, lead to successful changes in behavior: performance accomplishment, vicarious experiences, verbal persuasion, and lowered emotional arousal.[9] Performance accomplishment is perhaps the most effective type of external reinforcement; lowering the anxiety that might accompany performing certain actions is also important in successful behavior modification.

Rational-Emotive Behavior Psychology

Albert Ellis developed this approach, which not only is an outgrowth of his scientific research but also rests on his philosophy of life. Ellis was a student of philosophy and was influenced by the philosophies of Baruch Spinoza, Friedrich Nietzsche, Immanuel Kant, and Arthur Schopenhauer; he was particularly influenced by the Stoic philosophers.

Ellis believed with the Stoics that most problems in life arise not from things but from the way in which people view things. A major tenet of his approach deals with the pleasure principle. A major goal in life is pleasure. However, short-term pleasure that will ultimately produce pain is to be avoided; rather, responsible pleasure seeking maintains pleasure over the long term. Thus drug abuse and alcoholism ultimately produce pain even though there is short-term pleasure. He and the humanistic psychologists held similar views concerning the need both to view human beings from a holistic goal-directed perspective and to consider human nature as basically good. In achieving the good life, people must be efficient, flexible, and logical in their thinking. Ellis certainly did not discount the importance that biological, social, and psychological factors play in the life of an individual. However, his basic theory of behavior is predicated on rationalism, or the correct way of thinking.[10]

When a principal receives a number of complaints from parents about a particular teacher whom they believe does not have the skills necessary to effectively teach their children, the principal may need to attend not only to the parental criticisms but also to the way in which the teacher reacts to the criticisms. The correct way of thinking is for both the principal and the teacher to review the criticisms and to determine if there is a reasonable basis for the parental concern. Then both the principal and teacher can develop a problem-solving strategy, which might include attending staff development activities. If the criticisms are unfounded, then the principal and teacher can develop a strategy on how to correct the misperceptions of the parents. The inappropriate way of thinking would be for the teacher either to transfer the blame to the parents and become angry with them or to consider himself a poor example of a teacher, which could easily lead to frustration and depression.

Cognitive Psychology

The founder of this approach is Aaron Beck, who was influenced by Albert Ellis and Alfred Adler. Like Ellis, Beck was concerned with the impact of thinking on an individual's behavior. He was particularly concerned with automatic thoughts, which people may not be fully conscious of but which are an outgrowth of a person's cognitive schemata. A person uses these schemata in order to make choices and to draw inferences about life. Automatic thoughts occur spontaneously without effort; the basis for the thoughts is rooted in a person's experiences, beginning in early childhood and further developing throughout life. The thoughts produce emotional reactions, physiological reactions, and behaviors. There are two basic schemata: positive or adaptive and negative or maladaptive. However, what may be adaptive in one situation may be maladaptive in another.

A person who takes a superintendency in a large district after spending a long time as superintendent in a small school district may have serious problems adjusting to the need for sharing his responsibility with other administrators. In the small district, he would have been responsible for all central office functions, including hiring of teachers and staff members, curriculum development, budgeting, purchasing, transportation, and facilities maintenance. In the larger district, the superintendent could find himself with assistant superintendents who share his responsibilities. The positive schemata that made the person successful in the small district have changed and now have become negative schemata.

In order to be successful in the small district, the superintendent needed to be self-confident in his ability to perform many different functions and to rely totally on himself to produce results. In the larger district, the superintendent needs to be able to trust the abilities of his assistant superintendents and to rely on them to produce results while he is engaged in more policy-level activities.[11]

Reality Psychology

William Glasser developed an approach to help people control their behavior and make choices. He was particularly interested in education and wrote a number of books that have been of significant help to educators. Most noteworthy for educators are *Schools Without Failure,* written in 1969, and *Control Theory in the Classroom,* written in 1986.

His basic premise is that an individual's perception of reality determines his or her feelings, thoughts, and actions. It is not reality but rather the perception of reality that is important. There are four psychological needs that are important to people: belonging, power, freedom, and fun. Sometimes these needs are in conflict with each other. For example, the need for power might create a conflict in a principal who wants the teachers to like her and to consider her a colleague. A second premise concerns control, as stated by Glasser: "Control theory contends that our behavior is always our best attempt to control the world and ourselves as part of that world so that we can best satisfy our needs."[12]

People choose the way they will react to situations; this choice may be appropriate or inappropriate. They may choose to be depressed, angry, or anxious rather than accepting, understanding, or forgiving. Sometimes choosing to be depressed is a way to elicit the help of others and thereby experience a sense of belonging.

The assistant principal may choose to be a positive person when confronted by a multiplicity of responsibilities that infringe on her personal life. Instead of becoming bitter about the need to be on campus or in the high school three or four nights a week during certain seasons when the playing fields and gymnasium are constantly in use, the assistant principal may view this as an opportunity to visit with students and parents, which could result in creating more positive relationships with them. Or the assistant principal could complain that she is overworked and underpaid, which might lead to a reprimand by the principal. In the first reaction, the assistant principal is enhancing her need to belong, she could be having fun, and she is exerting her power of office. In the second reaction, just the opposite is occurring, and if her employment is terminated, certain freedoms are abrogated.

Human Relations Principles

There are nine principles emanating from the cognitive-behavioral approaches:

1. When positive consequences follow a behavior, the behavior is likely to be increased; when negative consequences follow a behavior, the behavior is likely to be decreased.
2. Performance accomplishment, vicarious experiences, verbal persuasion, and lowered emotional reactions are effective ways of increasing positive behavior.
3. Most problems in life arise from the way people view other people, things, and events.
4. To achieve balance in life, people must be efficient, flexible, and logical.
5. Rationalism, or the correct way of thinking, can change a person's behavior.
6. Everyone experiences automatic/spontaneous thoughts, which produce emotional reactions, physiologic reactions, and behaviors.
7. Although automatic/spontaneous thoughts constitute schemata that can be adaptive or maladaptive, a person can change the positive or negative dimension of schemata through reason.

8. In order to satisfy their needs, people attempt to control themselves and their world through their behavior.
9. People can choose their controlling behaviors.

DISCUSSION QUESTIONS AND STATEMENTS

1. What are the three major approaches to human relations?

2. Compare and contrast the psychodynamic approaches of Freud, Jung, and Adler.

3. What are the differences between the humanistic approaches of May and Rogers?

4. Compare and contrast the cognitive-behavioral approaches of Ellis, Beck and Glasser.

5. List and briefly explain the principles emanating from each approach to human relations.

EXERCISE **1.1**

Assessment of Human Relations Orientation

People develop an orientation toward themselves, others, and their professional responsibilities through their formal education, through dialogue and engagement with other people, through their professional study and reading, and through entertainment and the news media. The following is a brief assessment of your orientation toward your psychological disposition. This understanding should be helpful to you as you analyze your thoughts and feelings about colleagues and the people you supervise. On a scale of 1 to 3 (1 = disagree, 2 = partially agree, 3 = agree), rate the degree to which your ideas and behaviors conform to the three approaches to human relations.

Psychodynamic Orientation

Rating

_____ When I am having problems, it is important for me to reflect on my earliest experiences because the feelings associated with those experiences have an influence on my ideas and behavior.

_____ When I am having problems, I sometimes think that it would be helpful to seek assistance from a professional who will help me uncover my unconscious memories, feelings, desires, and impulses.

_____ At times I have a general feeling of anxiety about my life, which is probably the result of unconscious influences.

_____ I have developed certain defense mechanisms (rationalization, projecting blame on others, etc.) that help me cope with the stress of everyday living.

_____ The way I feel and think about other people is sometimes caused by my unconscious thoughts and feelings.

_____ As these thoughts and feelings break through into my consciousness, I tend to project them onto other people.

____ My ideas about birth, death, power, heroism, and many other things seem to be universal notions that have basically the same content in everyone's psyche.

____ Even though I do not always recognize or understand it, everything that I think and do has a purpose that is guided by my unconscious.

____ I can change the way I think and feel on the conscious level through reflection on the past.

____ Even though I am not fully aware of it all the time, many of my thoughts and actions are geared toward finding my place in the world.

____ Having a sense of belonging and developing a positive self-identity are driving forces in my life.

____ **Rating** (A maximum rating of 33 indicates that a person is significantly influenced by psychodynamic psychology. A rating of 17 can be used as a median score for purposes of analysis.)

Humanistic Orientation

____ I exercise control over my life through the decisions I make.

____ Because I am a free human being, the decisions and choices I make are affirmations or negations of my value system.

____ I am totally and personally responsible for the decisions I make.

____ It is only through relationships with other people that I find meaning and purpose in my life.

____ My relationship with another person is meaningful only if it is reciprocal in the sense that the other person actively engages in sustaining the relationship.

____ My search for meaning is enhanced through positive personal relationships.

____ For me, true relationships tend to transcend immediate needs and are meaningful only if they are grounded in unselfish concern for other persons.

____ I consider myself to be capable of self-actualization.

____ I believe that most people tend to be rational and realistic.

____ I believe that most people are cooperative and trustworthy.

____ I believe that most people are capable of developing good social skills.

____ I hold the position that everyone wants to become a fully functioning person capable of directing his/her own life.

____ Being considered in a positive way by others is important to my becoming a fully functioning person.

____ Developing a sense of positive self-regard is necessary for me to become a fully functioning person.

____ **Rating** (A maximum rating of 42 indicates that a person is significantly influenced by humanistic psychology. A rating of 21 can be used as a median score for purposes of analysis.)

Cognitive-Behavioral Orientation

____ I tend to repeat an action when it has a pleasing or positive effect on me, and I tend not to repeat an action when the effect on me is displeasing or negative.

____ The type of reactions that other people have to my behavior either encourages or discourages me from repeating the behavior in the future.

(continued)

E X E R C I S E   **1.1**   **Continued**

_____ Most of the problems that I encounter in life stem from my personal view of people, things, and events.

_____ In order for me to maintain my balance in life, it is important for me to be flexible.

_____ In order for me to maintain my balance in life, it is important for me to be logical and efficient in my thinking.

_____ By being rational in my thinking, I can change my way of perceiving people, things, and events.

_____ A significant challenge for me is to use my rational power to keep in check my automatic/spontaneous thoughts, which can produce undesirable emotional and physiological reactions.

_____ There is a cause-and-effect link between my rational thought and my behavior.

_____ If I use my power of reason, I can control my behavior.

_____ Positive behavior reinforces my rational thought.

_____ **Rating** (A maximum rating of 30 indicates that a person is significantly influenced by cognitive-behavioral psychology. A rating of 16 can be used as a median score for purposes of analysis.)

S U M M A R Y

There are three basic approaches to human relations. The first one is psychodynamic, which focuses on the structure of personality as well as on how personality affects perceptions, actions, and decisions. The ideas and concepts of Sigmund Freud are the basis of the psychodynamic approach. There are six principles that can help to explain his psychoanalytic psychology and its importance for human relations: The first six years of life are the most important in terms of personality development; the unconscious has a significant impact on human behavior; anxiety is a continual phenomenon of life; people protect themselves from threatening thoughts and feelings with ego-defense mechanisms; transference occurs when a person shifts his or her feelings toward an individual with whom he or she has formed a relationship; and countertransference is the projecting of feelings onto another person whom one is trying to help.

Carl Jung is a second contributor to the psychodynamic approach. Wholeness is the essential tenet in the psychology of Jung. During their life, people strive to develop wholeness through the self, which is the center and totality of their entire personality. A major contribution of Jung is his notion of the collective unconscious, which contains images and concepts that are independent of consciousness. It is called "collective" because the images and concepts are common and have significance for all humans. Human beings inherit a predisposition for some thoughts and ideas; humans also have similar physiology and similar environments that give them the capability to view the world in universally common ways. The collective unconscious contains instincts and archetypes. Archetypes do not have content but have form; archetypes represent the possibilities of certain types of perceptions.

Common archetypes include birth, death, the wise old man, the child, the persona, the anima and animus, the shadow, and the self.

Alfred Adler is the third contributor to the psychodynamic approach as set forth in this book. He emphasized the social rather than the biological determinants of life. From Adler's point of view, people are motivated by social forces and strive to achieve specific goals, of which the goal of significance is most important. Thus when people strive for power, superiority, and perfection, they are searching for their unique identity and their place of belonging.

The second approach to human relations is the humanistic approach. In a sense, all approaches are humanistic. However, this approach views the relationship that exists between people as the key factor in understanding human relations. Also, from this perspective people are empowered to such a degree that they can determine their own destiny. People's past history and environment do not play as significant a role in their decision making as do their personal capabilities.

Rollo May is a major contributor to the humanistic approach. He viewed people as responsible for their own mode of existence because they are choosing subjects. People are capable of reflecting on events and attributing meaning to them; thus, they are acutely conscious of their lives and the potential that their existence offers them to affect their individual direction in life. The notion of time is important because in the present a person is in the process of self-actualization, which will take him or her into the immediate future. This can create a sense of anxiety in a person, which offers that person the opportunity to find creative and meaningful ways of being. Loving relationships can help a person face the isolation that is inevitable in everyone's life.

A second major contributor to the humanistic approach is Carl Rogers. He viewed people as rational, socialized, forward-moving, and realistic. There are many negative reactions and frustrations in life that people encounter while trying to satisfy basic human needs such as love and security. Human beings are basically cooperative, constructive, and trustworthy. As such, people are self-regulating and will balance their negative impulses with positive ways of meeting their needs. This tendency toward adjustment is a manifestation of the human tendency of self-actualization.

The third approach to human relations is the cognitive-behavioral approach. Behavior is buffeted by an entire range of positive and negative experiences. The reactions of people to experiences are molded by their past reactions and by their processing of such reactions in order to modify future behavior. The basic principle of behavior is reinforcement: The consequences of behavior increase the possibility that a certain behavior will be performed again; without those consequences, the behavior could be extinguished. There are four types of reinforcement; taken together, the following lead to successful changes in behavior: performance accomplishment, vicarious experiences, verbal persuasion, and lowered emotional arousal.

A significant contributor to the cognitive-behavioral approach is Albert Ellis, who believed that people must be efficient, flexible, and logical in their thinking. His basic theory of behavior is predicated on rationalism, or the correct way of thinking. A second contributor is Aaron Beck, who also was concerned with the impact that thinking has on an individual's behavior. He was particularly concerned with the automatic thoughts people have that they may not be fully aware of because such thoughts are an outgrowth of cognitive schemata. Automatic thoughts occur spontaneously and without effort; the basis for these thoughts is rooted in a person's experiences, beginning in early childhood and further developing throughout life. These thoughts result in emotional reactions, physiological reactions, and behaviors; they have two basic schemata: positive or adaptive and negative or maladaptive.

William Glasser is also a recognized contributor to this approach. His basic premise stated that an individual's perception of reality determines his or her feelings, thoughts, and actions. It is not reality but the perception of reality that is important. The critical factor in this approach is the way people choose to react to situations, which may be either appropriate or inappropriate. People may choose to be depressed, angry, or anxious rather than accepting, understanding, or forgiving.

ENDNOTES

1. G. Corey, *Theory and Practice of Group Counseling,* 4th edition (Pacific Grove, California: Brooks/Cole Publishing Company, 1995), pp. 142–150.

2. R. Sharf, *Theories of Psychotherapy and Counseling: Concepts and Cases* (Pacific Grove, California: Brooks/Cole Publishing Company, 1996), pp. 87–94.

3. Corey, *Theory and Practice of Group Counseling,* pp. 187–192.

4. R. May, E. Angel, and H. Ellenberger, eds., *Existence: A New Dimension in Psychiatry and Psychology* (New York: Basic Books Publishers, 1958), p. 41.

5. Ibid., p. 63.

6. C. Rogers, *On Becoming a Person* (Boston: Houghton Mifflin Publishers, 1961), pp. 90–92, 194–195.

7. C. Rogers, *Client-Centered Therapy* (Boston: Houghton Mifflin Publishers, 1951), pp. 20–22.

8. S. Koch, ed., *Formulations of the Person and the Social Context,* Vol. 3 (New York: McGraw-Hill Publishers, 1959), pp. 194–212.

9. A. Bandura, "Regulations of Cognitive Processes Through Perceived Self-Efficacy," *Developmental Psychology,* 25 (1989): 729–735.

10. A. Ellis and M. E. Bernard, eds., *Clinical Applications of Rational-Emotive Therapy* (New York: Plenum Publishing, 1985), pp. 1–30.

11. A. T. Beck, "Cognitive Therapy: A 30 Year Retrospective," *American Psychologist,* 46 (1991): 368–375.

12. W. Glasser, ed., *Control Theory in the Practice of Reality Therapy: Case Studies* (New York: Harper & Row Publishers, 1989), p. 5.

SELECTED BIBLIOGRAPHY

Ansbacher, H. L., and R. Ansbacher, eds. *The Individual Psychology of Alfred Adler.* New York: Basic Books Publishers, 1956.

Ellis, A., and R. A. Harper. *A New Guide to Rational Living.* North Hollywood, California: Wilshire Books, 1975.

Freud, S. *A General Introduction to Psychoanalysis.* New York: Washington Square Press, 1917.

Glasser, W. *Control Theory: A New Explanation of How We Control Our Lives.* New York: Harper & Row Publishers, 1985.

Jung, C. G. *Memories, Dreams, Reflections.* New York: Pantheon Books, 1963.

Kazdin, A. E. *Behavior Modification in Applied Settings,* 5th edition. Pacific Grove, California: Brooks/Cole Publishing Company, 1994.

May, R., E. Angel, and H. Ellenberger, eds. *Existence: A New Dimension in Psychiatry and Psychology.* New York: Basic Books Publishers, 1958.

Rogers, C. R. *On Becoming a Person.* Boston: Houghton Mifflin Publishers, 1961.

2 Use of Power and Its Impact on Human Relations

Underlying the relationship that exists between supervisor and employee is the issue of power because the supervisor has the authority to affect the employee's job status. This, of course, can be a major obstacle to developing a trusting relationship. However, it is within the purview of all educational leaders to develop strategies for mitigating the negative dimension of the supervisor/employee relationship. In fact, it is necessary to develop such strategies in order to establish the helping relationship so important to effective human relations.

Nature of Power

In order to develop these strategies, it is important to understand the nature of power. At its most elementary level, power can be viewed as that capability a person has to influence the behavior of another person or persons. This implies that the person or persons being influenced are in a dependency relationship with the person who has power. It also implies that the person or persons being influenced have discretion to comply or not comply with the wishes of the person with power. Finally it implies that the person or persons who are being influenced would not usually behave in the manner desired by the person with power. The person with power forces the dependent person or persons to make a choice; thus there is always the element of freedom operational in such situations.

Power emanates from four bases: coercion, reward, persuasion, and knowledge. Coercive power has the key element of fear. A teacher may comply with the demands or wishes of a principal because noncompliance could bring about some sanction the teacher fears. Sanctions that are available to a principal, superintendent, or other administrators might include unpleasant work activities, embarrassing treatment, suspension, or even termination of employment.[1]

Reward power is the opposite of coercive power. A teacher may comply with the demands or wishes of a principal because he has the power to grant valued benefits to the compliant teacher. The circumstances within which rewards are exercised are similar to those within which sanctions are exercised: The principal may assign work activities the compliant teacher finds pleasant; the compliant teacher may receive complimentary treatment by the principal; or the teacher may even receive a job promotion. The biology teacher may become the chairperson of the science department because of her compliance with the wishes of the principal.

Persuasive power is the ability to allocate or manipulate symbolic coercion or rewards. The principal who can stir up the emotions of his faculty when budget cuts are required by the central office exercises persuasive power. The principal knows that the teachers will be speaking to parents about how the budget cuts will adversely affect the education of their children. In like manner, some parents will most likely complain to members of the board of education. Similarly the superintendent of schools who touts the successes of a teacher to her principal might be persuading that principal to give the teacher favorable treatment.

Knowledge power is predicated on having access to unique or valuable information that is not readily available to others. The financial data available to a school district's negotiating team give them an advantage in at-the-table bargaining with the teachers' union negotiating team. The casual conversations that principals have with parents usually provide them with information about teachers that can be used in a coercive or rewarding manner. Further, not well publicized information about school district policies and procedures gives principals an advantage in dealing with teachers and parents.

There are four sources from which power emanates: position or job, personal characteristics, special skills or knowledge, and opportunity. In school districts the most obvious power positions are superintendent of schools and principal. These positions are powerful because the people who occupy them have supervisory responsibilities over others and control functions that are critical to the operation of the schools. Depending on the school district, through influence superintendents and principals directly or indirectly have a significant impact on who gets hired; in like manner, through influence they can either directly or indirectly have a significant impact on employment terminations. In addition they have control over budgets and promotions, just to mention the most obvious areas of position power.[2]

Some administrators are more powerful than others, not just because of their positions within a school or school district but also because of their personal characteristics. Not all principals within a school district have the same level of influence with the superintendent or with assistant superintendents and other central office administrators. Of course not all assistant superintendents have the same level of influence with the superintendent, and so on. Administrators who are articulate, charismatic, or physically imposing, or those who have an aura or presence, tend to be more influential than those who lack these characteristics.

Superintendents, principals, and other administrators have expert power when they excel because of their skills or knowledge. The principal who has an exceptional understanding of how to implement technology in her school or who is exceptional at conflict management will command influence among colleagues, with her superintendent, and probably with the board of education. The principal with excellent human relations skills could find teachers and staff members from other schools in the district applying for vacancies in his school.

Opportunity power cannot be controlled or planned for; it is something that happens. However, what a person can do is to take advantage of the opportunity and use it as a power source. Desegregation orders emanating from federal district courts throughout the United States created magnet schools in the hope of attracting both African American and European American students into specialized programs operating in given school buildings. Mathematics, science, foreign language, technology, and performing arts magnet schools were established in all major segregated cities. The principals of the schools where these programs were introduced found themselves in a unique situation with a unique opportunity to gain firsthand experience in this new attempt to end segregation. Many of these principals gained local, state, and even national recognition for their success in implementing magnet programs. They gained influence and power because of an opportunity they had due to circumstances not of their making.

Power Tactics

There are several tactics used by power holders to influence others. Perhaps the most common are reasonable argument, friendliness, coalitions, enlisting of higher authority, negotiating of benefits or favors, and assertiveness.[3] Most people begin the process of influencing others through the use of reason, often formulated in a logical presentation of ideas. A principal may attempt to influence the teachers in his school to accept a more anecdotal approach to reporting student academic progress through an argument that sets forth the need to inform parents in a more detailed manner about the progress their children are making in academics. Teachers may view the approach as too time-consuming given the high pupil/teacher ratio and the lack of teacher assistants in a given school.

Administrators who foresee opposition to something that they want to initiate with those whom they supervise may attempt to set the stage by using flattery, being humble, and acting friendly. While this seems to be obvious manipulation, it is not easily perceived by employees if a given superintendent or principal is rather adept at this technique. Similarly a superintendent or principal may try to set the stage by using a coalition technique whereby she gets teachers or other administrators to support an initiative before it is introduced. This is allied to gaining support for an idea from people at higher levels in the school district. The principal who wants to initiate a new method of informing parents about student academic progress may try to get the support of the superintendent before introducing the idea to her faculty.

Negotiating benefits or favors is a much more cynical tactic used to influence others. A principal may send a teacher to a convention or an out-of-town professional meeting as a reward for promoting his ideas with other faculty members. It is always possible for a principal to manipulate the playground and cafeteria duty schedules in order to accommodate those teachers who are more supportive of him than others on the faculty.

The least effective tactic is assertiveness. Superintendents, principals, and other administrators who resort to demanding compliance or who order someone to comply will ultimately find themselves defending their actions. A much more subtle approach to assertiveness is to constantly remind someone about compliance or to point out what the policies or procedures require.

Teachers and other staff members usually learn behaviors that will mitigate the power that is exercised over them by principals and other administrators. The ultimate purpose of these behaviors is influence or control of the power holder. These techniques are employed not only when the use of power by a principal is abusive but also when it is justified. The most commonly used techniques are conformity, flattery, favors, acclamation, association, excuses, and apologies.[4]

A teacher utilizing the conformity technique will continually tell the principal that she agrees with what he is doing and will immediately comply with his requests. Such a teacher must be certain that her supervisor knows that she is conforming with the request or the technique will be ineffective. The principal who personally delivers a report to the superintendent when interschool mail could have been used probably has ulterior motives.

Conformity is usually accompanied by flattery and the doing of favors for the power holder. A teacher either publicly or privately praising the actions of a principal in order to gain favor is a common flattery technique while the doing of favors is usually more effective if it is unknown to others. A principal who offers the superintendent her tickets to an athletic event under the guise of being unable to use the tickets could be an example of doing a favor for personal advantage.

Acclamation of the power holder's or one's own accomplishments or activities is dependent on the impression of others. To be effective, the acclamation must create a positive impression; otherwise it will be counterproductive. In utilizing this technique, a teacher may make it known that his students scored extremely high on a standardized test or a principal may tell the superintendent that she has been elected to an office in the state principals' association.

Association is the technique that makes a connection with the power holder. The teacher who has the superintendent's daughter in his class may attempt to let it be known that he is in communication with the superintendent on a regular basis. The intention is to imply that he has some influence with the superintendent because of the relationship he has with the daughter. The teacher may try to use this relationship with the superintendent as a way of manipulating his principal.

The use of excuses and the use of apologies are sometimes two aspects of the same technique. A principal who does an inadequate job of creating a budget for her school may attempt to blame the large enrollment in her school. The excuse may follow this line of thought: She could have done a better job but for the fact that there are so many pupils in her school; because of the high enrollment, there are always teacher and student issues that take up most of the time, not only during the school day but also in the evening; and in most other school districts, schools with high enrollments have an assistant principal. If this line of excuse fails, the principal is likely to indicate that she is sorry and certainly understands the superintendent's disappointment. She will probably indicate that a revised budget will be forthcoming immediately. Some people would rather seek pardon from a forgiving power holder than attempt to do the best possible job on an assignment, especially if they are preoccupied with other problems or issues.

In themselves, the activities associated with these techniques are not inappropriate and can be positive reinforcements for the power holder. It is the intention of the person that makes the difference: If the intention is to compliment or reinforce appropriate behavior in the power holder, this is laudable; if the intention is to manipulate the power holder, the behavior is inappropriate.

Defensive Tactics

Most defensive tactics can be categorized under two aspects: those used to avoid action and those used to avoid blame.[5] The reasons for using defensive tactics will vary with each individual. However, it is reasonable to suspect that most superintendents, principals, and other administrators may use defensive tactics because they have neglected their responsibilities in some manner. This is obvious in relation to avoiding action and blame. Less obvious is the relationship of avoidance to change. It is the responsibility of every administrator to plan for change in order to meet the fluctuating needs of faculty and students. It is difficult not to recognize that change is inevitable. The tactics that are used to avoid action and blame basically accomplish the stalling of positive change; thus avoiding positive change is an outcome that always accompanies the avoidance of action and blame.

Avoiding action in a school district requires an administrator to give the appearance of performance, of doing something. The most obvious way to avoid action is to transfer the responsibility to another person or to a group of people. Under the guise of wanting to involve the faculty in decision making, a principal may allow the faculty to create the discipline policies for a given school. In removing himself from the process, the principal avoids the criticism that may be forthcoming from parents and students. This will also allow the principal to avoid making hard implementation decisions because he can say to parents and students that he is just applying the rules that were created by the faculty. Further, the principal can avoid taking into consideration the circumstances that may affect the application of a policy. Not being a part of the process gives the principal the excuse of being helpless in relation to policy implementation.

Another commonly used avoidance tactic is stretching out a task over a prolonged period of time. A principal may state to parents that she is working hard on revising the student progress report card while engaging in considerable footdragging because she knows that the faculty is not interested in revisions. If revising the student progress report card is a school district goal, the principal may be telling the superintendent that the work is underway while intending to stretch it out over the entire academic year, knowing that she could accomplish the task in a few months.

Avoiding blame is a tactic used by administrators when they have neglected to carry out their responsibilities or have carried out their responsibilities in an inappropriate or ineffective manner. Implementing the inclusion of children with disabilities in the regular classroom is a challenge in those schools where the children have been segregated in self-contained classrooms. When regular teachers are having problems with inclusion, a principal may use the tactic of requiring teachers to put problems in writing before he takes any action. This will demonstrate that he is not the problem; rather, the teachers who are not effectively implementing the inclusion policy are the problem. Further, a principal may publicly escalate his commitment to inclusion in order to cover up a poor beginning or a failing course of action. The principal may also develop an elaborate explanation of the actions that he has taken in order to implement the inclusion policy as a way of justifying his actions in the face of less than stellar outcomes. Of course a commonly used tactic is blaming circumstances for negative outcomes; the high pupil/teacher ratio, the lack of money, or the lack of training may become the rationale for the lack of progress in implementing the inclusion policy.

When the school buses are continually late in picking up the students or late in bringing them home, the director of transportation may avoid blame by withholding information about her inability to effectively schedule routes through embellishing or manipulating information about the number of miles that must be traveled and the need for more buses.

A superintendent of schools may play it safe by asking the board of education to approve a school/business partnership if he thinks that the project will not be successful and if he wants to avoid being blamed for the failure. The superintendent may also use qualifying expressions of judgment or take neutral positions on projects that have slim chances of being successful even if they are laudable.

In concluding this section on the use and misuse of power, it is important to recognize that there are two dimensions to using power: a negative dimension (associated with abuse) whereby educational administrators exploit others for their personal status or benefit and a positive dimension whereby educational administrators help others accomplish their personal goals and lead teachers and staff members in formulating and accomplishing school and school district goals.

Servant Leadership

The positive dimension of using power is closely associated with the notion of servant leadership, which also acts as a safeguard against the negative dimension. However, the concept of *servant leadership* is a paradox to many administrators because they are hampered by a mind-set that views servants as people who are not leaders or by the mind-set that views leaders as people who are served by those they lead. Furthermore the popular meaning of these two words reinforces these ideas. The concept of servant leader rests on a deeper understanding of the words. The notion of leader will be addressed first, and then that of servant.

When a person is hired or promoted as the principal of a school or the superintendent of a school district, the expectation is that he or she will be a leader and not just an administrator. Leadership is essentially dynamic.[6] A principal is a leader only when the teachers and staff members recognize and accept her as the school's leader. No one is a leader without a following. Not only is leadership dynamic, but it is also relational.[7] The mistake that some principals and superintendents make when they assume their position is isolating themselves from those they supervise. Engagement with others is the only way to exercise leadership. Administration without engagement is a static concept. It implies that an administrator is engaged in perfunctory duties. While it is necessary to carry out the day-to-day responsibilities of the principalship in an efficient and effective manner, this alone does not help teachers and staff members accomplish either personal or school-related goals. That requires leadership.

Educational leadership can be easily focused only on the educational segment of the community. It is much more comfortable to exercise leadership in this context because it prevents the principal or superintendent from confronting the needs of individuals within the whole community. It is a way of avoiding conflicts and confrontations. Yet it is in the context of engagement with individual teachers, staff members, students, parents, and members of the general community that an administrator exercises that form of leadership that ultimately best serves the community as a whole. Individuals constitute the elements of the whole; their welfare is endemic to the welfare of the entire community. It is impossible to have a well-functioning school when the members of that school are being neglected as individuals by the principal.

The idea of being a servant can imply a one-sided relationship to others. The popular notion of service is usually viewed as continual giving and establishes others only as recipients. This is not service in the correct sense of the term. The principal who views his role only as provider establishes a dependency that militates against the self-determination of teachers, staff members, students, and parents. Effective service empowers individuals to exercise their freedom as human beings who are capable of developing strategies and making decisions on their own behalf and for the welfare of those for whom they have responsibilities. The dignity of those who are considered only as recipients is undermined by that type of educational leader.

The initial requirement for effective educational servant leadership is mutual trust and cooperation between the leader and other members of the school community. That trust and cooperation are fostered through the actions of both the leader and the individual members of the community. The engagement of individuals is the essential ingredient in establishing trust. Without trust and cooperation, there can emerge a passive aggression by individuals and even by the community as a whole.[8]

Initially true leadership is freely conferred on the principal by the faculty, staff, students, and parents of a given school. In order to maintain this leadership imperative, the principal must demonstrate that she warrants this trust through performance. Of course this is the case with all educational administrators. Superintendents, assistant superintendents, coordinators, etc., must continually reinforce their leadership through their actions with individuals and with their respective communities. It is an ongoing process.

The basic approach that is necessary for all leaders is respecting the dignity of those whom they are expected to lead. Leading with dignity means respecting individuals as human beings with rights and responsibilities, fostering their rights and responsibilities through empowerment, and providing them with as much assistance as is necessary for them to exercise their rights and responsibilities.

DISCUSSION QUESTIONS AND STATEMENTS

1. Define the term power as it is applied to the supervisor–employee relationship.
2. What are the four bases of power?
3. Briefly explain the sources of power.
4. What are some tactics that a power holder can use to influence others?
5. Explain the tactics that can be used by a dependent employee to mitigate the power of a supervisor.
6. Compare and contrast the positive and negative dimensions of using power.

Assessing Leadership Style

The following three exercises are meant to provide you, the reader, with an opportunity to assess your use of power. Those who score on the negative use of power can use this information to reflect on their motivation and behavior in their exercise of educational leadership. Those who are not already administrators can use this information to be proactive in developing those attitudes that will lead to a more positive use of power.

EXERCISE **2.1**

Overt Administrator Power Tactics Assessment

On a scale of 1 to 3 (1 = never, 2 = sometimes, 3 = always), rate the degree to which you use overt power tactics to influence other administrators, teachers, and staff members.

Rating

_____ When I want people to accept my opinion, I develop a logical argument to support my position.

_____ When I want to influence others, I make an overt effort to meet and engage them in a friendly manner in the hope that they will support my position.

_____ I make a concerted effort to enlist the support of certain people for a position I am promoting before I make my position known to others.

_____ Before I present my position on an issue, I try to gain the support of my supervisor in order to state that he or she is in agreement with my position.

_____ I attempt to find out what people want in terms of working conditions, and I give it to them as a reward for supporting my position.

_____ I attempt to find out what people do not like in terms of working conditions, and I assign them those tasks or find a way to engage them in those activities as a punishment for not supporting my position.

_____ I utilize assertive speech and body language in order to coerce others into accepting my position on issues.

_____ **Rating** (A maximum rating of 21 indicates that a person always utilizes as many power tactics as possible in order to influence others. A rating of 11 can be used as a median score for purposes of analysis.)

EXERCISE **2.2**

Defensive Power Tactics Assessment

On a scale of 1 to 3 (1 = never, 2 = sometimes, 3 = always), rate the degree to which you use defensive power tactics to influence other administrators, teachers, and staff members.

Rating

_____ When I am confronted with accepting or rejecting the opinion of my supervisor, I conform to his or her position even if I do not agree with it.

_____ When I am asked by my supervisor why I did not perform a task or why I was in opposition to a certain position, I use an excuse to divert blame from myself.

_____ I utilize apology as a method of diverting my supervisor's concern about something I neglected or performed in an inadequate way.

_____ Acclaiming to others my success in carrying out my responsibilities is a method I use to mitigate my supervisor's concern about my performance.

_____ Acclaiming the accomplishments of my supervisor is a method I use to keep him or her from being concerned about my opinion and performance.

_____ I do favors for and give token gifts to my supervisor in order to influence his or her opinion about me and my performance.

_____ I form associations with people who are influential with my supervisor as a way of promoting my own welfare.

_____ I avoid the disfavor of my supervisor by transferring my responsibilities to others.

_____ I use footdragging as a tactic when I want to avoid a task that may not be in my own best interests.

_____ I utilize strict adherence to administrative procedures as a method of protecting my own interests when confronted with opposition to my position.

_____ I blame circumstances as a way of averting blame for my inadequate response or lack of performance.

_____ Withholding or manipulating information is a method I use to avoid responsibility for inadequate performance.

_____ I take no position on controversial issues as a way of avoiding the disfavor of others.

_____ **Rating** (A maximum rating of 39 indicates that a person always utilizes defensive power tactics in order to influence others. A rating of 20 can be used as a median score for purposes of analysis.)

EXERCISE **2.3**

Servant Leadership Assessment

Using 1 or 2 (1 = disagree, 2 = agree), indicate if the following statements reflect your leadership style.

Rating

_____ I continually try to engage others in positive discussions about the mission of my school/school district.

_____ I take every opportunity to speak before small and large groups of people about educational issues.

_____ When the occasion arises, I utilize contacts with stakeholders in order to develop support for the goals of my school/school district.

_____ I seek out meetings with diverse groups of people even if they are not strong supporters in order to promote the goals of my school/school district.

_____ I make an attempt to remove the causes of misunderstanding and dissatisfaction among all constituents of the school/school district.

_____ I believe that it is important to formulate and communicate core values to the entire educational community.

_____ I try to maintain a spirit of openness to criticism and the opinions of others.

(continued)

EXERCISE **2.3**   **Continued**

_____ When others find themselves in a stressful situation, I attempt to make them comfortable.

_____ When others have experienced a crisis in their lives, I try to create an atmosphere of understanding and healing.

_____ I place a high priority on respecting the dignity of every person with whom I come in contact.

_____ As an administrator, I try to develop an atmosphere of cooperation and teamwork within my school/school district.

_____ I use active listening in order to understand the challenges others are facing in their lives.

_____ I ask not only other administrators but also those whom I supervise for advice when I am uncertain about a course of action.

_____ I make every effort to be enthusiastic about my responsibilities, even when they present a certain amount of difficulty.

_____ I consider it a major responsibility to create an atmosphere of approachability so that others feel comfortable when meeting and talking with me.

_____ I try not to second-guess those people whom I supervise when I give them a task to carry out.

_____ When something does not work out the way I had anticipated, I can effectively change my approach or strategy.

_____ My first inclination is to trust the abilities of the people with whom I work.

_____ I consider it inappropriate to judge the motives of other administrators and those whom I supervise.

_____ I believe that it is inappropriate to make unilateral decisions that affect others without their input.

_____ **Rating** (A maximum rating of 40 indicates that a person can be considered a servant leader. A rating of 21 can be used as a median score for purposes of analysis.)

Case Study

The Newly Appointed Superintendent of Schools

After eighteen years of service, the superintendent of schools decided to retire. During that time he hired four of the six elementary school principals, the principal of one of the two middle schools, and the high school principal. In addition, he hired both of the assistant principals at the two middle schools and one of the three assistant principals at the high school. It was his administration in almost a literal sense. All the administrators in the district knew how he operated and what he wanted them to do. There was very little ambiguity in terms of what it meant to be an administrator in his school district.

The superintendent was a very directive person who viewed his role as analogous to that of a corporate president who ultimately had complete responsibility for success. This superintendent defined success to mean that the school district's administrative team was unified through policies and procedures he created. Furthermore, his interpretations of policies and procedures were the only acceptable ones.

He was extremely loyal to his administrators, teachers, and staff members, defending them in the face of all criticism from parents, community members, the news media, and even the board of education. Any attack on them was an attack on him. He was their leader, and everyone seemed to appreciate his earnestness and concern for their welfare.

The superintendent expected all members of the school community to accept his leadership; when he made a decision, he expected everyone to accept and defend it. Even though he seemed to be rather inflexible, most people liked him. He was a kind person who treated everyone in a courteous manner.

When he retired, the board of education conducted a national search for his successor. They hired a woman who was an assistant superintendent of a comparable-size school district. In her earlier career, she had been a high school principal. Her administrative style was quite different from that of the former superintendent. She created a cabinet composed of the assistant superintendents for human resources, curriculum and instruction, business, and facilities. They met on a weekly basis in order to discuss the issues facing the district and formulated administrative policies and procedures for central office functions. She also created an administrative council composed of all the administrators in the school district; she met with them on a monthly basis in order to discuss not only the issues facing the district as a whole but also those issues that affected the functioning of the schools. This body also formulated administrative policies and procedures for school operations. What really set her style apart from the former superintendent's was her practice of letting the staff create the agendas for the meetings and leading the two groups into consensus when developing policies and procedures.

Six months into her superintendency, she observed an uneasiness in the administrative staff concerning some of the decisions that had been made at cabinet and council meetings. The administrators began to rethink their decisions, and a sense of ambiguity began to overshadow the teachers and staff members in the schools. Many seemed to be worried about issues that had not surfaced before. There were major concerns about class size and teacher salaries. Parents began to openly question building and central office policies.

The board of education was perplexed and concerned about the decision they had made in hiring the new superintendent. Of course the board of education also had noticed that she was much more reluctant to give them direction in their deliberations but rather preferred to provide them with information and used the strategy of presenting them with a series of questions that she thought they should consider before making decisions about certain issues.

Eventually administrators, teachers, and staff members began to make excuses for the criticism that was leveled against them by parents, community members, the news media, and students. People felt betrayed by the lack of response from the superintendent to this criticism. There was talk in the school district community about her lack of leadership, and some people even suggested that she should resign.

Discussion

1. How would you describe the new superintendent's use of power? Distinguish between the sources and bases of her power.
2. What are the sources and bases of the former superintendent's power?
3. In terms of power, what has caused the change that has taken place in the school district community?
4. Which superintendent exhibited the tenets of servant leadership?
5. Explain how he or she practiced servant leadership.
6. What defensive power tactics were being used by members of the school district community?
7. What should the new superintendent do about the adverse reactions to her leadership style?

S U M M A R Y

Underlying the relationship between supervisor and employee is the issue of power because the supervisor has the authority to affect the employee's job. Superintendents, principals, and other administrators can develop strategies that will mitigate the negative dimension of power that is operational in the supervisor/employee relationship. In order to effectively develop such strategies, it is necessary to understand the nature of power. At its most elementary level, power is the capability of a person to influence the behavior of another person or persons. This implies that there is a dependency in the relationship and that the dependent person or persons have the discretion to comply or not comply with the wishes of the person with power. It also implies that the dependent person(s) would not usually behave in the manner desired by the person with power. The element of freedom is present because the person with power forces the dependent person(s) to make a choice.

Power is derived from four bases: coercion, reward, persuasion, and knowledge. The key element in coercion is fear that the person with power will do something to dependent persons that they do not want to happen if they do not comply with the wishes of the person with power. The opposite of coercive power is reward power. A person with power may grant benefits to dependent persons in order to influence those persons to comply with his or her wishes. Persuasive power is the ability to manipulate or allocate symbolic coercion or rewards. Knowledge power is based on having access to unique or valuable information that is not readily available to others.

The sources of power are position or job, personal characteristics, special skills or knowledge, and opportunity. Power positions or jobs are those that both have supervisory responsibilities over people and control critical functions. Those people who are articulate, charismatic, or physically imposing, or who have an aura or presence, can exercise power based on personal characteristics. People who excel because of their skills and knowledge have expert power. Those who take advantage of an opportunity and use it as a power source exercise opportunity power.

There are many tactics used by power holders to influence others. The most common include reasonable argument, friendliness, coalitions, enlisting of higher authority, negotiating of benefits or favors, and assertiveness. Dependent persons can also use tactics that will mitigate the power exercised over them by supervisors. The most common tactics are conformity, flattery, favors, acclamation, association, excuses, and apologies. In themselves, these tactics are not inappropriate and can be positive reinforcements. It is the intention of the person utilizing the tactics that makes the difference; if the intention is to manipulate, the behavior is inappropriate.

Defensive tactics are utilized either to avoid action or to avoid blame. It is reasonable to suspect that most people who use defensive tactics do so because they have neglected their responsibilities in some manner.

There are two dimensions to using power: a negative dimension (associated with abuse) whereby educational administrators exploit others for their personal status or benefit and a positive dimension whereby educational administrators help others accomplish their personal goals, which in turn will lead to the accomplishment of school and school district goals.

The positive dimension of using power in educational administration is closely connected to the concept of servant leadership. Educational leadership in this context is dynamic and relational. Such leadership requires the engagement of individual teachers, staff members, students, parents, and members of the general community. The notion of servant implies that the educational leader will empower individuals to exercise their freedom as human beings capable of developing strategies and making decisions on their own behalf and for the welfare of those for whom they have responsibilities. This requires mutual trust and cooperation between the leader and the other members of the school community. The basic element in the servant leadership approach is respect for people because of their dignity as human beings.

ENDNOTES

1. S. P. Robbins, *Organizational Behavior: Concepts, Controversies, and Applications,* 6th edition (Englewood Cliffs, New Jersey: Prentice-Hall, Inc., 1993), p. 409.

2. Ibid., p. 411.

3. D. Kipnis, S. M., Schmidt, C. Swaffin-Smith, and I. Wilkinson, "Patterns of Managerial Influence: Shotgun Managers, Tacticians, and Bystanders," *Organizational Dynamics,* Winter 1984: 56–67.

4. R. A. Giacalone and P. Rosenfeld, eds., *Impression Management in the Organization* (Hillsdale, New Jersey: Lawrence Erlbaum Associate Publishers, 1989), pp. 45–71.

5. Robbins, *Organizational Behavior,* pp. 428–429.

6. G. Wilson, "Leadership or Incumbency?" *Human Development,* 19, no. 3 (Fall 1998): 6.

7. Ibid.

8. Ibid., p. 8.

SELECTED BIBLIOGRAPHY

Baum, H. S. "Organizational Politics Against Organizational Culture: A Psychoanalytic Perspective." *Human Resource Management,* Summer 1989: 191–206.

Bhindi, N., and P. Duignan. "Leadership for a New Century: Authenticity, Intentionality, Spirituality, and Sensibility." *Educational Management and Administration,* 25, no. 2 (April 1997): 117–32.

Heifetz, R. *Leadership Without Easy Answers.* Cambridge, Massachusetts: Harvard University Press, 1994.

Krackhardt, D. "Assessing the Political Landscape: Structure, Cognition, and Power in Organizations." *Administrative Science Quarterly,* June 1990: 342–369.

McCormick, R. "Authority and Leadership: The Moral Challenge." *America,* 175, no. 2 (July 20–27, 1996): 12–17.

Wheatley, M. *Leadership and the New Science.* San Francisco, California: Berrett-Koehler Publishers, 1992.

3 The Empathetic Administrator

The underlying issue concerning empathy is easily conveyed in the following statement: "That person doesn't have a clue about how I feel." In developing and maintaining effective human relations, the most important consideration is empathy. It is impossible to establish meaningful relationships if a person has little or no idea how other people feel about concerns, problems, and issues. The vehicle for this understanding is the attitude that is commonly referred to as empathy.

As a personal quality of an effective administrator, empathy is practiced both on an individual level and in groups. Superintendents, principals, and other administrators have the opportunity to exercise empathy in individual conferences with students, teachers, staff members, parents, and other members of the community. There is also the little-recognized opportunity for these same administrators to practice empathy at faculty meetings, PTA/PTO meetings, board of education meetings, town meetings, and other small-group settings.

Nature of Empathy

Empathy is a process whereby an educational administrator attempts to perceive the world-view of others in such a manner as not to be influenced by his or her own perceptions. However, it is equally important to maintain a sense of separateness in order to avoid being caught up in the worldview of the other person or persons.[1] The following example of empathetic understanding concerns a middle school principal who is working with a student who started a fight with another student because the other student made a joke about his small stature:

P: "Jeff, why did you hit Frank?"

S: "It wasn't my fault. He's always making fun of me. I tell him all the time to stop or I'll get even."

P: "Well, I guess you got even this time."

S: "Yeah, I did."

P: "Do you feel better because you got even?"

S: "Of course."

P: "Will this end the problem, or could it happen again?"

S: "Sure it could, if he makes fun of me!"

P: "What does he say that makes you so angry?"

S: "He's always making fun of my size. You know I'm shorter than the other kids."

P: "Yes, but why does this make you so angry? Tell me how you feel about your size."

In this example, the principal is beginning the process of trying to understand not just what happened but also why it happened. He is trying to place the student at ease so that both he and the student feel comfortable discussing the underlying issue. In order to do this, the principal must be completely focused on the student, perceiving at every moment the feelings the student is experiencing during the conversation. It involves suspending value judgments about the student's behavior and trying to uncover the meaning that the behavior conveys. In all such situations, the principal is also trying to communicate to the student what he is sensing about the student's world in order to give the student a fresh perspective on the behavior.

Of course a principal may need to punish a student in some way for misconduct. However, because the principal is trying to understand a given student's behavior, this will make it easier for the student to believe that the principal cares about him as a person and that the principal really wants to help him.

Because empathy is an attitude and not a technique, it is a *way of being*. It is fostered through practice, but it will only be a technique unless an administrator genuinely has the intention of trying to unconditionally and uncritically accept the life-world of others. Viewed from this perspective, the empathetic administrator has the potential to empower others who are trying to make changes in their lives. Empathy promotes self-learning and self-determination. Thus the teacher, student, parent, or staff member is empowered to explore alternatives to the present issues or problems.[2]

The empathetic administrator also is in a position of trust. Those people with whom he or she is working will likely share more about themselves because of the empathetic relationship. When a person feels understood by another person, she is more trusting and open about revealing issues and problems. As such, an empathetic relationship can mitigate alienation, and those who receive empathy come to consider themselves as valued individuals. It is confirmation that they are appreciated and cared about.[3]

It is important for educational administrators to convey to others with whom they are working the value of communicating what they are feeling and thinking about issues and problems. This allows a superintendent, principal, or other administrators to more accurately understand the meaning of what people are communicating to them even when these others are not completely aware of their feelings and thoughts.[4]

In order to achieve the kind of empathy that will be most helpful to educational administrators, they will need to practice sensitive listening, which requires a genuine interest in making contact with the life-world of others. This involves not only the cognitive but also the affective dimensions of a person's life-world. These dimensions are conveyed through words and through nonverbal behaviors. Gestures, tone of voice, and posture can convey as much about a person as words.

The following dialogue between a principal and a teacher illustrates accurate empathy:

P: "Marina, I understand some of your students caused quite a disruption in your class this morning."

T: "Yes, that's why I wanted to talk with you. I took care of the problem, but something has to be done with those kids. Their parents need to take charge of them."

P: "Please tell me what happened."

T: "I have eleven rather large boys in that class who are always testing each other. They make obscene gestures to each other, call each other names, and push and shove each other when entering and leaving my classroom. They're real problems."

P: "What do they say and do when you correct them?"

T: "Well, it's difficult to correct them. They aren't responding to me the way they should. I think it's time for you to get involved."

P: "OK, but let's discuss this a little more so that I can understand how best to support you."

T: "I'm really happy to hear you say that. I've tried everything, and you know I'm a good teacher. These kids aren't typical. This is the first group of kids that has made me question my ability."

P: "You're right. I know you're a good teacher, and together we can handle this situation. Do you think the fact that they are much taller and bigger than you makes a difference in how they respond to you?"

T: "Yes. It always bothers me when students are bigger than I am, especially since my husband, Tom, got punched in the face by one of his students last month. Tom's even about the same size as my students."

The principal in this example is trying to establish rapport with the teacher through empathy for her situation, which has allowed her to be open and candid not only about the situation but also about her personal feelings. She is undoubtedly concerned about what her principal and colleagues think in relation to her ability to teach students because she is having trouble with discipline in her classroom. This has caused her to question her own ability as a teacher. Further, she is somewhat afraid of being injured by the students because of her physical size and the fact that there had been a recent incident with her husband, also a teacher, in a school where a student committed a violent act against him.

It is the ability of a person to experience common human feelings that facilitates the practice of empathy. Such feelings as love, hate, joy, sadness, anger, guilt, fear, happiness, agitation, contentment, and rejection accompany life experiences and become the avenue through which people can understand others who are having similar feelings. People who exhibit antisocial behaviors generally lack the ability to appreciate the fact that other people have similar feelings. However, empathy requires an active attempt to make this transference. Those who just wait for the insight to occur may never accurately and fully acquire the ability to be empathetic. The fact that the circumstances producing the feelings may be quite different from one person to another does not need to hinder appreciation for the feelings of others. It is the feelings and not the circumstances that facilitate empathy.

The following dialogue exemplifies the empathy that is present between a principal and a parent who is concerned about his daughter:

PAR: "Thanks for seeing me on such short notice. I'm really concerned about Kim."

PRIN: "She's missed a lot of school this quarter—twelve days so far. Why has she missed so much school? We know she hasn't been sick. Do you know?"

PAR: "No, not really. She leaves home in the morning but doesn't go to school. My wife and I think she's been spending most of her time with her friend, Joe."

PRIN: "He dropped out last year. What's he doing?"

PAR: "Hanging out with my daughter. He doesn't have a job, and as far as we can tell, he just doesn't do anything. My wife and I just don't know what to do. We've tried grounding her, taking away her use of our car, stopping her allowance. Nothing seems to work. She just gets angrier with us and less cooperative every day."

PRIN: "My sister had a similar problem with my nephew. He just stopped going to school and didn't say anything to her. She had to find out about his absence from the middle school counselor. My sister is a teacher, and she was extremely embarrassed about the entire situation. She thought that because she is a teacher, she should have recognized the signs. There are always signs, you know."

PAR: "What did she do? I mean, did your nephew finally go back to school?"

PRIN: "Eventually, but it didn't happen right away. They got some help from the Family and Children's Services Agency. It was short-term counseling, and they finally worked it out."

PAR: "Do you think they could help us?"

PRIN: "It's worth a try."

The principal and the parent immediately struck up a mutual relationship based on their personal experiences. There was no need for the principal to overemphasize her professional position because the parent was neither disputing her authority nor seeing her to complain about the school staff. Rather, the parent was seeking help and understanding. In this example, the principal knew about a similar problem with her nephew. However, the reason why she was able to empathize with the parent was because she felt the frustration of dealing with a problem that involved another person. Typically such frustration would be accompanied by anger with the child, fear of what was going to happen to him or her, helplessness at not finding a solution to the problem, and love for the child. The emotions of frustration, anger, fear, helplessness, and love are the genuine bases for empathy; they are the touchstones for empathy. Thus another principal who does not have a nephew who was in a similar situation can still empathize with the parent because of having experienced the same emotions in other circumstances or with other people.

DISCUSSION QUESTIONS AND STATEMENT

1. What is the underlining issue concerning empathy?

2. Define empathy.

3. Why is it important to be an empathetic educational leader?

Assessing Empathy

The following is an exercise to help administrators understand the importance of feelings in establishing helping relationships with others. Furthermore it is meant to give administrators the opportunity to practice empathetic understanding.

EXERCISE **3.1**

Empathetic Relationships Assessment

After reading each situation, identify the surface feelings being expressed, the underlying feelings, and the appropriate empathetic responses.

Example Situation
Student to principal: "I'm sorry I shoved Laurie. I didn't think she'd get hurt. I was only playing around. Are you going to call my mom and dad?"

Surface feelings: Guilt and fear about what is going to happen.

Underlying feelings: Disappointing the adults and family members, fearing rejection, losing approval and friendship or love of peers and adults, desiring forgiveness.

Response: "Let's try to figure out how you can prevent this from happening again as well as what you can do to make this right with Laurie. What caused you to shove her in the first place?"

Situation 1
Teacher to principal: "At the faculty meeting, you didn't mention anything about the workshop that Pam and I attended on the Reading Recovery Program. We thought you might have wanted us to tell the rest of the teachers about the program. It has great possibilities."

Surface feelings: _____

Underlying feelings: _____

Response: _____

Situation 2
Female principal to female principal: "I'm really getting tired of this. Every time we have an administrators' meeting, Ted wants to tell me an off-color joke. It makes me wonder if I've given him the wrong idea about myself."

Surface feelings: _____

Underlying feelings: _____

Response: _____

Situation 3

Principal to superintendent: "Did the parent complain about me? She's never happy about what we are doing with her son. She thinks the kid is a genius and that he's not being challenged. Her son's teacher is really very capable and says the student is just an average kid."

Surface feelings: _____

Underlying feelings: _____

Response: _____

Situation 4

Superintendent to superintendent: "My board is acting very strangely. These days none of the members seem to be very supportive of what I'm trying to accomplish. The troubling thing, however, is that they were the ones who helped me set my goals. I'm just trying to do what they said they wanted."

Surface feelings: _____

Underlying feelings: _____

Response: _____

Situation 5

Student to principal: "I don't care if my mom and dad are getting a divorce. I'm always with my friends anyway. They're the only people I really want to be with."

Surface feelings: _____

Underlying feelings: _____

Response: _____

Situation 6

Teacher to superintendent: "I think teachers want to support the tax-increase referendum, but we don't believe the board of education is going to use the money for what is really needed—higher salaries."

Surface feelings: _____

Underlying feelings: _____

Response: _____

Situation 7

School bus driver to principal: "Those three kids are the most disrespectful I've ever had on my bus. They don't do anything I say, and it's dangerous. One of them is going to either get hurt or hurt some other kid."

Surface feelings: _____

Underlying feelings: _____

Response: _____

(continued)

Situation 8

Custodian to principal: "Some of those teachers let those kids do whatever they want. Their classrooms look like pigpens. It takes me twice as long to clean those classrooms as some others, and I don't have time to do that. This is a big school for just one custodian to clean."

Surface feelings: _____

Underlying feelings: _____

Response: _____

Situation 9

Teacher to principal: "I don't like to do this, but I've got to complain about Margaret. She's never on time for cafeteria, playground, or bus duty. It places a lot of pressure on the rest of us when we have to supervise all the students without her help. It's not fair. You need to talk with her."

Surface feelings: _____

Underlying feelings: _____

Response: _____

Situation 10

Principal to superintendent: "I need at least two additional teachers in my building. Some of the grades have classrooms with more than thirty students. You know some of the families that these kids come from. They have a lot of problems, which they bring to school. The teachers think we don't care or understand how difficult it is to teach these students."

Surface feelings: _____

Underlying feelings: _____

Response: _____

SUMMARY

The underlining issue concerning empathy is learning how other people feel about the concerns and problems they are dealing with in their daily lives. As a personal attitude of an effective administrator, empathy is practiced both on an individual level and in groups.

Empathy is a process whereby an educational administrator attempts to perceive the worldview of others in such a manner as not to be influenced by his or her own perceptions. It is also important to maintain a sense of separateness in order to avoid being caught up in the worldview of other persons. Empathy is a quality and not just a technique; it is a way of being. It is fostered through practice. The empathetic administrator must genuinely have the intention of trying to unconditionally and uncritically accept the life-world of others. It is through this attitude that the administrator can empower others to make changes in their lives.

The empathetic administrator is in a position of trust, and as such, the relationship can mitigate alienation because those who receive empathy will have the opportunity to view themselves as being valued and cared about. Thus the administrator must convey to others the value of communicating what they are feeling and thinking about issues and problems. This can be accomplished through sensitive listening, which requires the administrator to make contact with the cognitive and affective dimensions of other persons' life-world.

It is the ability of people to experience common human feelings that facilitates the practice of empathy. However, empathy requires an active attempt to make the transference from one's own personal experiences to those of others.

E N D N O T E S

1. C. Rogers, "Empathic: An Unappreciated Way of Being," *Counseling Psychologist,* vol. 5, no. 2 (1975): 4.

2. Ibid., 4–9.

3. Ibid., 7.

4. P. Natiello, "The Person-Centered Approach: From Theory to Practice," *Person-Centered Review,* vol. 2, no. 2 (1987): 203–216.

S E L E C T E D   B I B L I O G R A P H Y

Barrett-Lennard, G. T. "Listening." *Person-Centered Review,* vol. 5, no. 3 (1988): 308–315.

Levant, R. F., and J. M. Shlien, eds. *Client-Centered Therapy and the Process-Centered Approach: New Directions in Theory, Research, and Practice.* New York: Praeger Publishing, 1986.

Rogers, C. "Empathic: An Unappreciated Way of Being." *Counseling Psychologist,* vol. 5, no. 2 (1975): 2–9.

Sharf, R. S. *Theories of Psychotherapy and Counseling: Concepts and Cases.* Pacific Grove, California: Brooks/Cole Publishing Company, 1996.

CHAPTER

4 The Genuine Administrator

The practice of educational leadership requires administrators to be psychologically active in the work of the school and school district. This implies that the administrator has a genuine enthusiasm for the role of leader. It is impossible for teachers, staff members, and other administrators to become effective members of a school and/or school district community if the leader is apathetic or uncommitted. Superintendents, principals, and other administrators must have a clear sense of who they are as persons; they must know who they are, what they believe, and how they feel.

The administrator comes to recognize that she is a facilitator who promotes the self-actualization of all members of the school and school district community. She understands that the personal qualities of a leader are more important than techniques of leadership. The principal or superintendent recognizes that most professionals can find their own way not only as individuals but also as a group in a more effective way with minimal direction but with maximum facilitation from an administrator.

When a principal or superintendent accepts a facilitative approach, he or she can move away from playing the role of leader and move closer to using a more direct way of self-expression, to becoming more tolerant of ambiguity, to becoming more aware of subjective experiences, to becoming more open with others, and to becoming more aware of internal resources in searching for answers to problems.[1]

The educational leader thus becomes a more congruent person. The more he becomes involved with others in a genuine way, putting up no professional front, the more likely that teachers, staff members, and others will take ownership of their responsibilities because they will be able to form a more trusting relationship with that educational leader. As a consequence, teachers and staff members are more likely to experiment with their creativity.

In essence the genuine superintendent or principal is a respectful person. While respect may appear to be rather elusive, respect can be conceived in the context of both giving and receiving it. In the practice of educational leadership, establishing genuine relationships is also dependent on other qualities and on the approach to administration. Those other qualities are congruency, positive regard, and warmth and trust; the administrative approach is empowerment.

Congruency

Congruency refers to an attribute an administrator possesses when her external expressions are in harmony with her internal disposition. Principals and superintendents who are congruent do not pretend to be interested when they are not, do not pretend to understand when they do not, do not say something they do not mean, and do not adopt a certain form of behavior just to win approval.[2]

Even though congruency is such an important attribute for a successful administrator, it is often neglected because it is difficult to achieve. Without congruency, administration tends to be more about technique and eventually becomes meaningless. Furthermore the incongruent administrator uses techniques to be controlling and manipulative.[3]

E X E R C I S E   4.1

Congruency Assessment

Answer the following questions, keeping in mind that the objective is to understand the degree of your congruency.

1. How often do I pretend to be interested in what the teachers and staff members are doing? _____

2. How often do I pretend to be interested in what students are doing? _____

3. Do I pretend to be interested in the opinions of parents? _____

4. Do I pretend to be a friend to others? _____

5. Do I pretend to appreciate the advice and counsel of the superintendent or school board president? _____

6. Do I pretend to like teachers, students, or parents? _____

7. Do I pretend to be interested because I believe it is my job to show interest? _____

8. What is really on my mind when I pretend to be interested? _____

9. How can I be more genuine in showing my interest in what teachers and staff members are doing? _____

10. How can I be more genuine in the way I feel toward others? _____

Positive Regard

The notion of positive regard is built around the idea of unconditional acceptance. The objective of educational leadership is to establish a climate in a given school or school district in which each person can freely express himself or herself as an individual and also to establish a climate in which groups of people can express their ideas, attitudes, and feelings in a collective manner.

Operationalizing positive regard involves a caring attitude on the part of the principal or administrator that is also nonjudgmental. The ideas, feelings, and attitudes expressed by teachers, staff members, students, and parents are not evaluated in relation to the principal's or administrator's values but rather accepted without stipulations or expectations. There is unconditional acceptance of other people. This can be very difficult for principals and administrators who consider it their responsibility to regulate the behavior and speech of those they supervise. Sometimes they confuse acceptance with approval or, more likely, believe that others will view their acceptance in this manner. However, what the principal or administrator is actually doing is asserting that he or she values others as people who have a right to their separateness. It is this receptivity to the subjective world of other people that gives rise to the impression that the principal or administrator is on the side of the teacher, staff member, student, or parent. Also, exhibiting positive regard does not mean that the principal or administrator cannot express concerns about the ideas or behaviors of others. Certainly inappropriate behavior cannot be allowed to continue. Respecting the notion that other people have a right to be different and even a right to make mistakes or to do something that is inappropriate is the key to demonstrating positive regard.

TABLE 4.1   Ways to Indicate Positive Regard

Greet teachers and students in the halls of the school, especially at the start of the school day.

Maintain an inviting atmosphere in the school that encourages parents and others to visit the school.

Invite board of education members to visit the school.

Send congratulatory notes to teachers, staff members, students, and colleagues who receive awards.

Have award ceremonies at the school building level and school district level.

Have service appreciation and retirement celebrations and dinners for teachers and staff members.

Go to parent and community meetings when attendance has not been requested.

Go to school athletic events when attendance has not been requested.

Take time to talk and visit with teachers, staff members, students, parents, and colleagues without interruption.

Be visible in and around the school just to provide support for the teachers and staff members.

Develop a school or district newsletter that highlights the accomplishments of teachers, staff members, students, and colleagues.

Vital to this attitude of positive regard is the attitude of caring, which is not dependent on the principal's or administrator's own personal needs but is a genuine concern for others as human beings. Any artificial attempt to express caring will make it difficult for others to trust the superintendent, principal, or administrator. Often a caring attitude can be expressed through gestures, tone of voice, and facial expressions. All of these expressions will be genuine only if the person truly has a positive regard for others. Fostering this type of attitude is certainly possible, but it requires a person to reflect on his or her thoughts, feelings, and attitudes for the purpose of channeling them in this direction. Selected reading, study, and staff development programs focused on personal growth are essential for people who tend to lack the attitude of positive regard. The attitude of positive regard also contributes to the personal growth of others. When people recognize that they are worthy of being valued, they also can see in practice the importance of developing in themselves an attitude of positive regard for others. See Table 4.1 for a list of ways to indicate positive regard for others.

In the principalship, these dimensions of positive regard are also extended in the aggregate to the school faculty, staff, student body, and parents. In like manner, in the superintendency these dimensions are extended in the aggregate to the faculty, staff, students, and parents of the entire district.

EXERCISE **4.2**

Positive Regard Assessment

On a scale of 1 to 3 (1 = never, 2 = sometimes, 3 = always), rate the degree to which you manifest positive regard.

As an administrator, I maintain a positive attitude about the persons involved in the following situations until I can talk to them about their actions.

Rating

_____ When a teacher comes late to school

_____ When a student does not carry through on a suggestion that I make

_____ When a parent who is often critical of the school makes an appointment to talk with me

_____ When a teacher has a discipline problem in the classroom

_____ When the superintendent of schools makes an unannounced visit to my school

_____ When a teacher does not carry out a directive I asked him or her to undertake

_____ When a student is sent to my office by a teacher

_____ When a group of teachers makes an appointment to see me

_____ When the school bus driver arrives with the children after the time to start school

_____ When there is a student disruption in the cafeteria

_____ When a student has a controlled substance in his or her possession

_____ When a student is involved in a fight

(continued)

_____ When a parent is late for an appointment to talk with me

_____ When a teacher is late in turning in a report or form that is a routine requirement

_____ When a central office administrator does not promptly return my telephone call

_____ When I see a group of teachers congregating in the teachers' lounge

_____ When student test scores do not meet my expectations

_____ When my secretary does not complete one of my assignments on time

_____ When the school building is in disarray after an outside group used the facility the night before

_____ When it appears that the custodian did not properly clean my office

_____ When there is a large number of students waiting to see me in my outer office

_____ When a colleague does not offer assistance with a problem I am having

_____ When a newspaper or electronic media reporter wants to talk with me

_____ When an outside organization wants to use the school building

_____ When the superintendent or board of education cuts the budget

_____ **Rating** (A maximum rating of 75 indicates that a person always maintains a positive attitude about people even in relation to possible unpleasant encounters until he or she receives further information. A rating of 38 can be used as a median score for purposes of analysis.)

Warmth and Trust

It is usually immediately obvious when a person has an aura of aloofness or coldness in relationships with other people. Such people have developed the *stance of observer* rather than the *posture of engagement.* This type of persona blocks genuine communication because other people have difficulty getting to know and understand the person with these characteristics. However, the effects of these characteristics are especially problematic for superintendents, principals, and other administrators. Most people attribute suspicion and a lack of trust to a person who is aloof or cold, and employees who do not trust a supervisor generally will not take risks. Some administrators tend to take on a business-like approach with teachers, staff members, students, and parents rather than use a close-knit, warm approach. The former approach does not require as much personal investment as the latter.

Even more important is the effect that lack of trust in an administrator has on school or school district culture. In a school setting, teachers and staff members may find it difficult to establish meaningful interactions and might be reticent to challenge each other to higher levels of performance. Furthermore teachers and staff members may believe that it is safer to keep their feelings about issues facing the school or school district hidden. People do not naturally trust one another just because they are working together in a given school or school district. It is the principal or superintendent of schools who must set the

TABLE 4.2   Indicators of Teachers' and Staff Members' Trust in Administrators

People express themselves more directly.

People tend to be more open in expressing their feelings.

People look for solutions to problems within themselves.

People give constructive criticism.

People readily form relationships with others.

People take responsibility for their own actions.

People are aware of their own subjective experiences.

People are more tolerant of others.

People deal more constructively with ambiguity.

People are more open to new experiences.

People are willing to challenge their own preconceived ideas.

People are willing to challenge the ideas of others.

People are more interested in the welfare of the school community.

People are more interested in the welfare of the school district community.

tone and establish the environment in which trust can flourish. The objective is for people to feel safe enough to be themselves, to reveal who they are as persons.[4]

Establishing trust rests on the principal's or superintendent's ability to be open and personable. The administrator must be capable of trusting himself or herself and, by extension, have faith in the abilities of the teachers and staff members. This is demonstrated when the administrator shows an interest in the welfare of individual members of the school or school district as well as the welfare of people in the community.[5] See Table 4.2 for indicators that an administrator is trusted by others.

Empowerment

Empowerment as an approach to administration has its origins in an historical reality: Teachers perform their respective responsibilities in relative isolation from each other.[6] On a daily basis, they make decisions about what occurs in their classrooms and are expected to be in control of student behavior, the content and structure of teaching, and the evaluation of student performance. However, teachers are often not involved in the decisions that affect school and school district operations and policies. Those types of decisions are often left to the discretion of principals and superintendents. Such a reality is self-reinforcing in the sense that teachers sometimes become rather defensive in relation to their classroom prerogatives and often set up in their own minds a false dichotomy between what they do and what administrators do. The attitude becomes one of noninterference: "Don't bother me, and I won't bother you."

Of course the role and function of both teachers and administrators are intertwined to such an extent that what teachers do significantly affects what administrators can do, and vice versa. There is reciprocity between teaching and administering; therefore, a sense of community must exist if both teachers and administrators are going to be successful in carrying out their responsibilities in an effective manner. This community spirit is fostered through commitment on the part of both teachers and administrators to assume collective responsibility for developing and implementing the overall goals and objectives of a given school and of the school district in general.

Empowerment is thus an attitude of mutual trust between teachers/staff members and administrators. The natural extension of this trust is shared decision making. Sustaining the notion of empowerment is essential to the concepts of both facilitative and inclusive leadership. Facilitative leadership recognizes that leadership does not necessarily reside in one person (for example, the principal or the superintendent of schools). Rather, leadership can come from teachers, staff members, students, parents, and community leaders. The principal or superintendent has the responsibility of enlisting and directing the talents and expertise of all those who have a stake in the success of both a given school and the school district in general.

Inclusive leadership recognizes that teachers and staff members are not merely employees but stakeholders who have a vested interest in the success of the school where they serve and the school district to which they are contracted. Inclusion implies that teachers and staff members have the information that is necessary to make decisions and that they are involved in decision making about significant issues, not just about mundane matters. Inclusive leadership complements facilitative leadership in the sense that people who come from different backgrounds and points of view can enrich the dialogue about both school and school district issues. Thus inclusive leadership gives credibility to the decision-making process.

Process of Empowerment

There are three areas of empowerment that foster respect for teachers and staff members: organizational impact, professional growth, and personal autonomy. Principals and superintendents who truly believe in empowerment must continually evaluate their commitment to this approach and need to develop a strategy for its implementation.

Before initiating a movement toward greater empowerment of teachers and staff members, it is important to remember that the involvement of teachers and staff members in the planning process is critical. Furthermore not every teacher or staff member wants to be empowered to the same degree. Some value the fact that they are left alone to work with their respective students and really do not want to be involved in decision making. These individuals have not been informed that such engagement is a responsibility that helps to enrich the school community.

Principals and superintendents can begin the planning process by eliciting information from teachers and staff members through a questionnaire. The following is a sample questionnaire that could be used by a principal that deals with the dimension of empowerment and its organizational impact.

EXERCISE **4.3**

Empowerment Process Assessment

In answering the following, please keep in mind that the intent is to gather information that can be used to develop a process for involving faculty and staff in more meaningful ways in the operations of your school.

Based on your professional experience, describe how teachers and staff members can be more effectively involved in the following:

Establishing a vision and goals for the school _____

_____

Developing the school budget _____

_____

Developing the organizational structure of the school _____

_____

Creating student rights and responsibilities policies and procedures _____

_____

Creating student assessment policies and procedures _____

_____

Creating problem-solving and event policies and procedures _____

_____

Developing curriculum, program, assessment, and instructional materials policies and procedures

_____

Creating policies and procedures for the inclusion of students with disabilities _____

_____

Developing a school community relations program _____

_____

Creating a staff development program _____

_____

Creating policies and procedures for the recruitment, selection, and assignment of teachers and staff members _____

_____

Creating policies and procedures for use and maintenance of school facilities _____

_____

_____

Please add other dimensions of school operations not covered above that you think should have teacher and staff member involvement: _____

_____

_____

_____

Signature (optional): _____

Assessment of Empowerment

The other two dimensions of empowerment, professional growth and personal autonomy, are more difficult to implement. The most effective way to bring about empowerment is to encourage teacher and staff member involvement in the areas set forth in the empowerment process questionnaire (Exercise 4.3). However, it is obviously important for a principal or superintendent to be continually vigilant in assessing the degree to which empowerment has been accomplished. Exercise 4.4 is a sample instrument that can be used to assess the perceptions of teachers, principals, and other administrators concerning empowerment. While this presentation has been focused primarily on empowering teachers and staff members, these same principles can and should be applied to principals and other administrators. Administrators also must be empowered if the education enterprise is to be successful.

E X E R C I S E   **4.4**

Empowerment Assessment

On a scale of 1 to 3 (1 = never, 2 = sometimes, 3 = always), rate the degree to which you believe that you have been empowered and have an effect on school and school district operations, your own professional growth, and your ability to be an autonomous professional.

Rating

_____ I have access to sufficient information in order to make reflective decisions.

_____ I have been granted sufficient time in my schedule to participate in decision making.

_____ I believe that my ideas and opinions are valued.

_____ Communication has been improved in the school and in the school district.

_____ I have been motivated by the administration to participate in the decision-making process.

_____ I feel that I can take risks in presenting unpopular ideas and opinions.

_____ Appropriate boundaries have been established in regard to my participation in decision making.

_____ I am allowed to experiment with different modes of instruction (teachers and staff members).

_____ I am allowed to experiment with different modes of leadership (principals and other administrators).

_____ I am involved in the establishment of my performance objectives.

_____ I consider myself to be a stakeholder in the school and school district.

_____ I feel comfortable using my personal resourcefulness in carrying out my responsibilities.

_____ My abilities and talents are recognized.

_____ My services are appreciated.

_____ My professional development is encouraged and supported.

_____ My status as a professional is recognized and respected.

_____ I have reasonable control over my daily schedule.

_____ My effectiveness is dependent on my personal motivation and performance.

_____ There is a reasonable expectation concerning the level of my performance.

_____ My assignment is intellectually stimulating.

_____ My abilities and talents are being utilized in my assignment.

_____ **Rating** (A maximum rating of 63 indicates that a person always perceives that he or she has been empowered to make a difference in the school or school district and is in control of his or her professional life. A rating of 32 can be used as a median score for purposes of analysis.)

DISCUSSION QUESTIONS AND STATEMENTS

1. How can an educational leader become a more congruent and genuine person?

2. Explain the concept of positive regard.

3. Compare and contrast the "stance of the observer" with the "posture of engagement."

4. What are the two notions of leadership that support the empowerment of others?

5. Explain the goal of the empowerment movement.

SUMMARY

The practice of educational leadership requires administrators to be psychologically active in the work of the school and school district. This implies that the administrator has a genuine enthusiasm for the role of leader. The administrator comes to recognize that he or she is a facilitator who promotes the self-actualization of all members of the school and school district community. When a superintendent or principal accepts a facilitative approach, that administrator moves away from playing the role of leader and moves closer to a more direct way of self-expression. Thus the educational leader becomes a more congruent, more genuine person. The personal characteristics that reveal the genuine administrator are operationalized through the administrative strategy of empowerment.

Congruency refers to an attribute an administrator possesses when external expressions are in harmony with internal disposition. The congruent administrator is a person who is not pretending either interest or understanding.

Positive regard is predicated on the idea of unconditional acceptance. Free expression of ideas, attitudes, and feelings, not only by individuals but also by groups of people, is cultivated primarily in a climate of positive regard. The operative expression of positive regard is a nonjudgmental attitude exhibited by administrators, teachers, and staff members. Sometimes people confuse acceptance with approval. However, what nonjudgmental administrators really are asserting is that they value the right that others have to their separateness. This receptivity to the subjective world of others demonstrates that a given administrator is an advocate for teachers, staff members, students, and parents. Superintendents, principals, and other administrators certainly can express their own opinions, and inappropriate behavior by teachers, staff members, students, and parents cannot be tolerated.

Vital to this attitude of positive regard is the attitude of caring, which is a genuine concern for others as human beings. A caring attitude can be expressed through gestures, tone of voice, and facial expressions.

When administrators exhibit an attitude of positive regard, they contribute to the personal growth of other people because they can see in practice the importance of developing in themselves an attitude of positive regard.

Aloofness or coldness in a person is usually immediately apparent. Such people have developed the stance of observer rather than the posture of engagement. Such a persona blocks genuine communication because other people have difficulty getting to know and understand the person with these characteristics. Such characteristics are particularly problematic in administrators because aloofness or coldness usually gives the impression that the administrator cannot be trusted. Trust is established through engagement whereby people get to know and understand each other. When teachers and staff members lack trust in a principal, they find it difficult to establish meaningful interactions and might be reticent to challenge each other to higher levels of performance. They certainly will not be open in expressing their feelings about issues facing the school and school district. Establishing trust is dependent on an administrator's ability to be an open and personable individual.

Empowerment is an outgrowth of an administrative movement to liberate teachers/ staff members from the isolation that can occur if they are not overtly engaged in the operation of the school and school district where they practice their profession. The role and function of teachers/staff members and administrators are so interwoven that what each does significantly affects the ability of others to carry out their responsibilities. Thus a sense of trust and community must exist between teachers/staff members and administrators if the goals of a school and school district are going to be effectively accomplished.

Empowerment is an attitude of mutual trust that naturally leads to shared decision making. Supporting the notion of empowerment are the two concepts of facilitative and inclusive leadership. Facilitative leadership recognizes that leadership resides not only in the principal or superintendent but also in teachers, staff members, students, parents, and community leaders. Inclusive leadership recognizes that teachers and staff members are both employees and stakeholders in the school and school district where they serve. Inclusive leadership implies that teachers and staff members are provided with the necessary information and opportunities to participate in the decision-making process regarding policy and procedure issues that affect a given school and school district.

There are three areas of empowerment: organizational impact, professional growth, and personal autonomy. Planning to initiate empowerment in these areas must be systematic and must give teachers and staff members the opportunity to participate in the planning process. Ongoing assessment concerning the progress in empowering teachers and staff members is a necessity.

ENDNOTES

1. G. Corey, *Theory and Practice of Group Counseling,* 4th edition (Pacific Grove, California: Brooks/Cole Publishing Company, 1995), p. 96.

2. Ibid., p. 267.

3. Ibid., p. 269.

4. Ibid.

5. Ibid., p. 96.

6. P. M. Short and J. T. Greer, *Leadership in Empowered Schools: Themes from Innovative Efforts* (Upper Saddle River, New Jersey: Merrill Publishing, 1997), p. 131.

SELECTED BIBLIOGRAPHY

Hamachek, D. F. "Evaluating Self-Concept and Ego Development Within Erikson's Psychosocial Framework: A Formulation." *Journal of Counseling and Development,* vol. 66, no. 8 (1988): 354–360.

Levant, R. F., and J. M. Shlien, eds. "Unconditional Positive Regard: A Controversial Basic Attitude in Client-Centered Therapy," in *Client-Centered Therapy and the Person-Centered Approach: New Directions in Theory, Research, and Practice.* New York: Praeger Publishing, 1984, pp. 41–58.

Rosenholtz, S. J. *The Teachers' Workplace: The Social Organization of Schools.* New York: Teachers College Press, 1991.

Short, P. M., and J. T. Greer. *Leadership in Empowered Schools: Themes from Innovative Efforts.* Upper Saddle River, New Jersey: Merrill Publishing, 1997.

Sirotnik, K. A., and R. W. Clark. "School-Centered Decision Making and Renewal." *Phi Delta Kappan,* 69, no. 9 (1988): 660–664.

PART TWO

Ethical and Philosophical Foundations of Human Relations

The effective superintendent of schools, principal, or other administrator will quickly realize that he or she cannot deal with the variety and intensity of issues in the leadership milieu unless he or she has an ethical and philosophical base from which to lead. Too often the general public and administrators themselves believe that leadership is a skill that can be learned best through task accomplishment. Such an approach will doom the administrator to failure.

All administrative decisions will have an effect on others—be they teachers, staff members, students, parents, colleagues, or taxpayers. Further, the effect that is produced will be beneficial or detrimental. Determining which course of action will have the most positive effect on people without hindering others is an ethical dilemma. It is only in decision making that an administrator can truly know who he or she is as a person. Decisions are the actualization of a person's core values.

Furthermore, in contemporary society no administrator will be able just to perform tasks without knowing and understanding why or how something is best practiced from a theoretical perspective. Therefore the philosophical dimension of educational leadership takes on a very important function. That function calls the administrator to reflection on the role and responsibilities of leadership.

Part Two consists of five chapters dealing with ethical and philosophical foundations: Human Relations in an Ethical Context; Transcendental Leadership and Human Relations; Administrator Responsibility and Effective Human Relations; Conflict, Pluralism, and Human Relations; Social Justice in a Human Relations Context; and Public Discourse in a Human Relations Context.

5 Human Relations in an Ethical Context

There is no way of knowing how humans dealt with human relations issues before the advent of writing, but they must have confronted difficult situations that required reflection about what was the most effective way to act. Of course human conduct is the subject matter of human relations and, as such, is extremely complicated. Human conduct does not just occur but rather emanates from the totality of a person's knowledge, experience, and relationships. People tend to react to situations rather than act from predetermined guidelines. At times everyone engages in the reactive type of behavior. However, putting thought and reflection behind actions is the only way human beings can maintain a stable and equitable society.

Reflection on the best way to maintain good human relations will become productive only if such reflection is driven by the following fundamental philosophical question: *What does it mean to be a human being?* It is impossible for this question to be explicitly set forth in every deliberation. Nevertheless, what it means to be human is fundamental to good relationships. The way people are treated in general and the formation of human relationships are significantly influenced by certain notions about humanity. Furthermore those notions are certainly influenced by the culture of a given society; societies are ever-changing for either better or worse. Finally, economics and scientific advances can have a significant influence on concepts about human nature.

Concepts about what it means to be a human being affect the manner in which people organize and deliver not only education but also health care and social services. When certain categories of people are devalued in society, other people abrogate their responsibilities to them. Human relations as a discipline is much more complicated that just making decisions about how to create effective relationships. From a philosophical perspective, human relations is concerned with how human reason can be used to acquire knowledge that can be used in forming relationships. In a true sense, the study of human relations is a search for the most effective way to establish relationships.

Human relations is also concerned with human conduct in the forming of relationships, in contrast with mere human behavior. Conduct implies that people have a choice in the way they will proceed to establish relationships; they can follow one course of action or another. By contrast, behavior is a descriptive term referring to human activities in general. The underlying assumption in human relations is that intentional conduct is rational conduct.[1]

There are two reasons why it is appropriate for principals and superintendents to utilize philosophical analysis as an ongoing way of thinking about human relations. First, the issues that philosophy explores are significant because they provide a framework for decision making and because these issues require reflection on human values that are at the core of all human enterprises.

Second, philosophical analysis offers administrators a unique kind of perspective on educational leadership issues. It is a different perspective from what would be expected if an administrator approached issues from a management viewpoint. Certainly it is important to analyze issues from a management perspective, but a philosophical or ethical analysis will enhance the strategies that are developed through these other approaches. A management approach to human relations answers the questions of *how* and *what* while the philosophical approach answers the *why* question.

Approaching Ethics

There are two traditional ways to study the ethics of human relations in educational leadership. The deontological approach is concerned with the rightness or wrongness of a given action and thus is usually considered within the context of duty (see Chapter Seven). What is the right thing to do in a given situation? Of course there are many interpretations of what is the right thing to do. One way of interpreting the *right action* is rooted in utilitarianism, which is a position that places the consequences of an action as the standard for what makes something right. Others indicate that a person's motivation or the nuances of the situation itself are the determinants that make an action right or wrong.

The teleological approach is concerned with the goals of an action in terms of goodness and badness. Naturally the questions arise as to what the meaning of goodness and badness is and whose definition of the terms should be used in making decisions. Both approaches are intermingled in this presentation so that a broader-based position can be utilized rather than a narrow position formulated by the exclusion of one or the other.

Norms

The ethics of effective human relations must be situated within the context of all other human activities because it is impossible to isolate the establishment of relationships in educational leadership from other human responsibilities. A principal or superintendent administers educational programs from the totality of who he or she is as a person. From this perspective, the insights of contemporary science have captured the imagination of many people. These insights have renewed an interest in the human genome and evolution.

An understanding of human evolution is an important component in understanding the ethical issues in human relations that will have a significant impact on the unsuspecting educational leader. To begin this presentation, it is important to remember that scientists have confirmed that evolution proceeds from the simple to the more complex: electron to atom, atom to molecule, molecule to cell, cell to organism, inferior organism to human. This is known as the *law of continuity.* In addition, the evolutionary process is governed by the *law of design,* which states that growth in complexity does not occur merely from an accumulation of elements but rather proceeds to a new plane when a certain degree of complexity has been reached. Evolution must proceed to a new plane in order for the process to continue. Therefore, a genuine metamorphosis occurs, which is a necessary discontinuity within the necessary continuity of evolution.[2]

The noted paleontologist and philosopher Teilhard de Chardin hypothesized *spirit-matter,* which was a stumbling block for many scholars during his lifetime. However, it is a notion that has gained much support since his death in 1955. Spirit-matter is the basic composition of everything in the entire universe. Further, matter and spirit are not two separate entities but rather inseparable and present at the most elementary physical level. For example, human beings possess the spiritual ability to exercise freedom of choice because of the continuity of the evolutionary process. In other words, these forms must have possessed elements of freedom.[3]

Of course the appearance of humans is the greatest discontinuity because it brought about the spirit endowed with thought, reflection, and liberty. Consequently human consciousness emerged and initiated a new evolutionary process tending toward ever greater complexity and consciousness. When this process began, it became irreversible and subject to the laws of continuity and design. Eventually the evolution of humanity will reach a critical point of complexity that will require the ascendance to a higher plane.[4]

Evolution produces a synthesis that safeguards previous stages of development. While speculation is only an educated guess, it seems probable that the social aspect of humanity will be affected by future evolution. The reason for this is consciousness necessitates a greater awareness of the interrelatedness of social experience and the need for better communication between human beings at all levels of relationships. This is the reason why communicative technology is such an important endeavor to the future development of humanity. Technology has either a direct or indirect effect on human communication, which in turn has a direct or indirect effect on human relations issues and problems.[5]

When humanity became a new form of biological life, it had certain characteristics: the emergence of internal arrangements above the factors of external arrangements in individual life; the appearance of true forces of attraction and repulsion (sympathy and antipathy); the awareness of an aptitude to foresee the future and thus the consciousness of a state of absolute irreversibility.[6] Teilhard de Chardin envisioned a future created through further human evolution centering on the socialization of humanity that is a map for the futuristic journey into the area of human relationships.

Worldview. From human consciousness emanates the context within which ethical norms are identified. Essentially consciousness consists of thought, reflection, and liberty. These components are operationalized through human experience, understanding, and judgment. Thus emerge ethical norms.

The evolutionary perspective and other scientific knowledge have created a new worldview and vision that compel humanity to reevaluate previous ethical norms. For this presentation, the previous worldview will be designated as classical and the current worldview will be designated as modern.[7]

The classical worldview sets forth the world as a finished product and holds that the experiences of people will allow them to have a clear understanding of immutable essences. People, therefore, can have a high degree of certitude about ethical principles that will remain forever valid. The only path to right conduct is formulated using universal principles in a deductive method that will yield secure and complete conclusions. People with this perspective emphasize the duty to adhere to preestablished norms and to comply with authority. Superintendents and principals agreeing with this worldview will probably find it difficult to accept unconventional values.

The modern worldview sets forth the world as dynamic and evolving. Progression and change are its hallmarks. The experiences of people allow them to identify individual traits within concrete and historical particulars. Thus the path to right conduct is primarily through induction from particular experiences. Some conclusions may change with an increase in knowledge. Incompleteness and error are possible, which could lead to a revision of principles. Adaptation to change and responsibility are characteristic of this worldview.[8] Superintendents and principals following this perspective probably would be more accepting of unconventional values.

Of course most people would agree that the prudent approach to developing ethical norms lies somewhere in the middle of these two divergent positions. Therefore, superintendents and principals should use kindness and understanding when dealing with people who do things that they consider inappropriate or wrong because circumstances could have diminished those people's culpability.

Natural Law.   The most misunderstood concept in ethics is the concept of the natural law because people tend to confuse the *natural law* with the *law of nature*. The natural law does not refer to a codified body of precepts but is constituted of those parameters that define the essential nature of humanity. Thus the natural law should not be identified with physical, chemical, or biological laws that explain how the natural world works.[9] Unfortunately, when some people observe nonhuman life, they project onto human life the laws governing these phenomena. Instead it is important to consider how human evolution has underscored the uniqueness of human life in the realm of nature. Therefore, to observe the behavior of primates, such as gorillas and chimpanzees, and then to project such behaviors onto humans is a mistake. In like manner, to project human characteristics onto primates and other animals constitutes a mistaken idea about the natural law.

Given the uniqueness of the human condition, it is extremely difficult to define natural law. However, it is possible to set forth certain notions that should help superintendents and principals as they make decisions that affect human relations. First and foremost, the natural law is discoverable through discourse, research, and reflection on humanity. This is possible because rationality is the foundation of the natural law, which is the hallmark of humanity. The values held by human beings are always affected by history and culture.[10]

Second, there are levels within the natural law. The most general level is "Do good and avoid evil," which for most people is self-evident. The more complex an issue is in the ethics of human relations, the more deliberation will be required. Such deliberation most likely will involve dialogue and study. For example, a conflict between a teacher and a principal over the teacher's evaluation will require dialogue between the two people and may involve a third person who acts as a mediator.[11]

Third, deliberation concerning the natural law must take into account the social dimension of humanity. Everything we do probably has some effect on others—if not immediately, then at some time in the future. The enactment of a zero-tolerance policy calling for the expulsion of students who possess, use, or sell drugs in school would probably keep drugs out of the hands of some students but would deprive the expelled students of an education if alternative school programs were not available.

Finally, using the notion of the natural law allows people to enter into rational debate concerning our collective humanity. This is particularly important in the United States because it is a pluralistic society. Thus human relational issues such as communication, school violence, rights and responsibilities of students, and rights and responsibilities of teachers can be publicly debated.[12]

As a consequence of this approach, the natural law concept extends beyond physical and biological precepts in order to consider the social, spiritual, and psychological aspects of human existence. Through the use of reason, people reflect on the requirement of the natural law in order to promote the well-being of humanity in general. Of course this approach must take into account those principles that are self-evident and necessary to human coexistence, such as mutual respect between people in the community in general and in a person's particular environment. It is also important to realize that the self-evident truths of human relations found in the natural law are under the creative control of people, resulting in diverse new avenues for establishing and maintaining effective human relations.

Knowing the natural law through the use of reason should be understood as the capacity within each person to reflect on human experience and to make judgments concerning the most appropriate way to establish relationships. The tools of reflection are observations, human testimony, research, analysis, logic, intuition, common sense, art, cinema, music, poetry, theater, and all other avenues available that lead to a better understanding of reality. Of course, it is important to keep in mind that discovering the precepts of the natural law and applying them to a particular relationship are always limited by the fact that humans only have a partial and limited grasp of reality because of any given person's capabilities, emotions, and cultural conditioning.

There are four ideas that must be considered when developing ethical norms that pertain to human relations, First, it is the responsibility of individuals and the aggregate community to pursue what is necessary to form ethically good human relations. Second, ethically good human relations should emerge from our experience of what it means to be fully human. Third, ethically good human relations must consider the unfinished evolutionary character of humanity. Finally, the principle of *proportionality,* which testifies that people are achieving ethically good human relations when they strive for the greatest possible proportion of good, should be observed.[13]

Social Ethics

The basic notion of social ethics is that good and sincere people may be implicated in structures, institutions, or systems that inflict injustices on other people. The underlying issue is that unethical actions by an individual can have a power that reaches beyond that individual to influence others to be unethical. It is a common experience to observe that unethical attitudes can be transmitted to children and other people in such a way that those attitudes become situated in their thoughts and actions, which can lead to their unethical treatment of others. From this perspective, people inherit the unethical actions of past generations. Women and people with disabilities are two groups that have personal experiences that validate the symbolic, mythic, and linguistic structures that perpetuate injustice. Thus the suffering that is caused by bigotry is much different from the suffering caused by disease or natural disaster. Bigotry is a learned attitude and is passed on from one generation to another. Therefore, individuals' actions that are unethical can eventually become embodied in institutions, structures, and systems. The segregation of African Americans in public schools is a good example of how the actions of individuals eventually became institutionalized in public education.[14]

The free decisions of people always place other people in situations in which they are required to make a decision. The decision is the link with the other person. He or she must decide to act or not to act. Hence an unethical decision invites other people to make unethical decisions also. From this perspective, life becomes a series of decisions and situations.[15]

Even though each person is unique, human beings can develop to their fullest potential only within the context of community. Principals and superintendents are usually aware of this reality and can take advantage of every opportunity to create learning communities where teachers and students can develop professional relationships.

A significant observation about unethical institutions is that changing them becomes extremely difficult because political and socioeconomic relationships and structures tend to take on a life of their own and become threatened by efforts to eradicate their unethical components. For example, federal laws concerning the treatment of people with disabilities in schools sometimes failed to bring about the needed changes because the laws did not solve the underlying issue. It is the attitudes of individuals that must be changed. In certain schools the full inclusion of children with disabilities into regular classrooms has not been very successful because some superintendents and principals neglect to provide teachers with adequate training, equipment, and supplies that are needed in order to facilitate the instruction of children with disabilities.

It is possible to understand personal and social unethicality only in relation to one another because they are dimensions of the same phenomenon. From a social perspective unethicality is experienced as external, inherited, overbearing, and seductive whereas from a personal perspective unethicality is freely chosen and incurs blame. Furthermore it is interesting to note that unethicality is powerful, fascinating, addictive, and alluring. Unethicality is often considered to be knowing ignorance that requires the active collaboration of individuals. There is a reciprocal relationship between human beings and society. As people create social institutions, structures, and systems, society is transforming human beings in either an ethical or unethical manner. Unethicality is a universal condition of humanity encountered through social relationships. Humanity creates society and society creates humanity.[16]

Human Consequences

The consequences of unethical actions do not vanish when the action is over. Rather they remain in its core. The milieu within which reason, and therefore freedom, is exercised is the ordinary circumstances of life. From one decision to another, the person further restricts himself or herself and therefore is always situated because of prior decisions. Thus each person is the ultimate cause of the kind of person he or she becomes. A superintendent who neglects to form effective relationships with his staff because he considers his present position as a stepping-stone to a larger district is an example of how a person is ultimately fashioning himself into a selfish individual.

After a person completes a number of unethical actions, the external consequences fade away. However, the person's attitudes and orientation remain. Eventually the superintendent could harden his attitude to the point of total selfishness, which in turn will affect all of his relationships with colleagues and even with people outside the professional milieu. When certain actions are repeated over an extended period of time, the person becomes more inclined in the direction of those actions.

Self-centeredness creates a unique response in other people. They do not change, but the meaning the unethical person imparts to them changes. For the self-centered person, others are seen more as objects to be manipulated than as persons to be encountered. It becomes easier to take advantage of other people because they are not perceived as persons with dignity but rather as a means or an obstacle to that person's self-interest. When other people are objectified, the self-centered person often experiences a profound sense of isolation and, because of this self-imposed loneliness, a sense of anxiety.

Thus people act from the totality of their being. Every action expresses a person's attitudes, dispositions, and powers. A person's actions also alert others about who he or she is at the very center of his or her being. Because of their positions, superintendents and principals become role models for others to emulate for appropriate or inappropriate reasons. Accepting a position of leadership imposes a responsibility on superintendents and principals to demonstrate appropriate ethical behavior. A most unfortunate situation occurs when a superintendent or principal involves a teacher or other administrator in an unethical action. Fear of losing a job or the amenities controlled by an administrator could create a situation in which the other person feels compelled to comply. In such a situation, the superintendent or principal not only abrogates responsibility but also inflicts an injustice on the other person. Finally, because of the administrator's position, the other person may experience a sense of uncertainty about the ethical issues involved; once again the possibility of emulating the unethicality is strengthened.[17]

Ultimately the goal of an ethical superintendent or principal should be the integration of all his or her attitudes, passions, powers, and tendencies in order to orient himself or herself toward ethical relationships with other people in both personal and professional life. The real obstacle to the conversion of a person who exhibits continual unethicality is the fact that she has hardened her heart, to use a popular phrase, and is not capable of seeing that she has changed into an unethical person.[18] For such a person, conversion can occur only through an event that enlightens her intellect, such as a serious illness.

Emphasizing the overall orientation of a person toward living either an ethical or an unethical life is called fundamental option theory. Conversely, it is an approach to ethics that deemphasizes the discrete actions of a person. Thus when a superintendent or principal tries to make good decisions in carrying out job responsibilities, he or she will be considered a good administrator by students, parents, and colleagues even if mistakes are made.

Contemporary society places considerable adulation on people who exhibit rugged individualism, which places ethical responsibility solely on each person and neglects the social aspects of individual actions and omissions.[19] Of course this is an opposing view of social ethics.

The Virtues

Superintendents and principals seeking to live an ethical life must eventually consider how certain virtues can help them. Prudence, justice, fortitude, and temperance are certainly the most important virtues for an educational administrator. A more contemporary understanding of the virtues places them in the context of human development, which must be understood as a process that begins in early childhood and extends into adulthood.

Erik Erikson and Lawrence Kohlberg are perhaps the two most noteworthy scholars of human growth and development. Erikson began his career with an orientation toward psychoanalytic theory but eventually developed his own approach. He was fascinated with certain aspects of human experience that are operational in the somatic, societal, and ego processes. He considered these processes to be interrelated and emphasized that all three must be taken into consideration when analyzing a particular human interaction.

A key concept to consider in understanding Erikson's stages of development is the principle of *epigenesis,* which is part of the somatic process. This principle states that even though a person develops in intervals, certain significant potentialities come to pass only during later intervals in life. Thus, even though developments that occur in the beginning of life are important, those that occur later in life are also important.

A second key concept in understanding Erikson's stages of development is the significant influence that the community has on the development of the individual and the strong influence that the individual has on the development of the community. In fact, that is why his theory is called a *psychosocial theory.* Further, this concept is the reason why he broke with the psychoanalytic school of psychology, which placed significant emphasis on inherent determinant characteristics.

In Erikson's theory, the ego process constitutes the organizing and balancing principle for the person. This process keeps everything in balance; it is critical to a person's individuality and is an integrating agent. The ego also helps a person maintain a vision of wholeness and keeps a person's instincts in check.

In his stages of moral development, Erikson elucidated the notion of crises of development, which are critical points during times of transition from one stage to the next. It is important for each person to resolve these crises during a given life period; this resolution prepares the person for the next stage. Transitioning to the next stage without a positive resolution of a crisis during a given period will be problematic in the further development of a person. It is not critical to good development, however, for the resolution to be totally positive. In fact, Erikson states that some negativity can be helpful as a person progresses through the life cycle. A principal or superintendent, for example, at times needs to be cautious in making decisions; thus a certain amount of mistrust is advantageous. The ultimate goal should be achieving a favorable ratio of the positive to negative.

Erikson's stages should be considered as a continuum rather than discrete periods, and a person may experience these stages in varying degrees of intensity. Individuals may even oscillate between the stages. Erikson's eight stages of development, with their corresponding crises and strengths that allow the stages to progress, are found in Table 5.1.

The second scholar to deal extensively with human growth and development, Lawrence Kohlberg, was greatly influenced by Jean Piaget. However, like Erikson, he developed his own approach to ethical development, which is commonly referred to as a *structural-developmental approach.* In conducting his research, Kohlberg presented subjects with a story that described an ethical dilemma. The subjects were asked to respond to the situation, after which Kohlberg probed and analyzed the reasoning behind their responses. Kohlberg's research resulted in the development of a paradigm that he called the *six stages of moral development.* It was his position that the stages are universal in all

TABLE 5.1 Erikson's Stages of Development

Stages	Crises	Strengths
Stage one: Infancy	Basic trust vs. basic mistrust	Hope
Stage two: Early childhood	Autonomy vs. shame, doubt	Will
Stage three: Play age	Initiative vs. guilt	Purpose
Stage four: School age	Industry vs. inferiority	Competence
Stage five: Adolescence	Identity vs. identity confusion	Fidelity
Stage six: Young adult	Intimacy vs. isolation	Love
Stage seven: Adulthood	Generativity vs. stagnation	Care
Stage eight: Old age	Integrity vs. despair	Wisdom

Adapted from John W. Crossin, *What Are They Saying About Virtue?* New York: Paulist Press, 1985, pp. 58–64.

human development, and when a person passes through a given stage, he or she will never regress. He also held the position that development of ethical principles is not related to specific religious beliefs but rather takes place through interaction with other people. This forces the individual to restructure his or her experiences in order to achieve ethical growth.

Justice is the key virtue for ethical growth at each stage of development, according to Kohlberg. He considered his research to be related to the philosophies of Emmanuel Kant and John Rawls, both of whom wrote extensively about justice. Kohlberg's notion of justice is concerned with equality and reciprocity. Each person has a responsibility to treat others as equals. Justice in this context is concerned with the dignity of all employees in schools and school districts. Educational administrators are expected to promote the welfare of staff members and students but to do so in such a way that no one receives an advantage because of someone else's disadvantage.

Utilizing a developmental approach to human growth, new definitions of virtues are required. However, the traditional approach to formulating definitions of the various virtues needs to be modified to include a functional perspective. Thus virtues can be conceptualized in the following manner:

- Virtues are qualities that shape the very core of who people are as persons.
- Virtues are flexible and adaptable to the milieu within which people must act.
- Virtues shape human beings inclinations and dispositions so they act in a certain way.
- Virtues integrate a person's emotional and intellectual life in such a way as to facilitate the person's arriving at ethical judgments with ease.
- Virtues must be cultivated over time in order to facilitate a certain way of acting.

Thus virtues are analogous to the abilities acquired by athletes or musicians who must practice certain skills over a prolonged period of time. In like manner, virtues can be strengthened through practice or weakened if neglected.[20]

Prudence.   This is the foundational virtue because it permeates all decision making and only operates in concrete situations. When prudence is practiced in its fullest manner, the following human operations are functioning: memory, foresight, imagination, and docility. Prudence requires a person to recall similar past experiences when he or she is facing an issue or problem that requires a decision. Further, the person also tries to predict the possible consequences associated with various options. Thus creativity and bold solutions are formulated to deal with issues and problems. A key aspect of prudence is docility, which is an openness to learn from others.

The threat of student violence requires more than just tightening and monitoring security in a school. It also requires open and frank dialogue with students and teachers about the root causes of violence and how such causes can be addressed through accessing school and school district human and financial resources.

Justice.   This virtue is concerned with an individual's relationship to others in the various communities to which he or she belongs. There are three types of justice: *distributive justice,* which is concerned with the obligations of society to individuals; *legal justice,* which is concerned with the obligations of individuals to society; and *commutative justice,* which is concerned with the relationships that exist among individuals. In practice these relationships create rights and responsibilities for each individual and the society to which he or she belongs. The key concept is that there is a corresponding responsibility for each right. Another key concept can be formulated in a question that sets the stage for ongoing discourse: "Upon whom does a given right place a claim?" From this perspective, there are two distinct kinds of rights: a claim to something and a claim against interference.

The rights of students to an education cannot restrict others from receiving an education. In the example about school violence, a superintendent or principal should not create policies that unjustly prevent some students from attending school. Zero-tolerance policies can exclude some students unjustly because there is no room for discretionary judgment. It is inappropriate for a student to give another student an aspirin, but it certainly does not qualify for exclusion under a drug policy that makes no distinction between legal and illegal drugs.

Fortitude.   The superintendency and principalship are certainly time-consuming jobs that also bring considerable demands and pressures on the individuals who occupy them. It is no surprise that these high-pressure positions often evoke anxiety and fearfulness in superintendents and principals. The virtue of fortitude helps people moderate their fear and anxiety in addition to helping people overcome their weaknesses in the pursuit of doing good in their private and public lives. A weakness that is manifested through fear of forming professional relationships can significantly hinder the effectiveness of a superintendent or principal. Thus fears of criticism, failure, disappointment, and humiliation by a superintendent or principal will have a negative effect on a school district or school community. It is impossible to always take the safe path in leading. The virtue of fortitude can help administrators overcome obstacles and can strengthen them to look beyond their fears as they carry out their responsibilities.

Temperance.   There are educational administrators who are on the other end of the scale, placing their professional responsibilities above everything else in their lives. They even neglect their own personal well-being and that of their families. Human pleasures and comforts are not incompatible with human relations. In fact, without such desires an administrator will eventually blunt his or her sensibilities for anything except knowing that job-related tasks have been completed. Of course the other extreme finds those administrators who indulge so much in pleasures that they neglect their responsibilities or perform them at a minimal level. As the most flexible virtue, temperance requires a superintendent or principal to learn limits in order to recognize when pleasures begin to obscure values.[21]

Ethical Decisions

Conscience is that human capacity that allows an administrator to make ethical decisions. There are two ways to describe conscience. First, it is an inclination or instinct that helps a person decide how to act in relation to a particular ethical dilemma. Secondly, it is a skill acquired through experience that a person can use to make an informed judgment. The first signs of conscience usually appear in children when they realize that a certain action, thought, or omission is either right or wrong. The former is more difficult to decide about because, in most situations, a person must choose among many different levels of rightness.[22] A superintendent may need to decide if he or she should replace a building principal who is doing a mediocre job with a person of great potential and promise. In the decision a superintendent must weigh the service and welfare of the principal with the needs and rights of the faculty and students. It is critical for educational administrators to develop a process that will provide them with the opportunity to consider the human relations ethicality of each situation that calls for a decision.

Of course there are many approaches to making ethical decisions that support good human relations. Three approaches have the greatest application to educational leadership: *strict consequentialism, mixed consequentialism,* and *deontologism.*

The best-known approach, situation ethics, was developed by Joseph Fletcher, who is a strict consequentialist. His approach to decision making is as follows:

- Identify the problem.
- List alternative courses of action.
- Predict the consequences for each alternative.
- Assign a value to the good produced by each alternative.
- Select the alternative that produces the greatest good.

Peter Knauer, Bruno Schuller, Josef Fuchs, and Louis Janssen are mixed consequentialists. The approach they developed is as follows:

- Identify the problem.
- Analyze the problem (who, what, the context).
- Analyze the values involved that are influenced by a person's beliefs and convictions.
- Identify norms that should guide the action that protects the person's values.
- Explore the consequences of the action.
- Compare the consequences with the values.

- Explore other alternatives, if the consequences and the values are inconsistent, and test them in order to provide feedback concerning the norms that protect the person's values.
- Perform the action if the consequences and the values are consistent.

The last approach is typically identified with the deontologists Germain Grisez, William E. May, and Paul Ramsey. The process is as follows:

- Identify the problem.
- Match up alternative courses of action with corresponding norms. (Comparing the alternatives with the norms should yield the following conclusions: one alternative consistent with the norms, several alternatives consistent with the norms, one alternative consistent with one or more norms but in conflict with one or more other norms.)
- Act on the highest norm.[23]

When formulating ethical decisions that support good human relations, sometimes people use local, state, and federal laws as norms that they assert are ultimate mandates. However, a superintendent or principal may follow all the provisions of the laws that apply to children with disabilities in terms of procedures but violate the spirit of the law. This is true because there is a certain amount of subjectivity in the implementation of all laws, and it is certainly possible for an administrator to manipulate the provisions of a law that will ultimately defeat the intention of the lawmakers.

Meaning in Life

Events such as birthdays, death dates, employment dates, graduation reunions, religious and national holidays, and wedding anniversaries bring back memories and evoke feelings. Of course some memories and feelings are pleasant while others are painful. A significant dimension of memories and feelings is how they figure in a person's perceptions of meaningfulness. People engage in reflection through memory and feelings in hopes of confirming that their lives have purpose and meaning.

What follows is a framework within which superintendents or principals, or those preparing to become educational leaders, can reflect on the meaning of their professional lives. Even though they were not written for this purpose, the writings of Viktor Frankl address a core question facing contemporary educational administrators: Has my professional career made a difference? As stated earlier, the demands made on superintendents and principals are awesome and range from simple administrative tasks to health and safety issues. Perhaps the most significant issues deal with the way students, faculty, staff members, and administrators are treated by other people—the quality of their professional relationships. Most teachers entered the education profession believing they could make a difference in the lives of students. It can be a rude awakening to realize that making a difference often has nothing to do with learning in the traditional sense of the word and may have everything to do with establishing relationships.

Viktor Frankl, the famous psychiatrist, exemplified in his own life the struggle that everyone faces to find meaningfulness. Frankl's entire family except for his sister were victims of the Holocaust. He wrote that he lost everything, including his human dignity, in the camps. According to Frankl, the search for meaning is the primary human motivator in life. Furthermore this unique human phenomenon can be found only through consistent individual efforts. Frankl used the phrase *the will to meaning* to identify his theory, which gives priority to a person's individual freedom to effect and sustain a direction in life that continually seeks out meaning not only in major life events but also in everyday living. This dimension of meaning is set forth in ideals and values.

Frankl believed that the search for meaning is related to each person's profession or occupation. Even though people engage in work to make a living, it is also obvious that, for many people, their profession or occupation is either a hindrance or a help in their search for meaning. Certainly some superintendents and principals have lost a sense of meaning in their lives to such an extent that they cannot detect the difference they make in the lives of those for whom and with whom they work.

Reflection, using the active imagination, is the tool that can help a superintendent or principal learn and acknowledge his or her contribution to the profession and overall meaning in life. Each educational administrator's abilities and talents cannot be duplicated by other people simply because each person is unique. Frankl was an existentialist in the sense that he believed the search for meaning must be grounded in the here and now. Thus it is not surprising that Frankl took the position that the real world, not a person's psyche, is the milieu within which the person will find the meaning of life.

It is important to know that Frankl held the position that interpersonal relationships shape a person's search for meaning. In the last analysis, the meaning of life is always about human relations. Superintendents and principals are fortunate in the sense that their entire professional careers are focused on actualizing human potential. Administrators, faculty members, staff members, students, and parents all participate in the attaining of educational goals and objectives. In spite of all the current difficulties that are present in education, teaching and learning change the lives of students and educators for the better.

Unfortunately human potentiality can easily diminish without being actualized. Frankl believed that actualizing potentiality is the only transitory aspect of life. However, when potentiality is actualized, it is irrevocably stored in a person's psyche and can be retrieved. This is a profound notion because it acts as an explanation of how a person makes progress, and in turn how people affect other people. This idea is certainly related to Carl Jung's collective unconscious theory and to Teilhard de Chardin's evolutionary theory. Superintendents and principals are in the business of actualizing potentiality, that of the students, faculty, and staff members. Furthermore they play a part not only in the actualization that takes place in schools but also in the actualization that occurs throughout individuals' lives.

Frankl held the position that people are capable of progressing beyond biological, psychological, and sociological constraints. In fact, he thought that people were capable of changing not only themselves but also their environment and even the world. Regardless of the circumstances of a person's life and the pain or guilt that he or she experiences, a person can use these situations to change for the better. Frankl called this phenomenon a tragic optimism.[24]

Because suffering is the most universal human experience and because no one can escape suffering, it provides a shared experience that can be a vehicle for human empathy and understanding. Suffering is also a very personal phenomenon because no one can alleviate the suffering of another person. In this context it is important to make a distinction between pain and suffering. Pain can be alleviated through treatment and medication, but not suffering.

Suffering emanates from personal experience or from symbiotic experience. It always brings with it reflection on one of the most fundamental questions of human existence: Why me? The real anguish of suffering lies in its external meaninglessness. Symbiotic suffering occurs as a consequence of empathy with other people who are suffering.

Superintendents and principals experience symbiotic suffering when a tragedy takes place involving a student or a colleague. When a student dies in an automobile accident, it creates a sadness that is shared by all members of the school community, even if they did not personally know the victim.

Thus people live on a continuum between meaning and happiness on one end and meaninglessness and sorrow on the other end. The search for meaning, which Viktor Frankl believed to be the major motivational force in life, is constantly being frustrated by suffering.[25]

In schools and school districts, the response that people have to suffering—whether it is their own suffering or the suffering of others—should be of concern to superintendents and principals because of the effect suffering has on the attitudes and behaviors of students and colleagues. A pointed example of why the response to suffering is so important is because either positive or negative responses become models of how others should respond to suffering. Suffering is a human relations issue.

An effective approach to suffering is the self-agency model, which focuses on the person's beliefs, intentions, and actions. In this approach, people are viewed as self-determining through their own personal life history, and the suffering experience changes them. This change can be enhancing or destructive, depending on how the individual perceives the suffering situation.[26]

The use of life narrative as a method for implementing the self-agency approach is viewed as an ongoing historical account of a person's successes, failures, happiness, and suffering. From this perspective, suffering is not considered to be an unexpected event with the hope that it will eventually disappear. Rather, suffering is seen as a condition of life that transforms people, that becomes a part of a person's life narrative.[27]

Some people take the position that life is good only when they are free from suffering. However, most people are capable of finding the meaning of life only when they are able to accept not only their own suffering but also the suffering of others.[28] It is only in the face of tragedy that some people are able to rise to heights they thought were impossible. The destruction caused by natural disasters such as floods, hurricanes, and tornadoes often creates a bond between people who share the experience of suffering that melts away self-interest in favor of the common good.

Freedom is not the first thought that enters the mind of a person when he or she reflects on responsibilities, and yet freedom is the basis upon which responsibility is founded. Without freedom of choice, there is no responsibility. No one is guilty of neglect of duty unless the choice of noncompliance is possible.

Certainly one of the most well-known proponents of the responsibility/freedom relationship is Jean-Paul Sartre. His work enhanced the self-agency concept. According to Sartre, human beings are the initiators of everything in the world and should not attempt to disguise the fact that they are also responsible for everything in the world. Sartre was an existentialist and was concerned about a worldview that placed blame for human misconduct on extraneous forces. He stated that people are capable of almost anything, including atrocities connected to waging war. Thus it is absolutely incorrect to classify some types of inappropriate behavior as nonhuman.

In order to argue his position, Sartre used the example of waging war. He set forth that participation in war is a deliberate choice because people could have done something else, even something as tragic as suicide or as difficult as desertion in order to avoid going to war. Of course most people would not accept these as possible alternatives, but his point is that people must take on themselves their share of the responsibility. It becomes a personal war through participation. It is not someone else's war that individuals wage; it is their war.

Perhaps the most important concept elucidated by Sartre is that everyone is ultimately alone in making decisions. Also each person is being formed by the decisions he or she makes. Therefore, the decisions that superintendents and principals make are free choices even though the choices are in keeping with the policies of the board of education. They are free choices because superintendents and principals assimilate the policies and make them their own policies when they choose to enforce them.

Ethical Principles of Human Relations

Here are nine ethical principles that sum up the dynamic process of human relations:

1. The social and physical sciences have discovered that the universe and humanity are much older and more interdependent than was once believed.
2. Humans gradually evolved onto higher planes of thought, reflection, and liberty.
3. Thought, reflection, and liberty are the necessary components of human experience, understanding, and judgment.
4. The conscious exercise of human reason is the context within which educational leaders can develop ethical norms.
5. It is the responsibility of educational leaders to continually search for what is ethically good in providing services for students and in supporting the activities of school district employees.
6. The virtues of prudence, justice, fortitude, and temperance are valuable aids in helping educational leaders exercise their responsibilities.
7. Utilizing a systematic approach to ethical decision making can help educational leaders confront the complex issues facing contemporary education.
8. Educational leaders can sustain an ethical direction in their professional lives only through striving to find meaning in their daily activities.
9. When educational leaders are faced with human suffering, they are presented with a choice to react in either a positive or negative way.[29]

DISCUSSION QUESTIONS AND STATEMENTS

1. What are the three major questions concerning the human phenomenon that is endemic to human relations considerations?

2. Explain how the notion of evolution can impact human relations.

3. Explain how the classical worldview and the modern worldview influence effective human relations.

4. Explain the difference between the law of nature and the natural law, and how they both impact human relations.

5. How are ethical norms influenced by human relations?

6. Explain how human relations is affected by social ethics.

7. Explain how practicing the virtues of prudence, justice, fortitude, and temperance can improve a person's human relations skills.

8. Explain how Viktor Frankl's concept of the will to meaning affects human relations.

9. Explain how Jean-Paul Sartre's notion of human freedom and responsibility can enhance human relations.

E X E R C I S E   **5.1**

Ethics of Human Relations Assessment

The purpose of this awareness instrument is to provide you with an assessment of your understanding of ethical principles as they influence your human relations skills. On a scale of 1 to 3 (1 = never, 2 = sometimes, 3 = always), rate the degree to which your actions comply with the following statements.

Rating

_____ I realize that the development of my ethical human relations perspective should be based on what it means to be a human being.

_____ I understand that following a set of ethical norms will help me establish meaningful relationships with people.

_____ I know that professional ethical relationships usually are developed in the context of carrying out my responsibilities as an administrator.

_____ In making professional ethical human relations decisions, I know that who I am as a person, both at work and in other settings, will influence what I decide.

_____ I believe that the human phenomenon is still evolving, and future human relations situations must take this into account.

_____ When considering the ethics of human relations, it is beneficial to engage in discourse with other people, study research, and spend time in reflection.

_____ The ethics of human relations is predicated on social interaction and engagement.

_____ The tool for establishing ethical human relations is human reason.

_____ I understand that my ethical human relations decisions will place other people in situations in which they are required to act in either an appropriate or inappropriate manner.

_____ I know that a person can only develop his or her ethical human relations response to situations through the engagement of other people connected with the situation.

_____ Because people act from the totality of who they are as people, ethical human relations is an expression of attitudes and dispositions.

_____ Exercising the virtues of prudence, justice, fortitude, and temperance will help me establish ethical human relations.

_____ A prudent person will be able to establish ethical human relations because he or she is open to learning from others about human circumstances.

_____ Treating people with fairness is essential to developing ethical human relations.

_____ The fearful person will have a more difficult time establishing ethical human relations.

_____ Establishing ethical human relations with colleagues will not occur if people neglect their personal well-being and the well-being of their family.

_____ In making ethical human relations decisions, it is helpful to utilize a method for analyzing ethical dilemmas.

_____ When faced with tragic events, a person often comes to terms with how meaningful his or her life has been.

_____ It is only through a continual search for meaningfulness, not only in his or her work but also in his or her private life, that an administrator will be able to establish ethical human relations.

_____ Human suffering is a common phenomenon that often leads a person to understanding the importance of ethical human relations.

_____ **Rating** (_A maximum rating of 60 indicates that a person always understands ethical principles as they relate to professional actions. A rating of 31 can be used as a median score for purposes of analysis._)

SUMMARY

Endemic to all human relations is the fundamental question: What does it mean to be a human being? The ultimate goal of human relations is to develop standards of conduct. Human conduct is different from human behavior. Behavior is descriptive of what humans do while conduct implies that they can choose one course of action or an alternative.

There are two reasons why it is important for educational leaders to incorporate philosophical analysis as an ongoing way of thinking: Philosophy explores important issues that act as a framework for decision making based on core values, and philosophy provides a unique kind of response to leadership issues.

Research revealed that the universe and humanity are much older, more dependent on each other, and much more complex than once believed. As a consequence, the question of evolution has been raised again but in a much more significant manner because this research has made it easier to catch a glimpse of the larger picture. The two laws of evolution related to an understanding of humanity are the law of continuity and the law of design.

Teilhard de Chardin's concept of spirit-matter is most interesting. He held that it is the stuff out of which everything is formed in the universe. In relation to the evolution of humanity, he hypothesized that because people possess the spiritual potential to exercise freedom and because humanity evolved from nonhuman forms, those forms must have possessed some elements of freedom. Humanity, of course, is endowed with thought, reflection, and liberty. With this consciousness emerged a new evolutionary process toward ever greater complexity; thus humanity will eventually reach a critical point of complexity that will require the ascendance to a higher plane. Consciousness makes people aware of the interrelatedness of social experiences and the need for better communication.

Human consciousness evolved from this and is the reason why people can develop ethical norms. The essential components of consciousness are thought, reflection, and liberty, which are operationalized through human experience, understanding, and judgment. The perspective on life that ushered in previous ethical norms is often referred to as the classical worldview. It perceives the world as a finished product and holds that the experiences of people allow them to obtain a clear understanding of immutable essences. With this viewpoint, people can have a high degree of certitude about ethical principles: They are valid forever. By contrast, the modern worldview depicts the world as dynamic and evolving. People interpret reality within concrete and historical particulars. Right conduct is formulated primarily through inductive reasoning.

As a consequence of this latter perspective, the distinction between the law of nature and the natural law emerges. The natural law is not a codified body of precepts but rather is used in its widest sense as those parameters that define the milieu of being. It is that which follows from the essential nature of humanity. Furthermore the natural law should not be identified with laws that explain how the natural world works.

The natural law can be discovered through discourse, research, and reflection on humanity. Human reason is the foundation of the natural law. There are levels within the natural law; the more complex the issue, the more deliberation, dialogue, and study will be required. The social dimension of humanity must be taken into consideration in all discussions about the natural law. Also, using the natural law as a basis allows people to enter into rational discourse concerning human conduct.

There are four aspects to the development of ethical norms: It is the responsibility of individuals and the community to search for what is ethically good; norms must emerge from human experience; norms should account for the evolutionary character of humanity; and the principle of proportionality should be invoked. From this point onward, it is possible for humanity to develop ethical norms not only in private matters but also in matters that impact human relations.

Social ethics postulates that the free decisions of a person can place others in situations in which they are required to make decisions. These decisions become the link with other people and may require them to act or not to act for good. Personal and social unethicality are thus truly dimensions of the same phenomenon. Unethicality is experienced as external, inherited, overbearing, and seductive.

People who act unethically incur a consequence that remains long after the execution of the action. The decision to act unethically becomes a core orientation, which in turn becomes the milieu in which future freedom is exercised. In making subsequent decisions, a person is restricted because of those prior decisions. In this sense each person is the ultimate cause of the kind of person he or she becomes. Thus people act from the totality of their being. A person's attitudes, dispositions, and powers are expressed in every action.

On the positive side of human conduct is the power of virtuous living that can strengthen an individual and even rectify wrongs committed by people against others. Thus an educational administrator can pursue ethical living through cultivating the virtues of prudence, justice, fortitude, and temperance. Contemporary understanding of the virtues is viewed in the context of human development, which is a process that begins in early childhood, extends into adulthood, and terminates at death.

Conscience is that human dimension that prompts a person to make ethical decisions. It may be described in two ways. First, it is that sensitive inclination that helps a person decide how to act in relation to a given ethical issue. Second, it is a skill acquired through experience that a person uses to make judgments. There are three common approaches to ethical decision making: strict consequentialism, mixed consequentialism, and deontologism.

Educational administration in contemporary schools and school districts is sometimes practiced under difficult circumstances, which cause administrators to rethink the value and meaningfulness of their professional lives. Viktor Frankl held the view that the search for meaning is the primary motivator in life for everyone. The term used by Frankl is the will to meaning, which gives priority to the personal freedom of each person to direct his or her life and to find meaning not only in major life events but also in everyday living. Viktor Frankl presented his concept of tragic optimism as a philosophy of life for people who have experienced tragedy. Optimism is not something that can be mandated; it can only be reached through personal suffering.

The beliefs, intentions, and actions of people are the elements that constitute the self-agency approach to suffering. People are changed by suffering, and it can be enhancing or destructive, depending on how the person decides to react. Everyone has the freedom to decide how to react.

ENDNOTES

1. O. A. Johnson, *Ethics: Selections from Classical and Contemporary Writers,* 8th edition (New York: Harcourt Brace College Publishers, 1999), p. 1.

2. B. de Solages, "Christianity and Evolution," trans. H. Blair, *Bulletin De Litterature Ecclesiastique,* 4 (1948): 7–8.

3. J. Hitchock, *The Web of the Universe: Jung, the "New Physics," and Human Spirituality* (New York: Paulist Press, 1991), p. 25.

4. de Solages, "Christianity and Evolution," pp. 7–8.

5. Ibid.

6. T. de Chardin, *The Phenomenon of Man* (New York: Harper & Row Publishers, 1959), pp. 302–303.

7. R. M. Gula, *What Are They Saying About Moral Norms?* (New York: Paulist Press, 1982), p. 18.

8. Ibid., pp. 18–21.

9. Ibid., p. 34.

10. C. E. Bouchard, *Whatever Happened to Sin?* (Liguori, Missouri: Liguori Publications, 1996), p. 23.

11. Ibid.

12. Ibid., pp. 24–25.

13. Gula, *Moral Norms,* pp. 35, 37, 39, 41–44, 44–47.

14. M. O'Keefe, *What Are They Saying About Social Sin?* (New York: Paulist Press, 1990), pp. 2, 7, 13, 16, 46–47.

15. P. Schoonenberg, *Man and Sin: A Theological View,* trans. J. Donceel (Notre Dame, Indiana: Notre Dame Press, 1965), p. 104.

16. O'Keefe, *Social Sin,* pp. 19, 20, 24, 35–39, 43.

17. Schoonenberg, *Man and Sin,* pp. 63, 76, 80, 89, 90, 91, 111–113, 115.

18. Ibid., p. 80.

19. O'Keefe, *Social Sin,* pp. 8, 12.

20. R. W. Rebore, *The Ethics of Educational Leadership* (Upper Saddle River, New Jersey: Merrill/Prentice Hall, 2001), pp. 28, 30.

21. Bouchard, *Whatever Happened to Sin?* pp. 35, 56–61.

22. Ibid., pp. 35–38.

23. Gula, *Moral Norms,* pp. 60–62.

24. V. E. Frankl, *Man's Search for Meaning: An Introduction to Logotherapy* (New York: A Touchstone Book, Simon & Schuster, Inc., 1984), pp. 101–136.

25. L. Richard, *What Are They Saying About the Theology of Suffering?* (New York: Paulist Press, 1992), pp. 1–2.

26. Ibid., p. 110.

27. Ibid., pp. 105–106.

28. Ibid., p. 115.

29. Rebore, *The Ethics of Educational Leadership,* pp. 45–46.

SELECTED BIBLIOGRAPHY

Cahoone, L., ed. *From Modernism to Postmodernism: An Anthology.* Cambridge, Massachusetts: Blackwell Publishers, Inc., 1996.

de Chardin, T. *The Phenomenon of Man.* New York: Harper & Row Publishers, 1961.

Copleston, F. *A History of Philosophy,* Vols. I–IX. Garden City, New York: Image Books, 1994.

Cottingham, J., ed. *Western Philosophy: An Anthology.* Cambridge, Massachusetts: Blackwell Publishers, Inc., 1996.

Ingram, D., and J. Simon-Ingram. *Critical Theory: The Essential Readings.* New York: Paragon House, 1992.

Frankl, V. E. *Man's Search for Meaning: An Introduction to Logotherapy.* New York: Simon & Schuster, Inc., 1984.

Lonergan, B. J. *Insight: A Study of Human Understanding.* San Francisco: Harper & Row Publishers, 1978.

Sartre, J.-P. *Being and Nothingness,* trans. H. Barnes. New York: Philosophical Library, Inc., 1956.

CHAPTER

6

Transcendental Leadership and Human Relations

There are several reasons why this chapter has been developed for this book. To begin with, there are certain observations about the current state of affairs in both the superintendency and principalship that have prompted the need to consider a different approach to leadership. These observations could rightly be considered signs of the times. Basically they are as follows:

- The milieu within which the superintendent of schools and principal functions is very complex, ambiguous, and stressful.
- Superintendents and principals are required to perform their responsibilities even though they may not have job security.
- Boards of education continue to cross the line between governance and administration.
- The superintendency and principalship are becoming more political.

In addition, superintendents and principals are often criticized for poor student performance on standardized tests, substandard teacher performance, outdated curricula, student violence, and lack of financial stewardship. While some of these criticisms are legitimate in some schools and school districts, it is not a widespread condition by any means. Superintendents, principals, teachers, and staff members are doing an excellent job in most schools and school districts. Furthermore most educators are genuinely concerned not only about their particular students but also about education in general and are usually on the front lines in the battle for educational reform. They are the hero archetype for the marginalized in society and advocates for equal educational opportunity for all children as a means of creating a just society. However, it is very difficult for most superintendents and principals to find adequate leadership theories that will help them initiate and implement educational reform, particularly from a human relations perspective.

In spite of all these difficulties, administrators, teachers, guidance counselors, and curriculum specialists are still working in school districts. Schools of education are still graduating people who want to be teachers and administrators. Accountants, computer programmers, human resources specialists, food service staff members, and all levels of pupil transportation personnel are also on the job. Of course competitive compensation packages that school districts offer and certain basic working conditions give some school districts an advantage over others in finding the best qualified people.

It is no secret that some superintendents and principals fail within the first few years of being an administrator. The pressures are extreme in many schools and school districts. Of course there is speculation as to the cause of such failures. In spite of the fact that there are problems, there are still people available to take positions when they are vacated. Some schools and school districts that have inadequate financial resources do have problems in finding both administrators and teachers to meet their personnel needs.

However, as set forth in the previous chapter, a major concern in the lives of most administrators is the search for meaning, which goes beyond the paycheck and prestige that come from being a superintendent or principal. The search for meaning may be identified in a very concise way as the transcendental dimension of leadership.

For this purpose, the term *transcendence* means a way of life dedicated to leadership within and on behalf of the academic community and profession, in contrast to finding an administrative position in order to just make a living. Obviously it is not being suggested that making a living is not an important consideration in the lives of everyone. However, without a sense of transcendency, superintendents and principals may concentrate on the performance of tasks and neglect reflecting on the overall reason why they became educational leaders. Without focused reflection, administrators are often concerned only with the requirements of a position in a given school or school district and neglect their responsibility to the academic community and profession at large.

Nature of Transcendental Leadership

Accepting the transcendence of leadership requires a person to undertake a lifelong process of discerning how to be of service to the academic community and profession while carrying out the tasks and responsibilities of the leadership position within a given school or school district. This sense of service is difficult to sustain unless a person has an agenda to be followed. Operating from such a theoretical base ensures that a person will develop and maintain effective human relations. For this presentation, that agenda consists of the elements in a transcendental model of leadership. The transcendental model has been repressed in Western society since the Enlightenment. However, in the last decade it has reemerged. This is demonstrated by the large number of books, centers of study, and popular publications that are constantly being marketed. In addition, technology has created a worldwide communications system that brings to our consciousness events as they occur in the most remote regions of the world. Thus people are introduced to the interrelatedness of every aspect of life, such as ignorance, injustice, and poverty. As a consequence, most people recognize that these issues are not location-specific and that they indeed do affect every person and nation on earth.

Because superintendents and principals are concerned with human growth and development, they are generally more open to the cultural differences that exist between people and nations. In like manner, they recognize that values and philosophies of other people can have a profound effect on them and the people they serve.[1]

In addition, during the last two decades a significant number of people have migrated from other countries into the United States. This has created a new challenge for superintendents and principals in terms of inculturation. The new immigrants must be able to interact effectively with other people in the United States. However, there is another important aspect to this wave of new immigration. It has brought a new georeligious perspective. There are now significant numbers of second-generation Buddhists, Hindus, Jains, Muslims, and Sikhs living in the United States. In addition, these religions are followed by people who are not from Western Europe; they are Cambodian, Chinese, Filipino, Japanese, Korean, Thai, and Vietnamese. Of course there are significant numbers of Hispanics and African Americans who have religious beliefs similar to those of Western Europe. Such diversity requires dialogue between the new immigrants and educators. It is the only way that true understanding can take place. The purpose of such dialogue is not to compromise beliefs but rather to examine and explain values in relationship to the values of other people.[2]

It seems to be a characteristic demonstrated by people from every generation to seek a relationship with something beyond their own personal existence. However, the transcendental is not easily understood and exists in the minds of many people as just a vague notion. It sometimes takes an event or an encounter for people to be conscious of this phenomenon. Thus a death in the family or of a friend, the loss of a job, or a divorce can sometimes make people more aware of the transcendental. Of course people have a choice when such an event occurs to either respond or not respond. People are free in their decisions even though they may be limited in the choices because of the circumstances. This freedom is the fundamental requirement for good human relations.

It may seem odd to connect such personal and solitary experiences with human relations, but sometimes people escape into inactivity when such events occur, and that type of response has a significant effect on the people with whom they work. Endemic to being a human being is the interconnectedness that people have with each other.

The popular and insightful tenets of depth psychology have significance for the way people react to such situations. The creator of depth psychology was Carl Jung. The most relevant insight of Jung's psychology for the present discussion is his emphasis on the primacy of the inner life that animates our external existence. This concept must be understood within the context of the limitations of human existence. People are capable of perceiving only a limited part of their world.

Consciousness is not a static phenomenon but rather a dynamic unfolding analogous to the process of waking up. Thus, with every new awareness and with every increase in psychic content, human consciousness is expanded by degrees; there is no termination point. Individuals must find a balance between their emotional and intellectual lives. This will bring self-knowledge, which in turn will facilitate human relations. However, it must be incorporated into every dimension of a person's life, both personal and professional. For Jung, the innermost center of a person was the self. The balance between the emotional and intellectual lives gives an authentic reality to the self—the person becomes wholly integrated.

Also according to Jung, the beginning of mature consciousness occurs when a person becomes conscious of the unconscious. This means that no meaningful change can occur in personality and consciousness until a person develops an appropriate attitude not only toward the unconscious but also toward the activities of the unconscious. Conflicts occur within the inner depths of the psyche. When they are resolved, a higher level of consciousness is reached. Of course most conflicts originate because of other people. Thus there is a reciprocity between consciousness and human relations: A change in one precipitates a change in the other. This perspective gives impetus to the need to be a reflective person. The quest for wholeness does not mean that opposites cannot be intermingled in the unconscious.[3] For example, a superintendent or principal can be understanding and tolerant at school but just the opposite in his or her personal life. These opposites can coexist in the unconscious and rise to the surface of consciousness from time to time. The true necessity, however, is the reflection, which helps a person resolve the conflict and eventually leads to a heightened consciousness. Conflict resolution in this personal context becomes a model for conflict resolution in the external professional situation.

These insights from depth psychology concerning the existence and functioning of the unconscious certainly have altered the way people approach and understand human relations. Everyone experiences events, the residue of which is absorbed into the unconscious. The feelings and emotions associated with these events often emerge from the unconscious later in life through intuition or during times of crises.

The awakening about the presence and power of the unconscious occurs when people overestimate their willpower and believe that nothing can affect their mind unless they intentionally cause it to do so by an act of the will.[4] Not only depth psychology but also common human experience continually verifies the fact that attitudes, images, instincts, intuitions, thoughts, and urges make themselves known to consciousness when nothing appears to prompt their appearance. In fact, this spontaneity is itself a result of other unconscious phenomena. Principals and superintendents sometimes place themselves in difficult circumstances in terms of human relations because they neglect to pay attention to the prompting of the unconscious.

Transcendental Leadership Premise

Thus the basic premise of transcendental leadership is that a person acts from the totality of who he or she is as a human being. Further, most administrators are generally aware of the fact that their decisions are influenced by more than just the immediate circumstances, and that the effects of those decisions can have an impact that goes beyond the present situation. When a superintendent presents a proposal to the board of education to increase the number of teachers and thereby reduce the pupil/teacher ratio, she knows that her decision is probably influenced not only by her cognitive understanding of the instruction process but also by the fact that she was a teacher and knows the psychological and physical strain that an overcrowded classroom can have on a teacher. The relationship the superintendent has with the board of education could significantly affect the way the board perceives the request for more teachers. In like manner, a principal who meets with a parent who is not happy with his child's teacher knows that there may be extenuating circumstances that are not immediately apparent in the relationship between the parent and teacher.

In these two examples, there are a number of psychological as well as theoretical aspects interwoven into the situations just because everyone involved is a human being who is influenced by many different personal forces. Thus the human relations dimension is always at play in educational administration, and the ramifications of the decisions people make will have both psychological and philosophical effects that could influence the way everyone will react to future situations. It is for these reasons that it is necessary to set forth a way to operationalize transcendental leadership.

Elements of Transcendental Leadership

Operationalization is a process that includes various elements that are activated in order to guarantee that a given leadership theory is properly practiced. Many different theories have similar elements, but it is the combination of elements and the disposition of the person using a theory that make it effective. There are seven elements to transcendental leadership. Exhibit 6.1 highlights these elements.

EXHIBIT **6.1**

Elements of Transcendental Leadership

Transcendental leadership

Utilizes a reflection paradigm.

Practices the principle of subsidiarity.

Acts from a political base.

Acts from a sense of duty and responsibility (see Chapter 7).

Respects the power of pluralism to resolve conflict (see Chapter 8).

Advocates social justice (see Chapter 9).

Formulates professional positions through discourse (see Chapter 10).

The first element of transcendental leadership, "utilizes a reflection paradigm," takes into account the importance of practice as the phenomenon on which theory and foundational values are based. Everything begins with practice. Knowing/understanding what is occurring in schools and school districts is the only way to evaluate effective leadership. Leadership cannot be a top-down phenomenon but rather must begin with what is taking place on or in the classroom, corridor, cafeteria, media center, parking lot, and playground. It also means knowing/understanding what is going on with the physical systems of the facilities. Finally it means knowing/understanding the attitudes, emotions, and opinions of all stakeholders. Administrators, teachers, staff members, students, parents, and the public at large reflect in their daily lives the values, accomplishments, issues, and problems of public education as well as the educational practices of particular schools and school districts.

It is from this base that school administrators can ascertain if what they believe in terms of educational theory really works. Does block scheduling work? How successful is teacher empowerment as a management strategy? What about the effectiveness of helping students develop critical thinking skills? The common mistake that many superintendents and principals are guilty of in relation to school reform is making decisions about what will work just by *fiat*. There is no question about the value of educational theory. Practice without theory is chaos. Superintendents and principals move from one approach to a different one in the hope that something new will work better than what is currently being tried. This is a regular occurrence in some schools and school districts, particularly where well-intentioned but ill-informed non–educational reformers with influence and an agenda can capture the attention of school board members.

All theory is predicated on a system of values and beliefs. Teacher empowerment is based on the belief that professional educators are skilled and dedicated professionals capable of making their own decisions about what works best not only in their classrooms and disciplines but also in education in general. At the school and school district level, this means sharing the leadership responsibility with teachers and staff members. Thus theory without values and beliefs is chaos. Not making the connection that theory is founded on values and beliefs is the same problem that arises when practice is not viewed as emanating from theory.

There is another important aspect to the reflection paradigm: There is a reciprocal relationship between practice, theory, and philosophy. Not only does everything begin with practice, but in fact practice can change theory, which in turn can change a superintendent's or principal's philosophy. Such a change in philosophy can further alter a person's theory, which will ultimately affect practice. Figure 6.1 presents a diagram of this observation.

For purposes of discussion, practice can be considered the first level of reflection, theory the second level, and philosophy the third level of reflection. Reflection is the process and paradigm is the method. This is a rather easy paradigm to understand but can be a difficult one to implement because reflection takes time and energy. Time and energy are commodities that most administrators do not have in abundance. Reflection requires a superintendent or principal to hesitate before making commitments and decisions. That is often very difficult to do when conflicts occur. But more important than the mechanics of reflection is the disposition of superintendents and principals to search for the relationship between practice, theory, and philosophy.

This search takes self-knowledge and commitment. It also takes the willingness to ask the question, "Where doesn't my practice, theory of leadership, and personal philosophy match up?" It further requires a superintendent or principal to bring these three elements into synchronization, which in some instances could cause discontent on the part of faculty and staff. A principal who believes that he needs to empower his faculty to take more leadership responsibility for the instructional program may find a certain degree of resistance because the faculty might view such a position as encroaching on their already overcrowded schedules.

The second element states that transcendental leadership "practices the principle of subsidiarity." The principle of subsidiarity has a unique history that originated in social ethics and social economics. The principle states that decisions should be made at the low-

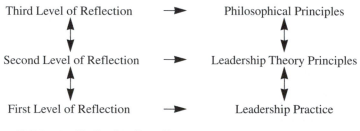

FIGURE 6.1   Reflection Paradigm

est possible level in a given school or school district. There is no question as to the relevance of allowing teachers and staff members to do their jobs without interference from administrators. There is also no question about the firsthand knowledge and experience that teachers and staff members have that make them eminently more qualified to handle issues and problems. It is in the way that superintendents and principals implement the principle of subsidiarity that problems occur. The application of this principle empowers all other staff members as they carry out the responsibilities of their respective positions. Thus decisions about budgeting, curriculum development, maintenance of facilities, public relations activities, technology implementation, etc., are shared responsibilities. As an example of empowerment, the superintendent becomes a consultant and mentor to assistant superintendents, directors, and principals; the principal becomes a consultant and mentor to teachers and other staff members. Furthermore the mentor responsibility of the superintendent or principal is sometimes adaptive rather than technical. He or she must help others recognize how their values influence their behaviors in the face of new realities.

Finally, the process of debureaucratization can lead to a better utilization of human, financial, and material resources. In this context debureaucratization means the simplification of the organization of schools and school districts. The term originated in the business sector and referenced the downsizing of many businesses and companies in the United States. Debureaucratization might even lead to the establishment of units within a school or school district that will give administrators, teachers, and other staff members direct control over the resources of the school and district.

The overarching concern is maintaining quality while debureaucratizing schools and school districts. Streamlining the organizational structure means having the minimal number of administrators necessary to ensure quality service. In turn this means changing the role of superintendents and principals in accordance with the principle of subsidiarity.

In terms of decision making, the principle of subsidiarity requires superintendents and principals to develop a comprehensive monitoring system whereby they will be able to know and understand the status of their schools or school districts to such a degree that they will be able to make informed decisions about which school, department, administrator, teacher, or staff member needs mentoring and/or consultation. While that may seem obvious, it is an issue that arises in medium to large school districts. In a small school district, the superintendent of schools and building principal probably will not have assistants and therefore are responsible for performing daily tasks that put them in direct contact with data. The larger the school or school district, the more the superintendent and principal must depend on others to carry out necessary responsibilities.

Appendix A, Monitoring Reports, provides a lengthy listing of reports that can be used by superintendents or principals to perform the monitoring function. Such reports will allow the superintendent or principal to ask questions that can uncover the reason why a given report contains information that is unexpected. Comparing reports from one time period to another will help the administrator establish a benchmark from which to analyze the reports. It should be noted that this is a rather exhaustive list; no school or school district will have all of these reports. The size of the school or district is a major determining factor. The more a superintendent or principal is removed from the front lines, the more different types of reports will be necessary. The contents of a report will also vary with the particular situation. For medium to large schools or school districts, the contents of the Human Resources Annual

Inventory should include the employee's name, age, date employed, sex, ethnic background, job title, placement, and education and/or training (along with the completion dates, special skills, and certification).[5]

This information will allow the administrator to compare how many new employees were hired during the last year, what the turnover rate is, when employees might retire, who has dual certification, the number of males who are teaching in elementary schools, etc. It is important to know the number of males teaching in elementary schools because of staff balancing. The ideal faculty is made up of both men and women, beginning and experienced teachers, and teachers from various ethnic backgrounds. It is for this reason that the content of the reports should be tailored to meet the needs of individual schools and school districts. The contents of most reports are obvious. However, a brief description of the contents of each report is also given following the title of the report.

The third element of transcendental leadership is "acts from a political base." For this presentation, "political base" refers to the human phenomenon whereby people try to manage the impact that their actions and decisions will have both on the actions or decisions of others and on institutions. The conceptualization of what constitutes a political base can be understood in a series of tensions. The first is *the responsibilities of the national government versus the responsibilities of the state government.* The role/function of superintendents, principals, and other administrators in this arena is to lead the school or school district so that there is no confusion on the part of other administrators, teachers, staff members, students, parents, and the general public about the responsibilities of both federal and state governmental agencies. Thus an issue that involves a student with disabilities may come under the jurisdiction of federal agencies. The concern is to clarify who has what responsibilities for children with disabilities.

The second tension is *the rights of the national government versus the rights of the individual.* The role/function of administrators is to ensure that the rights of individual teachers, staff members, students, parents, etc., are not in conflict with the rights of the national government. To continue with the example of students with disabilities, it is important that students who are not disabled receive the same type and quality of services from other financial sources as those mandated by the federal government for children with disabilities.

The third tension involves *the rights of the state government versus the rights of the individual.* Thus funding from the state for gifted programs must not set aside the rights of other students to a quality education through significant depletion of the general pool of money available for education. The role/function of the administration is to advocate for adequate funding of educational programs for all students.

The fourth tension is *constitutional rights versus ethical rights.* It may be constitutional to expel a student for having an illegal drug at school, but it might be an ethical issue if the school district does not provide an alternative educational program for such a student. Students who are free to be on the street instead of in school could be a threat to the general public, especially if these students cannot get meaningful work. Robbery is a common activity for those who are without hope.

The fifth tension, *the rights of the general public versus the rights of special-interest groups,* is always a problem when superintendents, principals, and boards of education react only to the loudest voices of the community or when the legitimate concerns of advocates are neglected. It is the responsibility of educational leaders to strike a balance between the rights of both the general public and advocates. Zero-tolerance policies concerning violence at school are such an issue. Expelled students who commit violent acts at school and who then are removed to situations without proper supervision or alternative programming could be a threat to the general public.

The last tension is *the rights of the marginalized versus the influence of the decision makers.* There is no question about the great influx of immigrants into some school districts. These people generally are not the decision makers in most school districts, and their plight can often be desperate. As marginalized people, their educational rights can sometimes be easily overlooked when a school district is experiencing financial difficulties.

The remaining elements of transcendental leadership require more extensive treatment and are covered in the following four chapters of Part Two: acting from a sense of duty and responsibility (see Chapter 7); respecting the power of pluralism to resolve conflict (see Chapter 8); advocating social justice (see Chapter 9); and formulating professional positions through discourse (see Chapter 10).

DISCUSSION QUESTIONS AND STATEMENTS

1. Describe the current state of affairs in educational leadership and how it affects the human relations skills of administrators.

2. How can the ideas of Carl Jung affect the human relations dimension of the superintendency and principalship?

3. What is transcendental leadership, and how is it related to effective human relations?

4. What are the essential elements of transcendental leadership?

5. Explain the reflection paradigm.

6. What is the principle of subsidiarity?

7. Define political base.

8. How does subsidiarity lead to debureaucratization of schools and school districts?

9. How is practice related to theory and philosophy?

10. Set forth and explain political tensions.

EXERCISE 6.1
Political Tensions Assessment

The following is a brief exercise to help you understand political tensions and the political consequences of those tensions.

1. Situation: Because of a zero-tolerance policy, a high school student is suspended for ten days for giving an aspirin to another high school student.

   Political tension issue/s: _____

   Political consequences of the action: _____

(continued)

2. Situation: The school district has an ineffective record of affirmative action in the hiring of women and members of minority groups for administrator positions.

    Political tension issue/s: _____

    Political consequences of the action: _____

3. Situation: The board of education has passed a policy charging fees for extracurricular activities because of the school district's dwindling financial resources.

    Political tension issue/s: _____

    Political consequences of the action: _____

4. Situation: The state legislature has lowered the age limit to twelve for certifying children as adults when they commit crimes at school using weapons.

    Political tension issue/s: _____

    Political consequences of the action: _____

5. Situation: The U.S. Congress has authorized genetic engineering that has the potential to produce children with predetermined intellectual characteristics.

    Political tension issue/s: _____

    Political consequences of the action: _____

S U M M A R Y

The current state of affairs in educational leadership has prompted a need to rethink the importance and value of leadership theory. Superintendents, principals, and other administrators work in an atmosphere that is complex, ambiguous, stressful, lacking in job security, and very political. Further, boards of education may drift into the realm of administration.

Administrators continue to seek positions in schools and school districts in spite of these concerns. However, there is a continual need for most administrators to search for a sense of meaningfulness in their profession. Transcendental leadership theory offers administrators the opportunity to practice their profession using an ongoing process of discernment that emphasizes the transcendental nature of leadership. This theory is founded on the premise that it is a human characteristic for people to seek a relationship with something beyond their own personal existence.

In order to prevent people from retreating from reality in this pursuit of the transcendental, the theory must be founded on the necessity of human relations as an anchor. A cornerstone for such an approach can be found in the psychology of Carl Jung. Jung's emphasis on the importance of the inner life becomes the focal point for transcendental leadership. Consciousness is the designation given to the phenomenon of educational leaders becoming aware of the relationship between their profession and their psychic life. Furthermore this consciousness becomes fully operational when a person becomes conscious of the unconscious nature of his or her psyche. It is the power of the unconscious to interfere with the conscious life that should prompt administrators to consider the unconscious as a determinant in decision making. Thus the basic premise of transcendental leadership is that a person acts from the totality of who he or she is as a human being. Administrators should be aware of the fact that their decisions are influenced by more than just immediate circumstances and that their decisions can have an impact that goes beyond the present situation.

Operationalization is the process that includes various elements that are activated in order to guarantee that a theory is properly practiced. The elements of transcendental leadership include utilizing a reflection paradigm, practicing the principle of subsidiarity, acting from a political base, acting from a sense of duty and responsibility, respecting the power of pluralism to resolve conflict, advocating social justice, and formulating professional positions through discourse.

The reflection paradigm is designed to help the administrator understand the reciprocal relationship between practice, theory, and philosophy. Reflection is the process and paradigm is the method. The principle of subsidiarity basically states that decisions should be made at the lowest possible level in a given school or school district. The application of this principle empowers other people as they carry out their responsibilities. Thus superintendents and principals become mentors and consultants. The ultimate consequence of this approach is the debureaucratization of schools and school districts, which also requires much more monitoring by administrators. The third element, "acting from a political base," refers to the human phenomenon whereby people try to manage the impact that their actions and decisions will have on the actions and decisions of others. This is played out in the way administrators handle certain tensions that arise between individuals and institutions in our society.

The remaining elements of transcendental leadership are explained in Chapters 7, 8, 9, and 10.

ENDNOTES

1. C. Gratton, *The Art of Spiritual Guidance: A Contemporary Approach to Growing in the Spirit* (New York: Crossroad Publishing Company, 1995), pp. 2–3.

2. D. L. Eck, "Challenged by a New Georeligious Reality: U.S. as a Hindu, Muslim, Buddhist, Confucian Nation," *In Trust,* 8 (1997): 10–12.

3. J. Hitchcock, *The Web of the Universe: Jung, the New Physics, and Human Spirituality* (New York: Paulist Press, 1991), pp. 50, 64, 71, 74–76.

4. C. G. Jung, ed., *Man and His Symbols* (New York: Dell Publishing, 1968), pp. 5, 24.

5. R. W. Rebore, *Human Resources Administration in Education: A Management Approach,* 6th edition (Boston: Allyn & Bacon, 2001), p. 39.

SELECTED BIBLIOGRAPHY

Hitchcock, J. *The Web of the Universe: Jung, the New Physics, and Human Spirituality.* New York: Paulist Press, 1991.

Jung, C. G. *Modern Man in Search of a Soul.* New York: Harcourt Brace Jovanovich Publishers, 1933.

———. *Man and His Symbols.* New York: Dell Publishing, 1968.

———. *Psychology of the Unconscious: A Study of the Transformation and Symbolism of the Libido,* Bollingen Series XX. Princeton, New Jersey: Princeton University Press, 1991.

Singer, J. *Boundaries of the Soul: The Practice of Jung's Psychology,* revised and updated. New York: Doubleday Anchor Books, 1994.

A P P E N D I X   A

Monitoring Reports

The following reports should always be presented in a format that makes a comparison with the last one or two years. These reports are generated by assistant superintendents and assistant principals. They are both qualitative and quantitative assurance documents. The process by which they are developed can also become an internal control mechanism.

Human Resources

Human Resources Annual Inventory
> Name, age, date employed, sex, job title, placement, education/training, special skills, certification

Affirmative Action and Equal Employment Opportunity Annual Report
> Name, ethnicity, age, sex

Annual Enrollment Projection
> Enrollment by grade level using historical data with cohort survival data

Annual Security Audit
> Number of critical incidents, location, people involved, disposition

Quarterly Fringe Benefits Usage Report
> Name, type of claim, actual cost, projected cost for medical, hospitalization, dental, etc.

Monthly Litigation Report
> Names of people involved and type of litigation

Monthly Human Resources Vacancy Report
> Position and location of vacancies due to resignations, deaths, etc.

Monthly Attendance Report
> Attendance by grade level and location

Annual Employee Relations Report
> Summary of process and issues involved in collective bargaining

Monthly Employee Grievance Report
> Name, type of grievance, disposition

Risk Management Incident Report
> Names of employees or students involved in accidents or critical incidents and whether insurance claims were required

Monthly Workers' Compensation Report
> Name, type of injury, disposition

Annual Workers' Compensation Report
Yearly summary of types of injuries and dispositions

Monthly Human Resources Employment and Termination Report
Name, position, and location of employees who resigned, retired, or were terminated and reasons for disposition

Annual Staff Development Report
Summary of types of staff development programs, program objectives, attendance, summary evaluation of the programs

Annual Teacher Evaluation Report
Name, placement, location, and evaluation status of teachers

Annual Employee Evaluation Report
Name, position, location, and evaluation status of noncertified employees

Annual Administrator Evaluation Report
Name, position, location, and evaluation status of administrators

Administrative Services

Monthly Budget Report
Revenues received, expenditures made, balances, cash-flow needs

Monthly Investments Report
Types, maturity dates, amounts

Annual Bonded Indebtedness Report
Status of bond retirement

Annual State Finance Report
Status of state aid anticipated and received

Average Daily Attendance Report
Summary of amount of state aid and state funding formula

Monthly Budget Development Report
Status of budget process in terms of calendar guidelines

Annual Budget Development Calendar
Objectives, process, methodology, and deadlines

Annual Vehicle Maintenance Report
List of district-owned vehicles, type of maintenance problems, cost

Annual Vehicle Replacement Report
Schedule of vehicle replacement

Annual Purchasing and Bidding Calendar
Process and dates for purchasing supplies, materials, and equipment

Annual Asset Inventory Report
List of items, location, value

Monthly Insurance Claims Report
Type and number as well as insurance companies to which claims were made

Annual Insurance Claims Report
    Summary of type and number as well as insurance companies to which claims were made

Monthly Accounts Payable Report
    List of accounts by type, vendor, and amount paid

Monthly Accounts Receivable Report
    List of accounts by type, source, and amount

Monthly Payroll Report
    List of employees, monthly salary, deductions

Annual Bank Depository Review Report
    List of banks, type of account, interest received, type of service, amount deposited

Annual Certified Public Accountant Audit Report
    Report from external auditing firm on internal financial controls and financial transactions

Annual Internal Controls Audit Report
    Report on internal financial controls and procedure modifications

Monthly Pupil Transportation Incident Report
    Accidents and critical incidents before, during, and after student transportation times

Annual Transportation Services Report
    Number of students transported, accidents and critical incidents, cost

Annual Facilities Maintenance Report
    Number of projects, location, cost

Annual Capital Improvements Calendar
    List of projects, starting and anticipated completion dates, cost

Annual Housekeeping and Custodial Report
    Number of custodians, position, location, evaluation, cost

Annual Food Services Report
    Number of students served, number of employees, position, location, evaluation, cost

Commodity Purchasing Calendar
    When and from which companies food products purchased, projected costs

Annual Property Zoning Changes Report
    List of properties in the school district with zoning changes and new zoning designation

Annual Commercial and Residential Building Report
    List of building starts in school district

Annual Technology Improvement Report
    List of technological improvements completed

Annual Telecommunications Report
    Location, type, and cost of telecommunications

Annual Community Access Report
Name of organization, location, retail fees, cost of using school facilities

Curriculum and Instruction

Annual Student Achievement Report
Standardized test scores and grade point average by grade level and location

Annual Student/Teacher Ratio Report
Number of teachers, teacher assistants, and students by grade level and location

Annual Technology Implementation Report
Type, grade level, and location of technological enhancements for instruction

Annual Instructional Supplies and Materials Replacement Report
Status of purchase and delivery of supplies and materials

Annual Instructional Equipment Replacement Report
Status of purchase and delivery of instructional equipment

Monthly Critical Incidents Report
Names of staff and students involved, location, issues, disposition

Monthly Instructional Supplies, Materials, and Equipment Availability Report
Status of new and replacement supplies, materials, and equipment requests

Annual Special Education IDEA Compliance Report
Status of compliance with federal guidelines for special education

Annual Federal Programs Compliance Report
Status of compliance with federal guidelines for federally funded programs

Annual Free and Reduced Lunch and Breakfast Report
Number of students served, location, revenue, cost

Annual Community Education Report
Number of students served and type of services received

Annual Pupil Personnel Services Report
Number of students served and type of services received

Annual School Calendar
Beginning and ending dates of academic year, holidays, other important dates

Community Relations

Annual Community Relations Report
Number of contacts, type, evaluation of involvement of community

Administrator Responsibility and Effective Human Relations

It is not as easy as it sounds to know one's responsibility. In fact, for superintendents and principals it can be difficult and at times ambiguous. In the most sweeping context, people have responsibilities to themselves and their families, friends, colleagues, neighbors, and acquaintances in addition to their communities, state, and nation. For superintendents and principals, there is even ambiguity in relation to the responsibilities they have to their profession, their school district, and those whom they supervise.

This section explores the concept of responsibility as a fundamental aspect of human relations through the eyes of five individuals who have shaped the milieu of the Western world, and particularly the United States, even though all of them were from Europe and all lived in either ancient or early modern times (except John Dewey, who was a contemporary). For this chapter, it is important to know that the terms *duty* and *responsibility* are used interchangeably. Each of these five treats responsibility from a perspective that is certainly relevant to human relations.

Categorical Imperative

Immanuel Kant lived a rather uneventful life for having such a profound effect on Western civilization. He was born in 1724 in the city of Königsberg, where he attended grammar school and its university. He lectured at the university and eventually became a professor, a position which covered most of his professional career. He never married and spent his entire life in the pursuit of knowledge. He was well educated in ancient and contemporary literature; he had no interest in the fine arts. Throughout his life, he demonstrated a keen interest and understanding of mathematics and physics. These studies acted as a diversion from his intense interest in philosophy. Kant was also interested in the political events of his time and was a strong supporter of both the American and French Revolutions.[1]

Kant practiced good human relations. He was a likable and kind person who was concerned about the social situation of other people and who gave financial assistance to many people. He was a loyal friend and treated other people with courtesy and respect. However, Kant's character is best understood in relation to his obsession with the idea of duty.[2]

Kant's concepts and ideas are found in three works: *Grounding for the Metaphysics of Morals* (1785), *Critique of Practical Reason* (1788), and *Metaphysics of Morals* (1797).

In the Preface to his *Grounding,* Kant set forth that the purpose of the treatise was to establish a supreme principle, which is his categorical imperative: Always act in such a way that you can also will that the maxim of your action should become a universal law. Thus Kant thought that his principle was applicable to all aspects of life, from politics to the moral requirements of duty both to oneself and to others.[3]

Both his *Grounding* and his *Critique* establish the foundation and method of Kant's ideas, which are contained in his *Metaphysics.* As previously stated, his *Grounding* set forth that pure reason is the supreme principle; in his *Critique,* Kant justified this a priori principle as the fundamental principle of the autonomy of reason in action. His *Metaphysics* treated judgments in concrete situations.[4]

Kant's ideas were influenced by rationalism and empiricism; particularly the rationalism of Gottfried Leibniz and the empiricism of David Hume. In his *Critique,* Kant elucidated his synthesis of rationalism and empiricism. The synthesis is truly a synthesis and not merely a combination. His position was that rationalism and empiricism, when separately considered, gave a distorted view of human knowledge.[5]

Kant's logic is interesting. After presenting the categorical imperative, he then tried to explain his idea of universal law in combination with what he thought was a willed idea of the natural order of life. Kant used four examples to explain his idea of duty based on the categorical imperative, which also establishes how the categorical imperative influences effective human relations. The first example dealt with the internal conflict of a person contemplating suicide. He tried to explain that self-love, which would eventuate in the self-destruction of a person's life, contradicts a willed universal law of nature because the purpose of nature is to further the cause of life.

The second example dealt with borrowing money when the person knows that paying back the loan would be impossible. Kant stated that such an action could not become a universal law of nature because it would lead people into distrusting the promises of others.

The third example was of a person who has many talents that could be useful. If the person neglects developing those talents because he or she wants to live a life of enjoyment, Kant stated that this could not become a law of nature because it contradicts the natural instinct of a person to develop all his or her faculties. Talents are meant to be developed for many different purposes, not just narcissistic ones but also those for the benefit of all members of society.

The fourth example is the most interesting in terms of human relations. It began with the idea that everyone should be left alone to deal with his or her own problems or good fortune, an approach which would also prevent people from taking advantage of others. However, willing that this approach become a law of nature would keep a person from receiving the assistance that he or she might need when troubles and problems do arise.

Kant wanted people to reflect on the categorical imperative using these examples in the context of how the principles are applicable to all situations. Of course, in times of crisis the reflection that is needed to analyze the potential human relations consequences of an action in relation to a universal law of nature presents a challenge to superintendents and principals. However, because superintendents and principals have the education and experience to utilize their intellectual abilities, Kant's approach is most appropriate.

In addition, superintendents and principals have the setting to utilize this method. Other than when dealing with crisis situations, educational administrators can find some time in their office to reflect on the human relations situations that are calling for a decision. Further, Kant's examples are relevant to the practice of educational leadership. The demands and stress placed on superintendents and principals can have a significant impact on those administrators' professional and personal lives. It is very difficult to find accurate statistics on how many superintendents and principals experience some form of job-related depression. Most administrators do not want to admit that they suffer from depression because of the potential effect that may have on their careers. Of course administrators are not a species set apart from the general population. Thus it is reasonable to assume that they suffer from depression and burnout as often as other professionals. Administrators must continually keep before themselves the need to maintain a healthy balance between their professional and personal lives.

Of course trust is an important element in developing and maintaining effective human relations. The entire school community—faculty, staff members, students, parents, and members of the board of education—must trust the superintendent and principal. This trust extends to all phases of their responsibilities. Without trust, the entire structure of a school or school district breaks down.

However, the most tragic situation occurs when a talented superintendent or principal neglects to grow and develop in his or her profession. It is absolutely critical for a professional to see the necessity of improving his or her skills and talents. It is sometimes very easy to become complacent with life's routine and to become completely involved in the tasks of a job position to such an extent that nothing else matters. Of course the challenge is to recognize and incorporate growth activities into professional and personal schedules. The objective is to become a better principal or superintendent, which in turn will benefit faculty, staff members, students, and parents, even if there is no immediate recognition of how this will take place.

Another situation that is troublesome occurs when a superintendent or principal encounters a situation in which he or she could be of assistance but neglects to provide it. There are many reasons for such behavior. Some parents become unreasonably demanding; in such a situation, a principal may conclude that their problems are their problems and not his or hers. The parents must come to terms with their unreasonableness, and it is not the principal's responsibility to find an answer for their every question. Some principals and superintendents even think that they will use such situations to teach parents a lesson on who is really in charge. This same attitude is sometimes used with teachers and others when they become uncooperative. Obviously this is not a good human relations approach to problem solving. The profession of educational administrator is first and foremost a people profession, and any behavior that portrays anything else is inappropriate.

The motivation that should drive a superintendent or principal is simply the responsibility he or she has to treat all members of the school community in such a manner that they will know their needs are being addressed. People are entitled to know that the educational administrator cares about them, even if he or she does not comply with their requests or meet their demands. Good human relations is founded on the trust people have in the superintendent or principal that he or she is doing a good job. Kant made an important point about duty when he stated that everyone may need assistance at some time in his or her life.

Philosophy of Right

Georg Wilhelm Friedrich Hegel was an idealist who was born in Stuttgart, Germany, on August 27, 1770. He did not distinguish himself as a student in grammar school. During that time, however, he was greatly influenced by the plays of Sophocles, particularly *Antigone*. In 1788 he enrolled in the University of Tübingen, run by the Protestant Theological Foundation. It was there that he met and became friends with Friedrich Schelling, who also was to become a famous author. They studied the works of Rousseau, and both men had a great admiration for the spirit of the French Revolution. Just as in grammar school, Hegel was not an exceptional student at the university. When he finished his studies at the university, Hegel supported himself first as a tutor but soon through his writings. Eventually he held many different university positions, including the chair of philosophy at the University of Berlin. He died in 1831 and by that time had earned a reputation that placed him within the ranks of influential Western philosophers.[6]

In 1821 Hegel published the *Philosophy of Right*. It is very clear in his writings that he considered duty to be a universal characteristic that liberates people from performing their responsibilities just to reach a particular end or objective. Rather he admonished everyone to carry out their responsibilities for the sake of duty alone. It is from this perspective that Hegel developed his fundamental principle about duty and responsibility: Do what is right and strive after welfare. Hegel's use of the term *welfare* applied not only to the individual's own welfare but also to the welfare of others.

For Hegel, duty is a transcendental reality even though it is founded on the principles of doing what is right and striving after welfare. Furthermore duty is the essence of self-consciousness, and the concept of good is an abstract notion that is subjective, unique to each person. In this context subjectivity is the inward certainty of a person that gives rise to the particular. It is a determining dimension of a person's psyche.

The will to do what is good is derived from a person's conscience. A person's conscience has no specific content; it is only in living life that people become aware of the objectivity of their responsibilities to themselves and to others. It is this same objectivity that allows a person to make judgments, and it is through this process that people realize their potentiality to make appropriate judgments.

Exercising responsibilities also provides people with an understanding of their freedom. This freedom is experienced as liberation from natural impulses and from the threat of self-absorption. The performance of duty is the way in which people become self-actualized.

An interesting point about Hegel's philosophy is his notion that private rights and the welfare of people are subordinate to the rights and welfare of the state. Duties to a person's family are also subordinate to those duties people have to the state. However, it is important to understand this notion in the context that the rights of the state are directed toward and in complete unity with the welfare of individuals. The litmus test is the degree to which the state provides for the welfare of people. Hegel asserts that people have duties to the state in direct proportion to the claim of rights they have against the state.

Hegel's position asserted that the state must create a legal structure that will provide for the well-being and happiness of people by providing them with services. Therefore, the state should enact laws that deal both with private rights and with rights of communities, corporations, and organizations. Hegel made an interesting observation about human services when he stated that they should be considered in terms of money in order for them to be justly distributed. He held the position that it is only when a person performs a service for money that he or she is capable of exercising free will.[7]

On first reading, it may seem difficult to see how Hegel's approach to the exercise of duty is applicable to human relations. However, his approach is not only theoretical but also practical. The theoretical dimension conceives of duty as springing from within a person, as directed by a person's will; from Hegel's position, that duty should be performed for its own sake. Hegel's approach is practical because it states that when a person carries out responsibilities, it is a liberating experience because it forces a person to leave the comfort of self-absorption through the self-actualization of decision making.

Of course the reasons why Hegel's philosophy is important for superintendents and principals lie in its mingling of the theoretical and practical. Because principals and superintendents are public figures, they exert significant influence by the positions they take on issues. Thus administrators should make decisions that emanate from their core values. Also, because education is a function of the state and superintendents and principals are state employees operating at the local level, educational leaders should keep their personal lives from affecting their professional decision making. This is often very difficult for some administrators. Hegel's idea that the happiness or welfare of the individual is the proper object of legislation can also become a guideline for superintendents and principals when they formulate school and school district processes and procedures.

Hegel's idea about money must be viewed within the context of social justice in order for it to make sense in contemporary society. His insight is proven from human experience. The abstract notion of justice is made tangible only through such items as money. His understanding of how financial compensation influences human motivation and actions is worthy of emulating. Teachers and administrators can make a decision based on their personal needs and values when they either accept or reject a job offer.

Duty of Citizens

Aristotle was born at Stagira, Greece, in 384 B.C.E. and was the son of a physician. He was one of Plato's students at the Academy. After Plato's death, Aristotle left Athens and was invited by King Philip of Macedonia to become the teacher of his son, Alexander the Great. Eventually Aristotle returned to Athens and founded a school, which was called the Lyceum.

The reason why Aristotle founded the Lyceum was to develop his own ideas about how education should be organized and to refine his philosophy. The Lyceum was organized like a union or society in which mature thinkers could engage in scholarship and research. In this respect, his school, having a library and teachers who regularly gave lectures, had some of the characteristics of a modern university. Aristotle picked the name for his school, Lyceum, from its location in the northeast section of the city, the precinct of Apollo Lyceus. However, the school was soon to become known as the *Peripatos,* which is the Greek word for walk, because the teachers carried on discussions with their pupils while walking up and down a covered ambulatory. When Aristotle had to leave Athens for political reasons, he retired to Chalcis in Euboea, where he died in 321 B.C.E.[8]

In reading this section, it is important to understand why it is presented here. It constitutes a theoretical base on which human relations can be developed and practiced within a school or school district. For Aristotle, the ultimate purpose for the existence of the state is the promotion of the supreme good, which he defined as the moral and intellectual development of its citizens. Historically the most important community is the family; when several families come together to provide for daily needs and other considerations, a village is formed. The state is an accumulation of villages that have joined together for the common good of their members. However, the state is different from the family and the village in both a quantitative and a qualitative manner. Because of the breadth of services that can be offered by the state, the quality of life is better, and a person can experience the good life to the fullest extent possible. Further, because the good life is the natural purpose of life, the state is a natural society.[9]

Athenian democracy was the base from which Aristotle developed the qualifications for citizenship. Athenian democracy was very similar to a representative form of government. Citizens were both rulers and those ruled; they participated in the creation of laws and the administration of justice.[10] All citizens had the same goal in life, which was the preservation of the state. In terms of virtues, Aristotle believes there is no distinction between the duty of a good person and that of a good citizen. Furthermore the virtues of a ruler do not differ from those of a citizen. Aristotle believed that it was proper and good that a person learn both how to rule and how to be ruled. In terms of supervising others, he held that the person who has never learned how to obey cannot know how to command. Thus the good citizen must know how to do both, which Aristotle considered to be the virtues of a citizen.

Principals and superintendents certainly know the importance of the family unit as the basis of the school community. Without this understanding, it would be difficult for the school and the parents to collaborate at a level endemic to good education. In terms of responsibility, the superintendent and principal must make a significant time commitment for interacting with parents. This can be a major challenge in a large school or school district. Of course the principal or superintendent cannot accomplish this alone but must enlist the support and help of teachers and other administrators. The quality of the relationship between parents and the teachers and administrators is dependent on the human relations skills of the professional staff.

Aristotle's notion of citizenship is important for all those who work for the welfare of children. As citizens of the school community, all are responsible for assuming the roles of ruling and being ruled, of supervising and being supervised, of being a good person and being a good citizen. Thus the notion of being an educational leader is certainly not restricted to educational administrators. Teachers, guidance counselors, and all staff members are called on to lead students and, at times, other colleagues. Administrators assume the formal position of leadership because schools and school districts are organizations, but the informal exercise of leadership is required of all members of the school community.

Aristotle's ideas about how learning occurs are consistent with the philosophy of experiential learning. Thus a person cannot know how to lead others unless he or she has learned how to follow others. Some first-time superintendents and principals tend to forget this tenet of human nature and neglect to give others the opportunity to be leaders in the school community. It is a responsibility of all administrators to prepare others to take their place when they retire or leave a school or school district for another position. This responsibility to help others assume responsible positions in the community also applies to parents who need to exercise leadership in relation to their position as parents. All members of the school community need to exercise trust in the abilities and intentions of others. Good human relations is predicated on trust. It is impossible to give others responsibilities that will allow them to become fully contributing members of the school community and yet be mistrustful. Sometimes the inability to trust is an externalization of an egotistical attitude that requires a superintendent or principal to micromanage everyone.

Meditations and the Stoics' Approach

Marcus Aurelius Antoninus was born in Rome in 121 C.E. during the reign of the Roman emperor Hadrian. His parents gave him the name Marcus Annius Verus. When he was very young, they died and Marcus was adopted by his grandfather, who provided him with a number of excellent tutors. The Roman emperor Aurelius Antoninus then adopted Marcus when he reached the age of seventeen; the emperor was Marcus's uncle through marriage. The emperor had no heir, which was the reason he adopted Marcus. Thus Marcus assumed the name of the emperor and eventually was persuaded to marry his daughter, Faustina. Together they had five children, and Marcus was succeeded by his son Commodus.

When Antoninus died in 161 C.E., Marcus succeeded him and did something that was unique in Roman history: He appointed Lucius Verus, who was another adopted son of Antoninus, to be coemperor with him. The Roman Empire was experiencing a number of natural disasters, including famine, floods, and plague, at that time. Furthermore barbarian tribes were invading the territories of the Empire. Marcus was leaving Rome to take command of the legions on the Danube in order to fight the barbarians when he composed his reflections, which eventually became titled *Meditations*. Marcus died in 180 C.E.[11]

Marcus adhered to the Stoic tradition, which is attested to in his writings. He was also a person who exhibited both profound understanding of the human condition and great humanity. Stoic philosophy originated in the writings of Zeno, who was a native of Citium in Cyprus. He taught at the colonnade, or *stoa*, in Athens, where his philosophy received its name. At various times in history, Stoic philosophy has been misunderstood. In essence it has three major ideas: Everything in the universe, even time and thought, is composed of physical matter; everything can ultimately be reduced to a single unifying principle; and everything is in the process of becoming something else.[12]

Marcus's writings are the private meditations of a great person. The content is philosophical, deals with human relations, and has proven to be of great assistance to many people, including public officials. The form of his *Meditations* is such that a reader may choose any one part without hindering the understanding of the content. Marcus considered philosophy to be a medium that could rightfully expound on the unseen powers behind creation and on the purpose and nature of human existence, as well as on how people should live their lives and interact with others.

The reason that *Meditations* is included in this chapter is because Marcus was a dutiful person whose personal reflections on life were influenced by his experience as a civil leader.

In *Meditations,* Marcus stated that reason can help a person lead a life that will provide self-control and courage in the pursuit of truth and justice. Furthermore he believed that such an attitude will provide a person with peace of mind in the face of tribulations that are beyond his or her control. In this sense, Marcus believed that destiny and duty are one and the same.

Clinging to destiny with zeal and truthfulness will give a person purpose in life, which will help that individual fulfill his or her duty. Marcus went on to explicate the role reason plays in human relations. Human reason is the common bond that unites all people in the pursuit of goodness because it is through the use of reason that universal laws of conduct are enacted. Thus rational beings, by their very nature, are required to help each other and in no way harm one another. Truthfulness is required by reason; therefore, to deliberately lie or even to involuntarily lie will bring discord to that nature, which is the source of reason and which gives order to the entire universe.

Marcus also expounded on a perennial enigma: Why do bad things happen to good people, and why do good things happen to bad people? His conclusion was that nature makes no distinction between good and bad people when bestowing pleasure or pain, life or death, fame or dishonor. Thus it is important for a person to live with a type of disinterest and to pursue duty without regard to these conditions of nature.

Superintendents and principals who measure the value of their professional performance against such criteria as being liked, receiving honors, or being happy will certainly encounter despair. The way to counterbalance these possibilities is the rational approach to carrying out responsibilities with courage, self-control, truthfulness, and trustfulness. Destiny as duty can also be a helpful concept for superintendents and principals, utilized by developing a healthy indifference to the actions of others and a continual striving to develop good human relations.

Pragmatism

John Dewey (1859–1952) is one of the most important individuals in American educational history. He was a prolific writer who published several hundred articles and approximately forty books. Dewey was concerned that the psychological and social dimensions of child growth and development were not being taken into consideration in the instructional process. He also understood the importance of the cultural context of education and viewed schools as the place where the fundamental principles of American democracy should be transmitted. Consequently his three factors in a good education were the child, society, and subject matter. The influence that Dewey had on education in the United States cannot be overestimated.

In order to instill the ideals of democracy in education, Dewey called for the active participation of students in the schools. Students should be expected to assume leadership roles in school or they will be unable to know and understand the requirements of citizenship.

An important notion that Dewey taught was that even though the majority rules in American democracy, it is critical in retaining democracy that the majority does not nullify the rights of the minority. An equally important notion is his understanding that truth is relative to time and place. Programs that are effective in a certain time period in a particular school may become ineffective at a later time. The manner in which superintendents and principals handle disciplinary issues can either enhance or negate student participation. Dewey held the position that disciplinary rules should not be overly restrictive, which is what he meant by being permissive.

Dewey spoke out against many educational systems in other countries that predetermined the educational future of children based on their performance in elementary school. Furthermore he viewed education as a lifelong process that did not end at adulthood. He considered the child a self-contained totality. No child can be dissected into component parts but rather must be considered in terms of his or her totality as a person. Every child should be considered in terms of their intellectual, social, physical, and emotional needs.

Dewey knew the importance of human relations even in the instructional milieu. He believed that the content of instruction and the instructional strategies should be developed with significant input from students. Human interaction plays such an important part in his philosophy that problem solving became the basis for instruction. Thus the curriculum should include not only general educational requirements but also vocational and practical arts courses in order to meet the diverse needs of students.[13]

There is general agreement among educators that teaching is most complex in the contemporary school and often brings a sense of isolation, especially because many teachers have little meaningful contact with colleagues. As a consequence many teachers have little input into school policies and procedural issues. In terms of human relations, this is not just an unfortunate situation but one that requires a solution.

A significant implication of Dewey's philosophy is empowerment—the empowerment of administrators, teachers, staff members, students, and parents. All segments must be empowered or no segment is truly empowered. In the practical realm, empowerment can mean something different in different schools. However, real empowerment must recognize that members of the school community have the right to direct their own lives, that they are provided with the means and opportunity to solve their own problems, that they can make short- and long-term plans, and that they can direct their own growth and development.

Empowerment becoming operational requires teachers and other staff members to be able to make decisions that have an impact and to have a certain degree of autonomy in providing professional services. Superintendents and principals should provide the organizational structure to allow teachers to participate in the decision-making process. There are two important conditions to empowerment: First, people must be allowed to make decisions about significant issues; second, people must have sufficient time and information to do this. Without these requirements, they will not be able to make informed decisions. Probably the most common obstacle is lack of information. Having information is a source of power, and people often do not want to share this power. Further, in order for the process to be effective, the level of participation must go beyond just making suggestions and should involve setting priorities.

Policies and procedures that affect the delivery of services are of primary concern to teachers. Imposing policies and procedures without significant participation by teachers in developing such policies and procedures will certainly elicit an unfavorable response from teachers because such an action implies that the administration does not value the dignity and expertise of the faculty. In addition, without such involvement the policies and procedures might not address the real concerns of those involved in the delivery of services.

The empowerment of students is similar to the empowerment of administrators, teachers, and staff members. Of course, student involvement will be determined by the level of students' maturity. In keeping with the philosophy of John Dewey, it is important to begin the empowerment process in elementary school because students will be unable to assume their rightful responsibilities in middle school and high school without such preparation. Empowerment is the best way to help students recognize that they are valued members of the school community. Furthermore it helps them understand that they have personal responsibilities, not only for their self-determination but also for others in the school community. Empowerment also affects the school and school district culture. Some of the elements that support empowerment are an intense focus on students, flexibility and resourcefulness, risk taking, and experimentation.[14]

A school culture that considers administrators, teachers, staff members, students, and parents as team members rather than as discrete and separate players in the educational enterprise is certainly a perspective that will encourage empowerment. In order to implement this perspective, all members of the school community must recognize that they have a stake in the success of the school. This gives everyone a sense of ownership in the school and will increase their understanding of their responsibilities. Of course, participation in decision making about important issues is the major element in helping people recognize their importance to the school community. The participation in decision making should extend not only to the instructional program but also to the operation of the school.

An adjunct focus on empowerment is the need for staff development. Administrators, teachers, staff members, students, and parents need to develop or enhance their problem-solving and leadership skills. Good human relations does not just happen because of noble intentions but rather must be inaugurated through a strategy. Courses, workshops, and mentoring are only a few of the many possible avenues for implementing human relations strategies. Self-evaluation skills are needed by all members of the school community so that they will be able to ascertain their effectiveness not only in promoting empowerment but also in implementing empowerment.

As elements that support empowerment, flexibility and resourcefulness are not common characteristics in many contemporary school communities. There are a tremendous number of requirements and tasks that are imposed on schools by local, state, and federal laws and guidelines. Time is extremely difficult to manage when superintendents and principals are dealing with large numbers of faculty, staff members, and students. However, without time to engage in meaningful discourse, true empowerment cannot be accomplished. Making mistakes and experimenting with new ideas are absolute requirements for effective empowerment. Developing a culture that encourages risk taking by both educators and students helps to develop leadership skills. This attitude can exist only if it is practiced by the superintendent and the principal. Teachers, staff members, and students will not feel comfortable becoming involved in creative activities unless they are convinced that the educational leadership values their involvement and will not be critical if they fail.[15]

As a final note, the empowerment of all students means that even those students who are underachieving or who exhibit unusual behavior are also provided with the opportunity and encouragement to become active members of the school community. Their unconventionality will not be an obstacle to their participation.

Human Relations Implications

The following is a list of seven human relations implications of administrator responsibility:

1. How a principal or superintendent carries out responsibilities will have a significant human relations effect on all members of the school community.
2. The manner in which an educational leader exercises responsibilities is indicative of his or her inner life and the true meaning of who he or she is as a person, as well as an indication of how effective he or she will be in establishing good human relations.
3. A good self-evaluation measurement of a superintendent's or principal's human relations effectiveness is that he or she would wish that everyone would act the way he or she does.
4. For principals and superintendents, duty is best understood if they learned how to follow the leadership of others when they were teachers or staff members.
5. Professional responsibilities are founded on reflective human reason.
6. Performance of duty has a social, and therefore a human relations, dimension.
7. Trusting other members of the school and school district community is the foundation of both effective human relations and effective performance of duty.

D I S C U S S I O N   Q U E S T I O N S   A N D   S T A T E M E N T S

1. Describe the kinds of human relations responsibilities that are typical of the superintendency and principalship.

2. Explain how the categorical imperative of Kant can help a superintendent or principal develop effective human relations in the discharge of responsibilities.

3. Explain what Hegel meant when he stated that a person can understand his or her freedom only in the exercise of duty. How does this affect human relations?

4. Discuss Aristotle's idea that a person cannot understand how to give commands if that person cannot obey commands. What are the implications for effective human relations in educational leadership?

E X E R C I S E   **7.1**

Assessment of Duty in Human Relations

The following is a brief assessment of your awareness of how duty affects human relations. On a scale of 1 to 3 (1 = disagree, 2 = partially agree, 3 = agree), rate the degree to which your understanding and feelings conform to the statements.

Rating

_____   When I make a decision required by my duty, I am aware of the fact that the decision will have a positive or negative human relations consequence depending on the manner in which I implement the decision.

_____ I understand that the manner in which I carry out my responsibilities will have a human relations effect on teachers, staff members, students, parents, and others.

_____ When I exercise my duty in creating administrative policies or procedures, I know that the way others view the quality of my human relations will have either a positive or negative effect on the way the policies or procedures are accepted.

_____ I recognize that exercising my duty does not mean that I should not elicit the help and advice of others.

_____ I think it is important to have a definite approach to exercising my duty that will also help me establish effective human relations.

_____ I should always act in human relations situations so as to will that everyone would act in the same way.

_____ An effective way to exercise my duty and create effective human relations is to carry out my duty for no other reason than it is the correct way to act.

_____ I believe that circumstances sometimes place people in situations they cannot control; thus the most effective way to carry out my duty so that I also create effective human relations with others is to act with indifference to consequences.

_____ A practical way to learn effective human relations skills in leadership positions is to practice these skills in relation to those who are in leadership positions to which I report.

_____ An approach to human relations that is most effective is to empower others in the performance of their duties.

_____ The human relations aspect of carrying out my duty must apply to all members of the school community, regardless of their influence or power to affect my professional or personal well-being.

_____ **Rating** (A maximum rating of 33 indicates that a person is significantly aware of duty issues. A rating of 17 can be used as a median score for purposes of analysis.)

SUMMARY

Everyone has a multitude of duties that are sometimes difficult to identify but generally can be classified into the following: duties to oneself as well as one's family, friends, colleagues, neighbors, acquaintances, employer, profession, and country. This concept of duty is explored in light of the perspectives of five philosophers, each of whom had a different approach to the subject.

The first is Immanuel Kant, whose thought was influenced by two philosophical streams—rationalism and empiricism. Kant's approach to duty originated in his categorical imperative: Act only in such a way that you can will that your action should become a universal law. He proceeded from this principle to identifying it with a willed universal law. Based on his categorical imperative, Kant gave four examples of how this principle can be utilized as a willed universal law of nature. It is clear from his presentation that Kant intended the categorical imperative to be applicable in all situations. The key to utilizing the categorical imperative is the practice of reflection in the decision-making process.

The second approach to duty is found in the philosophy of Georg Wilhelm Friedrich Hegel. His notion of duty is transcendental in the sense that it is abstract and universal.

Accordingly people are liberated from performing their duty in order to obtain a particular end but are admonished to carry out their duty for its own sake. In contrast with Kant's philosophy, Hegel's universal principle is: Do what is right and strive after welfare. Of course Hegel was referring to the welfare of other people. For Hegel, duty was the essence of self-consciousness; striving after welfare implied that people must decide for themselves the goodness aspect of welfare. This subjectivity is the inward certainty of a person that gives meaning to particular actions and becomes the determining dimension of his or her conscience. However, it is only through life itself that a person becomes aware of the objectivity of his or her duties, and it is his or her objectivity that allows a person to make decisions. Furthermore Hegel believed that it is only in the exercise of duty that a person comes to understand his or her freedom. Finally Hegel held the position that private rights are subordinate to the rights of the state, but the state in turn is responsible for enacting laws that both provide for the well-being and happiness of individuals and provide services for them.

The philosophy of Aristotle speaks to the duty of citizens and the purpose of the state. The purpose of the state is the fostering of the supreme good. In his approach to the good, Aristotle viewed the natural end of a person to be the good life; thus the state must be a natural society. A key to Aristotle's philosophy is his idea that citizens are both rulers and subjects vested with the right to participate in making laws and the right to participate in administering justice. He also raised the question of the relationship between the virtues of a good person and the virtues of a good citizen. According to Aristotle the virtues of a ruler do not differ from those of the citizen. In relation to the tenet of governing, the person who has never learned how to obey cannot know how to command. Thus the virtues of a good citizen lie in knowing how to rule and obey.

The fourth philosopher is Marcus Aurelius Antoninus, who used his *Meditations* to expound on the unseen powers behind creation and on the purpose and nature of human existence, as well as on how people should live their lives. He was a dutiful person, and the perspectives he shared were driven by his experience as a civil leader. For Marcus, destiny was synonymous with duty, which signals that a person may not have the luxury of deciding his or her duty but may have it thrust upon him or her. His basic principle appeared to be that experiencing life will give a person self-control and courage in the pursuit of truth and justice. The tool for this pursuit is reason. If a person channels zeal and energy with truthfulness into fulfilling his or her duty, no other power will be able to divert him or her from this purpose. It is through reason that people are capable of establishing universal laws of conduct, which are the common bond that unites all people in the pursuit of goodness. His *Meditations* also addressed the perennial enigma of why bad things happen to good people and why good things happen to bad people. Marcus held the position that nature makes no distinction between good and bad people when bestowing pleasure or pain, life or death, fame or dishonor. Thus people should live their lives with the same indifference and perform their duty without regard to these conditions.

The fifth philosophy dealing with school leadership is pragmatism, particularly the strand developed by John Dewey. Many school practices are attributed directly to him, and Dewey's influence continues to be felt in contemporary education. Dewey considered the psychological and social dimensions of child growth and development as important aspects of the instructional process. He further recognized the importance of the cultural context of education and the need to transmit the fundamental principles of American democracy in schools. In addition, he called for the active participation of students in school because they need to assume leadership roles in school if they are to understand the requirements of citizenship. Another of his mandates for education centered on the need for caution concerning majority rule. The rights of minorities must not be nullified through the rule of the majority. Change is supported by Dewey through his belief that truth was relative to time and place. In relation to student discipline, he advocated a permissive approach.

Dewey believed that education was a lifelong process and that instruction should be developed along thematic and problem-solving lines. Finally, he was also an advocate for a comprehensive educational curriculum.

One of the most important implications for educational leadership coming forth from Dewey's philosophy is the need for the empowerment of administrators, teachers, staff members, students, and parents. Teacher empowerment calls for them to be active participants in the decision-making process regarding policy and procedural issues that affect the entire school organization. Further, teacher empowerment means providing teachers with the means and opportunity to solve their own problems, to make short- and long-term plans, and to direct their own growth and development.

The empowerment of students has some of the same elements as the empowerment of teachers. Student empowerment emanates from a school culture that promotes an intense focus on students, flexibility and resourcefulness, risk taking, and experimentation. A school culture that considers students as team members rather than as products of the educational enterprise fosters an attitude that will permit the empowerment of students. In order to be active members of the school community, students must be given the opportunity to develop problem-solving and leadership skills. In addition, true student empowerment will be ineffective unless such empowerment opportunities are extended both to students with disabilities and to those students who do not fit the mainstream model.

ENDNOTES

1. J. O. Urmson and J. Rée, eds., *The Concise Encyclopedia of Western Philosophy and Philosophers* (Boston: Unwin Hyman Ltd., 1991), p. 156.

2. Ibid., pp. 213–214.

3. I. Kant, *Grounding for the Metaphysics of Morals* and *On a Supposed Right to Lie Because of Philanthropic Concerns,* 3rd. edition, trans. J. W. Ellington (Indianapolis, Indiana: Hackett Publishing Company, Inc., 1993), p. v.

4. Ibid., pp. v–vi.

5. Urmson and Rée, *The Concise Encyclopedia,* pp. 156–157.

6. F. Copleston, *A History of Philosophy, Volume VII: Fichte to Nietzsche* (Westminster, England: Newman Press, 1963), pp. 159–161.

7. G. W. F. Hegel, *Hegel's Philosophy of Right,* trans. T. M. Know (London, England: Oxford University Press, 1942), pp. 89–92, 107, 161, 194.

8. Urmson and Rée, *The Concise Encyclopedia,* pp. 23–24.

9. Copleston, *A History of Philosophy,* p. 92.

10. Ibid., p. 95.

11. M. A. Antoninus, *Meditations,* trans. M. Staniforth (New York: Penguin Books, Inc., 1964), p. 1.

12. Ibid., pp. 9–10.

13. P. D. Travers and R. W. Rebore, *Foundations of Education: Becoming a Teacher,* 3rd edition (Englewood Cliffs, New Jersey: Prentice-Hall, Inc., 1995), p. 64.

14. P. M. Short and J. T. Greer, *Leadership in Empowered Schools: Themes from Innovative Efforts* (Upper Saddle River, New Jersey: Prentice-Hall, Inc., 1997), p. 160.

15. Ibid., pp. 160–163.

SELECTED BIBLIOGRAPHY

Antoninus, M. A. *Meditations,* trans. M. Staniforth. New York: Penguin Books, Inc., 1964.

Aristotle. *Nicomachean Ethics,* trans. T. Irwin. Indianapolis, Indiana: Hackett Publishing Company, Inc., 1985.

Beiser, F. C., ed. *The Cambridge Companion to Hegel.* Cambridge, Massachusetts: Cambridge University Press, 1993.

Guyer, P., ed. *The Cambridge Companion to Kant.* Cambridge, Massachusetts: Cambridge University Press, 1992.

Hegel, G. W. F. *Philosophy of Right,* trans. T. M. Know. London, England: Oxford University Press, 1942.

Kant, I. *Grounding for the Metaphysics of Morals* and *On a Supposed Right to Lie Because of Philanthropic Concerns,* 3rd edition, trans. J. W. Ellington. Indianapolis, Indiana: Hackett Publishing Company, Inc., 1993.

Krackhardt, D. "Assessing the Political Landscape: Structures, Cognition, and Power in Organizations." *Administrative Science Quarterly,* June 1990: 342–369.

MacIntyre, A., ed. *Hegel: A Collection of Critical Essays.* Garden City, New Jersey: Anchor Books, 1972.

McKeon, R., ed. *Introduction to Aristotle.* New York: Random House, Inc., 1947.

O'Sullivan, R. *An Introduction to Kant's Ethics.* Cambridge, Massachusetts: Cambridge University Press, 1991.

Paton, H. *The Categorical Imperative: A Study in Kant's Moral Philosophy.* London, England: Hutcheson Press, 1947.

Rist, J. M., ed. *The Stoics.* Berkeley, California: University of California Press, 1978.

Ross, W. D., ed. *The Works of Aristotle.* Oxford, England: Clarendon Press, 1925.

8 Conflict, Pluralism, and Human Relations

The United States remains a nation of immigrants; that has been its hallmark from the very beginning. However, no longer are the immigrants coming only from Western Europe. Although there has been a definite influx of immigrants from Eastern Europe in the last decade, the most significant numbers of immigrants come from Asia and the Americas. This phenomenon is changing both the ethnic composition of the population and the religious orientation of the United States. It is no longer a nation of Christians and Jews but also a nation of Muslims, Hindus, and Confucians. The United States is now the most religiously diverse country on earth. Islam is the fastest-growing religious faith. In fact there are probably more Muslims than Episcopalians or Presbyterians, and perhaps more Muslims than Jews. In Chicago there are more than 1 million Muslims. The Council of Islamic Schools in North America counts approximately 180 full-time private Islamic schools operating in the United States.[1]

This religious diversity must be considered along with the ethnic pluralism of the population because within each ethnic group people embrace various religions. The issue of social justice is easily evoked with such diversity and pluralism. The rights and responsibilities of people as individuals and in the aggregate as members of various groups bring into play certain tensions, which are often manifested through intolerance and discrimination. Thus racism in the United States is a problem that affects the lives of not only African Americans but also Chinese, Filipino, Hispanic, Korean, and Indian Americans.

Of course discrimination based on age, disability, gender, illness, or lifestyle is further complicated by religious and ethnic pluralism. Thus the most important current issue facing many superintendents and principals, particularly in metropolitan areas, is providing effective leadership in schools and school districts of tremendous diversity. Such diversity extends not only to students and parents but also to diverse groups of teachers and staff members. Of considerable concern is recruiting administrators, teachers, and staff members from these religious and ethnic groups.

Such religious diversity prevents the use of religious norms as standards for human interaction. However, it is possible to utilize philosophical ideas about humanity as guides in developing human relations in schools and school districts and in preparing students to live in a diverse society. Therefore, there is a need to develop ideas about human relations that can become an orientation around which superintendents and principals can exercise their leadership.

There is another phenomenon that requires mentioning. In the present, as in the past, immigrants tend to congregate in neighborhoods where others share their customs, language, and traditions. However, there is a difference between the immigrants of contemporary times and those of past generations in that early immigrants were extremely motivated to become assimilated into the general population as soon as possible. They believed that such assimilation would give them and their children the opportunity to participate more fully in the American dream. Today immigrants from Asia and the Americas are more reluctant to seek complete assimilation and often take deliberate steps to preserve their heritage, not only for their own satisfaction but more importantly for the sake of their children. Thus, when considering assimilation, it is better to think of it as a continuum, with nonassimilation on one end and complete assimilation on the other. Nonassimilation implies a conscious rejection of other heritages in developing human relations norms while total assimilation implies a conscious rejection of personal heritage as a norm for human relations. Of course it is impossible for a person or a group of people to be completely unaffected by the heritage surrounding them or to totally dismiss a heritage shared by the majority of people.

This situation constitutes an additional reason to develop guidelines that can be used to develop effective human relations. A basic consideration has to be the engagement of people in dialogue about how to proceed and dialogue about how to deal with the issues and problems endemic to such engagement.

Aspects of Pluralism

The phenomenon just described is the situation in which many administrators will find themselves in the near future. There are three aspects to pluralism that will influence the future. The first aspect deals with the fact that values are conditional. The question of values has captured the attention of philosophers in every age. The responses to the question of values have been varied, but most people believe that there are a multiplicity of genuine values, which are different from one culture to another and from one generation to another. All values are worthy of consideration and must be contemplated from a perspective that understands the significance of diversity. It is also important to make a distinction between those values that produce a benefit and those that produce a harm.

Values can be thought of as either naturally occurring or humanly caused. Health and disease, of course, are naturally occurring; kindness and cruelty are humanly caused. Humanly caused values can be desirable or not, depending on the benefit or harm they produce. In like manner, love and respect are desirable and produce a benefit; humiliation and exploitation are undesirable and produce harm. Humanly caused values are generally considered to be universal and therefore applicable to all cultures, generations, and societies. Because of this, they are considered to be primary values.

Superintendents and principals certainly can model a humanly caused and desirable primary value when they treat other administrators, faculty, staff members, and students with respect. They model a humanly caused and undesirable primary value when they ignore or intimidate those whom they supervise. A superintendent who is recovering from a heart attack has experienced a naturally caused undesirable primary value while a healthy superintendent is experiencing a naturally caused desirable primary value. These distinctions become important only when people are in the process of discerning the various aspects of their personal responses to daily occurrences.

In addition to primary values, there are secondary values that vary with historical periods, cultures, individuals, and societies. The reason why they vary is the diversity in opinion as to what constitutes the good life. Social roles, a person's profession or occupation, personal aspirations, and personal preferences contribute to secondary personal values.

Primary values are subject to secondary values in the sense that there is significant variation in the way people seek the benefits of primary values and the way they avoid the harm of primary values. For example, seeking nutrition through eating is a primary value, but the way in which food is prepared and served is subject to individual and cultural differences.

The way in which superintendents and principals carry out their responsibilities is significantly influenced by their primary and secondary values. There is usually minimal conflict between people concerning primary values because they are universal. Conflicts usually occur over how primary and secondary values are implemented. When a school is experiencing an influx of teachers, staff members, or students from a different culture, the principal should reevaluate school policies and procedures because it can be disastrous for a principal to impose his culturally biased concepts of appropriate interpersonal behavior and relationships on others. Teachers, staff members, and students return to the culture of their homes and neighborhoods after school hours; therefore, the imposition of an artificial school culture is doomed to failure because it is a humanly caused undesirable secondary value. Because values are open to interpretation, they are conditional.[2]

A second aspect of pluralism concerns the observation that conflict is unavoidable because what constitutes life requirements and the values that facilitate them are diverse and varied. These perspectives and values are often pitted against each other in such a way that the realization of one prohibits the realization of others. It is for this reason that conflicts are unavoidable. Leading a good life thus includes coping with conflicts that arise because others have perspectives and values that they consider essential but that are incompatible with a given understanding of life requirements. This is why there never will be an effective compromise between those who are active in the pro-life movement and those who are active in the abortion movement. This is also the case when a person may want to enjoy something that has a value incompatible with her other values.

The notion that conflicts always arise from incompatible values is easily seen from these ideas. It is possible, however, to rank-order values in order to arrive at some reasoned decision. However, this rank ordering is necessary in each particular situation. Thus a reasoned decision involves accepting any one of a plurality of equally reasoned values.

A person cannot realize all the possibilities he or she values. For example, most people value both fairness and friendship. The notion of fairness requires impartiality and the notion of friendship requires partiality.[3] For example, a common issue facing neophyte administrators is the realization that they cannot treat those they supervise with fairness and be friends with them at the same time. The strain on a personal relationship between a principal and a friend who is a teacher often leads to loss of the friendship. In like manner, that same principal may quickly learn that some values of teachers, staff members, and parents may be different from his values which will inevitably lead to conflict.

A third aspect deals with the necessity of developing an approach to resolving conflicts. The conditionality of values will significantly influence the way conflict resolution is carried out. The key element is the desire of participants to arrive at a reasonable settlement. However, these conflicts arise in particular situations that require a practical and reasoned resolution, which usually occurs through a compromise. In other words, one side must abandon certain values. An effective approach to conflict resolution centers on the perspective that views conflicts as unavoidable given that values are conditional and incompatible. This approach contradicts common assumption that conflict is a crisis produced by the stupidity or perversity of the adversary. In addition, this approach posits that a particular conflict over a value can result in a more significant conflict or a series of conflicts because the value at hand is truly part of an entire system of values.

Because conflicts usually occur within particular traditions and between particular individuals, it is often thought that an entire system of values lies behind a given situation. Thus the disputants will have a deep-seated and vested interest in the conflict. When the conflict over values involves one individual, it usually centers on what the disputant holds dear in relation to life values. From this perspective, the entire value system of a person or a tradition will be greater than the particular conflict.

Objectivity is a requirement in conflict resolution because a person must be able to stand apart from the conflict in order to evaluate how the resolution of the dispute will ultimately affect the entire value systems of the disputants. The beginning attempt at resolution should focus on the values shared by the disputants. This will move the conflict from values to the means that will be used to reach a resolution.

The level of primary values is the place where shared values intersect. This is not to say that identifying secondary values will not lead to conflict resolution. The resolution of all conflict must rest on the quality of reasonableness. Thus, if a disputant gets the impression that a personal or political advantage can be gained by being unreasonable, she could hinder the resolution process. A certain value may be the pivotal point of an entire system of values, and there will be no resolution unless the focus of the conflict can be shifted to the means of implementing shared values. Flexibility and hospitableness are also key characteristics of disputants that help to facilitate resolution because hostilities can be mitigated and the real issues will likely emerge.[4]

Values are the constituents of a person's life requirements. The idea of the good life is also based on actualizing possibilities, but because many different possibilities may be incompatible, the good life involves selecting some possibilities and neglecting others. This situation requires a person to compare, balance, and ultimately rank-order the possibilities that he or she values most.

In order to carry out the selection, certain conditions must be met. The first condition rests on the quality level of the tradition within which a person lives. A person must have choices. A second condition is an active imagination so that people can consider how each possibility would enrich what he or she believes to be the good life. The third condition is the freedom to make choices, which depends on a person's experience and psychological well-being.

As people live out what they consider to be the good life, the possibilities for others are expanded. However, the notion of pluralism must not be misunderstood as requiring a common end for each person living in the same tradition because people have individual goals.

In summary, conflicts are unavoidable for four reasons: Many values are incompatible; there are many different valued possibilities; people can exercise their active imaginations; and people have freedom. Certainly this type of pluralism is cause for rejoicing because it makes life much more interesting and is a necessary attitude for tolerating the differences in other people.

In order to promote pluralism, it is important to understand that certain values are extremely important. It is also important, however, to understand there is probably no single value that always overrides all other values. Thus a distinction should be made between deep and variable convictions. Deep convictions are the safeguards of the good life, regardless of how they are conceived. Variable convictions indeed vary with traditions and conceptions of the good life. When considering deep convictions, it is important not to identify them only with primary values because secondary values can also have such a deep impact on a person that they are considered essential to the kind of life he or she wants to lead.

Because primary values are universal to all people, they satisfy basic physiological and sociological needs. However, the way in which these primary values are understood and maintained varies, depending on the context in which they are found. Thus it is important to view primary values as having significant content whereas secondary values are more concerned with context. There is an exception to this classification. Some secondary values are context-independent, and they always represent the manner in which primary values are implemented. For example, pro-life advocates may be against not only abortion but also euthanasia and capital punishment. Pro-life is the primary value, and the secondary context's independent values are against abortion, euthanasia, and capital punishment.

Acknowledging pluralism means accepting the fact that deeply held convictions are essential to what a person may hold as a life requirement. Of course some deeply held convictions are universal to all reasonable people and provide the base on which people can agree. For example, child abuse, slavery, and torture are unethical for all reasonable people. The news media are vigilant in keeping before the public incidents of child abuse in schools because they are such a betrayal of trust on the part of adults. All reasonable people recognize that such behavior is reprehensible because of deeply held convictions about trust and protection of children.

As a final note, superintendents and principals should develop a strategy that will recognize pluralistic, conditional, and incompatible values without advocating some specific value. Perhaps the safeguard of these values is the support of individual freedom to make defining decision in all areas of human interaction as long as these decisions do not compromise the integrity of other people.[5]

DISCUSSION QUESTIONS AND STATEMENTS

1. How do diversity and pluralism affect good human relations?

2. Explain the difference between primary and secondary values and how they impact human relations.

3. Because value conflict is unavoidable, how can effective human relations exist in such a milieu?

4. Explain how conflicts can be resolved.

5. What are the human relations implications of the fact that people experience content and context values?

6. Because some values are incompatible, what human relations approach can be utilized by a superintendent or principal?

EXERCISE **8.1**

Assessment of Conflict Resolution Awareness

The following is a brief assessment of your conflict resolution awareness, which should be helpful to you in analyzing your understanding and feelings about how conflict resolution strategies influence your professional conduct. On a scale of 1 to 3 (1 = disagree, 2 = partially agree, 3 = agree), rate the degree to which your understanding and feelings conform to the statements.

Rating

_____ When I make a decision, I am aware of the impact that the plurality of cultures in the school/school district community has on the consequences of that decision.

_____ I understand that cultural values are conditional in the sense that there are genuine values that differ from one culture to another.

_____ When I create administrative policies or procedures, I take into consideration the primary values of the members of the school/school district community.

_____ When I create administrative policies or procedures, I also take into consideration the secondary values of the members of the school/school district community.

_____ I understand that conflict is unavoidable because of differences in cultural values held by members of the school/school district community.

_____ I recognize that the reason why conflict is unavoidable is the incompatibility of cultural values held by members of the school/school district community.

_____ Because I recognize that conflict is unavoidable due to incompatible cultural values, it is sometimes easier to find a resolution to conflicts that arise between members of the school/school district–community.

_____ I understand that the key to conflict resolution is reasoned compromise, which requires those on one side of the conflict to abrogate certain values.

_____ I try to convey to those involved in a conflict that the reason for it is the incompatibility of values, not the perversity of either side.

_____ I am aware that behind each value there is most likely an entire system of cultural values that plays a significant role in the lives of the people involved in a conflict.

_____ I am also aware of the fact that there can be deeply held convictions that may be supported by either primary or secondary values that are pivotal in the lives of members of the school/school district community.

_____ **Rating** (A maximum rating of 33 indicates that a person is significantly aware of conflict resolution. A rating of 17 can be used as a median score for purposes of analysis.)

S U M M A R Y

The United States is a nation of immigrants, with most of them coming from Asia and the Americas. Because of this phenomenon, the United States is now the most religiously diverse country on earth. It is a country of Christians, Jews, Muslims, Hindus, and Confucians, among others. This religious diversity is compounded by the ethnic plurality of the country. This diversity and plurality preclude using religious or cultural norms as standards of human interaction.

There are three aspects to pluralism. The first deals with the fact that values are conditional. Values can be classified as either primary or secondary. Values produce either a benefit or a harm in people, and they are either naturally occurring or humanly caused. Primary values are generally universal and humanly caused. Secondary values vary depending on historical periods, cultures, individuals, and societies. Primary values are subject to secondary values because there are various ways in which people seek the benefits of primary values. Thus primary values are interpreted and, as a consequence, conditional.

The second aspect of pluralism is the fact that conflict is unavoidable because of the various perspectives of what constitutes life essentials. The realization of a given value may prohibit the realization of others. Also, some values are incompatible with other values; therefore, conflict always occurs between incompatible values. The resolution of conflict requires a reasoned approach that will consider a plurality of values because a person cannot realize all the possibilities he or she values.

The third aspect deals with how conflicts can be resolved. The conditionality of values will significantly influence the way in which conflict resolution is carried out. The key element is the desire of participants to arrive at a reasonable settlement. An effective approach to conflict resolution centers on the perspective that conflict is unavoidable given that values are conditional and incompatible. Objectivity is a requirement in the resolution of conflicts because a person must be able to stand apart from the conflict in order to evaluate how the resolution of the dispute will ultimately affect the entire value systems of the disputants.

The level of primary values is the place where shared values intersect. A certain value may be the pivotal point of an entire system of values, and there will be no resolution unless the focus of the conflict can be shifted to the means of implementing shared values. Flexibility and hospitableness are also key characteristics of disputants that help to facilitate conflict resolution.

The idea of what is essential to a certain type of life is based on actualizing possibilities, but because many different possibilities may be incompatible, the good life may involve selecting some possibilities and neglecting others. In order to make choices, a person must understand the quality level of his or her tradition, use an active imagination, and freely make choices based on personal experience and well-being.

In order to promote pluralism, it is important to understand that certain values are extremely important. This is best accomplished through recognizing that some values are deeply held convictions. When considering deep convictions, it is important not to identify them only with primary values because secondary values also can have such a deep impact on a person that they are considered essential to the kind of life he or she wants to lead. Although primary values are universal, they are understood and maintained based on the context in which they are found. Primary values have significant content; secondary values constitute the ever-important context. Some secondary values are also context-independent because they always represent the manner in which primary values are carried out.

It behooves superintendents and principals to develop a strategy that will recognize pluralistic, conditional, and incompatible values without advocating some specific value. Support for individual freedom to make defining decisions in all areas of human interaction would constitute a safeguard of values.

E N D N O T E S

1. D. L. Eck, *Challenged by a New Georeligious Reality, In Trust,* 8, no. 2 (1997): 10–12.
2. J. Kekes, *The Morality of Pluralism* (Princeton, New Jersey: Princeton University Press, 1993), pp. 17–21.

3. Ibid., pp. 21–23.
4. Ibid., pp. 23–27.
5. Ibid., pp. 27–37.

S E L E C T E D   B I B L I O G R A P H Y

Baier, A. *Postures of the Mind.* Minneapolis, Minnesota: University of Minnesota Press, 1985.

Habermas, J. *The Structural Transformation of the Public Sphere: An Inquiry into a Category of Bourgeois Society,* trans. Thomas Burger with the Assistance of Frederick Lawrence. Cambridge, Massachusetts: MIT Press, 1989.

Harvey, D. *The Condition of Postmodernity.* Cambridge, Massachusetts: Blackwell Publishers, Inc., 1995.

Kekes, J. *The Morality of Pluralism.* Princeton, New Jersey: Princeton University Press, 1993.

Moon, D. J. *Constructing Community: Moral Pluralism and Tragic Conflicts.* Princeton, New Jersey: Princeton University Press, 1993.

Williams, B. *Moral Luck.* Cambridge, Massachusetts: Cambridge University Press, 1981.

CHAPTER

9 Social Justice in a Human Relations Context

Pluralism can produce conflict, conflict can lead to injustices, and injustices always produce ineffective human relations. Thus there is a need to know and understand some basic notions about justice. *Justice* is the guide that regulates how people live out their lives as members of a community. Commutative justice involves the responsibilities existing among individuals. In contemporary society, everyone is a member of some society, even if he or she tries to live life as a hermit. Computer technology and space satellites make it possible to locate virtually every person on the planet. There are no places where a person can hide or neglect obligations to society. The choice either to live in society or to retreat from it by living a solitary life no longer exists. The very fact of *being* brings with it social obligations and the need for effective human relations.

Justice is one of the most important human relations issues in contemporary society because the actions of people can have an effect on others with an immediacy unknown in previous societies. This immediacy leaves little time to ponder the far-reaching consequences of actions, and actions can affect many more people than in the past. For example, the sophistication of communications has significantly altered the way people receive information. Information itself is always filtered through human perspectives.

The idea of justice implies that someone or a group of people can be treated fairly or unfairly. The content of justice is often referred to as entitlement. From this perspective, people have human relations claims properly due them. The most obvious social claims are services, goods, or money, but fidelity and respect are also entitlements. This is the locus of human relations because entitlements affecting an individual are present in almost every dimension of human interaction. For superintendents and principals, acknowledging and respecting personal entitlements are essential to the practice of leadership.

There are two aspects of respect as an entitlement. First, all people have an entitlement to basic respect because they are human beings. Not only people but also governments and institutions must afford others this type of respect, which entails personal integrity, liberty, and equality of opportunity. A second aspect of respect as an entitlement is that due a person because of a leadership position. This second aspect brings with it the expectation that superintendents and principals will perform their responsibilities with regard to faculty and students. Effective human relations cannot exist unless these entitlements are operationalized.

The responsibilities and obligations of a given society to people, called distributing justice, are met in the rendering of social services. In contemporary society these services include education, medical care, and police and fire protection. However, the economic principle of scarcity states that there will be more needs than resources. Thus, determining the scope of services and the processes for prioritizing and distributing services is of utmost importance. Of course there are differences of opinion about these variables, which give rise to the need for more effective and efficient means of arriving at decisions. In education, these responsibilities rest with the board of education, the superintendent of schools, principals, other administrators, faculty, and staff.

When a person becomes a member of a given society (such as the educational community), that person assumes certain responsibilities, which are summed up in the term legal justice. Education is a service that affects the entire society to such a degree that it is the responsibility of all citizens to support the efforts of superintendents and principals even if those citizens do not have a child attending school. Education is a necessity in a democratic society, and the type of education affects not only the kind but also the quality of service that is provided to society. Thus an important responsibility of each citizen is to pay taxes, which finance the necessary resources for a quality education; public schools are financed primarily through property, state income, and state corporate taxes.

In summary, the responsibilities and obligations that exist among people are referred to as commutative justice. Distributive justice consists of those responsibilities society has to the individual; legal justice consists of those responsibilities the individual has to society. These definitions set forth the responsibilities that superintendents and principals have to faculty, students, colleagues, and the community.[1]

The human relations and social justice issue of equal educational opportunity for children of color has been a consistent concern in public education. The following landmark U.S. federal court cases illustrate the magnitude of this social justice issue.[2] First, the Supreme Court ruled that racial segregation violated the equal protection clause of the Fourteenth Amendment in *Brown v. Board of Education,* 1954. This ruling resulted in the following court challenges:

Challenges to Desegregation
Cooper v. Aaron, 1958
United States v. Louisiana, 1960
Griffin v. County School Board, 1964
Alexander v. Holmes County Board of Education, 1969
Carter v. West Feliciana School Board, 1970
Northcross v. Board of Education, 1970
Dandridge v. Jefferson Parish School Board, 1971
Guey Heung Lee v. Johnson, 1971
Gomperts v. Chase, 1971
Columbus Board of Education v. Penick, 1978

Challenges to Busing Students for Integration
North Carolina State Board of Education v. Swann, 1971
Drummond v. Acree, 1972
Bustop Inc. v. Board of Education, 1978
Board of Education of City of Los Angeles v. Superior Court, 1980
Washington v. Seattle School District Number 1, 1982

Challenges to Integrating Faculties
Rogers v. Paul, 1965
Bradley v. School Board I, 1965
Bradley v. School Board II, 1965
U.S. v. Montgomery Board of Education, 1968
Davis v. Board of School Commissioners, 1971

Thus distributive justice has been played out in these court cases. However, the identification of social justice responsibilities is not always so easy to discern. Yet the human relations issue is always present. Superintendents and principals are responsible for ascertaining who or what agency has the responsibility in a particular circumstance because the problems facing every member of the school community are the concern of educational leaders as they carry out their human relations responsibilities. Human relations and social justice are truly one and the same. Considering entitlements apart from corresponding responsibilities is futile and precipitates many difficulties in the realm of educational leadership.[3]

The notion of justice also has another dimension—*restitution.* It is recognized that unjustly depriving someone of an entitlement does not nullify the responsibility but rather requires the implementation of the entitlement in addition to restoring what was withheld. Of course this is easily accomplished in relation to services and goods, but it is more difficult to implement in relation to personal qualities. Thus a student who was not provided with remedial reading services because she was not properly assessed should receive not just remedial reading services but a level of remedial reading services that will make up for the delay in receiving those services. This is not a common practice in most schools and school districts.

In order to better appreciate the responsibilities of superintendents and principals in relation to social justice, it is important to understand a human relations approach to justice that permeates the system of government in the United States. This is contractarianism, which sets forth that a political society should be designed by the very people who live in it. The needs of citizens become the parameters within which services are designed and delivered. Thus schools and school districts come into existence through a contract or agreement among the people to be governed. The purposes of the agreement are to provide educational services and to solve problems that are inevitable when numbers of people come together so that there are opportunities that will result in a better quality of life.

It is important to remember that specific governmental services are not natural to the human condition but rather take on a specific form through an agreement. There are many variations on this theme that have been analyzed and developed by many philosophers. However, only the contractarian philosophy of John Rawls will be considered here.[4]

A Theory of Justice

John Rawls is an American political philosopher who wrote *A Theory of Justice,* explicating his human relations notion of fairness.[5] The influence of Rawls has been extensive; he is considered to be a major defender of the social contract theory, which can be found in the writings of Immanuel Kant, John Locke, and Jean-Jacques Rousseau. Rawls's basic premise is that the best principles of justice for the basic structure of any society are those that would be the object of an original agreement in the establishment of a society that are derived by free rational persons from an initial position of equality. This principle forms the basis for all future agreements and should specify how human relationships form.

This notion becomes a guide for evaluating the fairness of educational services. In all Western societies, the original agreements were initially derived through many different means, some of which were violent; they were never neatly formulated through purely rational discourse. In fact, the murky remnants of the past are maintained only in a given society's collective consciousness. Of course the original conflicts were eventually reduced to writing and have come down to us through time as constitutions. Nevertheless, in subsocieties there is the possibility of observing or even participating in formulating an agreement. The policy formulations process used by boards of education and the administrative policies of superintendents and principal are examples of how original agreements live on in contemporary society. They are the original agreements of equality. Of course it is true that local ordinances, state and federal laws, and governmental agency regulations have established boundaries within which these policies are formulated. However, the manner in which superintendents and principals implement and interpret these policies can be guided by the principle of fairness. This is easily seen in school district administrative policies dealing with the rights and responsibilities of faculty, staff, and students. Perhaps the area most vulnerable to the fairness principle is the human resources function, particularly in regard to affirmative action and equal employment opportunity.

At the building level, a newly appointed principal will want to review and possibly change policies that deal with the human relationships among all members of the school community. Of course effective human relations is always a consideration in all regulatory policies. The importance of this perspective is in the realization that it is analogous to all original agreements on equality. The democracy that functions in the United States rests on the assumption that decisions are made by free rational persons. These same conditions set forth by Rawls are implemented as superintendents and principals enter into dialogue with members of the school district and school communities when formulating administrative policies.

Like all other institutions, public education goes through periods of time when it needs to reevaluate policies and practices for the purpose of renewal and reform. As the process of reevaluation is carried out, there arises the opportunity to examine individual school policies and the policies of a given school district in light of the human relations notion of fairness.

Rawls set forth two principles that he believed people in the initial situation would choose as a means of implementing the notion of fairness. The first principle is concerned with basic rights and duties, and the second principle states that inequalities can exist only if they result in compensating benefits for everyone, particularly for the least advantaged people in society.

The first principle sets forth that each person is to have an equal right to a system of liberties that is compatible with a similar system of liberties available to all people. The concept of a total system, of course, is an essential component of this principle because it establishes that the exercise of one liberty may be and probably is dependent on other liberties. Furthermore Rawls stated that the principles of justice are to be ranked, and he cited the example that liberty can be restricted only for the sake of liberty. Thus the liberties enjoyed by teachers cannot hinder the liberties enjoyed by students. One group or person cannot have a liberty that restricts the liberties of others. Teachers and students have the right to self-expression through the use of language. However, abusive language can be prohibited because it lessens the dignity of the person against whom it is used. Restricting the type of language that can be used by all members of the school community in essence supports the dignity of all members. Thus everyone has the liberty of self-expression, but only within the parameters of appropriate speech.

The second principle asserts that social and economic inequalities must benefit the least advantaged and that equal opportunity to secure offices and positions must be open to all. This principle of justice must also be ranked so that the principle of efficiency does not occupy the position of first priority. Affirmative action and equal opportunity in employment legislation and court decisions, along with legislation and case law that ensure equal opportunity to run for public office, help to secure the second part of this principle. The following federal legislation exemplifies how this second principle has been operationalized in our American society:[6]

Civil Rights Act of 1964 (as amended)

Title VII of this act provides that people cannot be denied a job or unfairly treated during employment because of race, color, religion, sex, or national origin. This act also established the Equal Employment Opportunity Commission (EEOC), which monitors and prosecutes violations of this law.

Age Discrimination in Employment Act of 1967

As amended, this act promotes the employment of older workers based on ability rather than age by prohibiting arbitrary discrimination. This law protects individuals who are at least forty years of age; it applies not only to employers but also to employment agencies and labor organizations. It is against this law for an employer to refuse to hire or otherwise discriminate against older workers in terms of compensation and working conditions.

Title V of the Rehabilitation Act of 1973

This law prohibits recipients of federal financial assistance from discriminating against people with disabilities in relation to the following employment practices: recruitment, selection, compensation, job assignment/classification. Employers are also required to provide reasonable accommodations for employees with disabilities.

Americans With Disabilities Act of 1990

This is a very comprehensive law meant to protect the rights of individuals with disabilities. This law is set forth under five titles: Title I regulates employment practices; Title II regulates services, programs, and activities of state and local governmental agencies; Title III applies to public accommodations provided by the private sector; Title IV requires telecommunications companies to provide telecommunications relay services for people with hearing or speech disabilities; and Title V contains a number of provisions including one prohibiting retaliation against persons seeking redress under this act.

Rawls's principle of just savings must be invoked when considering how inequities can benefit the least advantaged. Therefore, a school district that needs to raise the level of teachers' salaries because the superintendent is finding it difficult to recruit and hire quality teachers may place before the voters a referendum that will increase the amount of property taxes each property owner will pay in future years because this increase in taxation will benefit not only the present generation of students but also future generations.

The application of Rawls's just savings principle in this example demonstrates that the present generation of taxpayers will bear the burden of higher taxes in order to enhance the opportunities of upcoming generations. If there is a lack of quality teachers, the educational programs will continue to deteriorate, and ultimately the cost to bring programs back to the appropriate level will be much higher. In addition, salaries will have to be raised to the point at which it will be necessary to significantly increase the amount of taxes in order to attract the caliber of teachers required by the educational program needs of the students. Consequently future generations are saved from becoming the least advantaged through the present generation of taxpayers.

In the United States, these principles of justice are embodied in certain documents that are the cornerstones on which the United States was founded. In addition to the Constitution of the United States, the Bill of Rights and the Declaration of Independence contain the principles concerning justice set forth in this chapter.

DISCUSSION QUESTIONS AND STATEMENTS

1. Describe the various forms of social justice.

2. How do these various forms of social justice affect human relations?

3. What did John Rawls mean when he asserted that justice is fairness?

4. Elucidate Rawls's principle of justice as it affects human relations.

EXERCISE 9.1

Assessment of Social Justice Awareness

The following is a brief assessment of your social justice awareness, which should be helpful to you in analyzing your understanding and feelings about how social justice influences your professional conduct. On a scale of 1 to 3 (1 = disagree, 2 = partially agree, 3 = agree), rate the degree to which your understanding and feelings conform to the statements.

Rating

_____ When I make a decision, I am aware of the fact that the consequences of that decision could have far-reaching effects on the rights of other people.

_____ In all my interactions with people, I am always cognizant of the right they have to be treated fairly.

_____ When I create administrative policies and procedures, I am aware of my responsibility to protect the rights of other administrators, teachers, staff members, students, and parents, even if it means making my job harder.

_____ I recognize that everyone has a right to respect, even when someone has violated a school or school district policy or procedure.

_____ Because of my contractual obligation to the school district, I realize that I have a responsibility in justice to perform my responsibilities to the highest level possible.

_____ I always consider the right of taxpayers to full disclosure of the school district's use of tax money.

_____ I understand that the community has a right to use school and school district facilities for appropriate purposes, even when this inconveniences the staff or myself.

_____ When I consider the level and scope of services available to other administrators, teachers, staff members, students, and parents, I recognize that they have a social justice right to these services.

_____ I am comfortable with the notion that all the assets of the school district are owned by the taxpayers in the aggregate and that I am the custodian of those assets.

_____ I completely subscribe to and, when possible, model the idea that all people have a right to equal opportunities in the school or school district.

_____ The people who are least advantaged in a particular area of their lives have a right to assistance in order to help them achieve equality with those who are advantaged.

_____ **Rating** (A maximum rating of 33 indicates that a person is significantly aware of social justice issues. A rating of 17 can be used as a median score for purposes of analysis.)

SUMMARY

Justice is the human relations guide that regulates how people live out their lives as members of a given community. The substance of justice is entitlement, which refers to those rights to which individuals and groups of people have a claim. Commutative justice involves those responsibilities that exist among individuals. The responsibilities of society to the individual are called distributive justice. The responsibilities of each person to society are termed legal justice. Justice also involves restitution, which is the right of a person to have a withheld entitlement restored.

Contractarianism is a political philosophy that sets forth the notion that society should be designed by the very people who live in it. Thus government comes into existence through a contract or agreement among the people to be governed.

John Rawls is a contemporary contractarian. In his book *A Theory of Justice,* he described justice in terms of fairness. His basic premise is that the best principles of justice for the basic structure of any society are those that would be the object of an original agreement in the establishment of a society. These principles would be derived by free rational people from an initial position of equality. Rawls elucidated two principles he believed people would choose in the initial situation in order to implement the notion of fairness: The first principle asserts that each person is to have an equal right to a system of liberties that is compatible with a similar system of liberties available to all people; the second principle asserts that social and economic inequalities must benefit the least advantaged and that equal opportunity to secure offices and positions must be open to all. In explaining how present inequities may benefit the least advantaged, he developed the principle of just savings.

E N D N O T E S

1. R. W. Rebore, *The Ethics of Educational Leadership* (Upper Saddle River, New Jersey: Merrill/Prentice Hall, 2001), pp. 227–238.

2. Ibid., p. 230.

3. C. E. Bouchard, *Whatever Happened to Sin?* (Liguori, Missouri: Liguori Publications, 1996), p. 59.

4. J. O. Urmson and J. Rée, eds., *The Concise Encyclopedia of Western Philosophy and Philosophers* (Boston: Unwin Hyman Ltd., 1991), pp. 250–251.

5. J. Rawls, *A Theory of Justice* (Cambridge, Massachusetts: Belknap Press of Harvard University Press, 1971), pp. 11–12, 14–15, 61, 302–303.

6. Rebore, *The Ethics of Educational Leadership,* p. 233.

S E L E C T E D   B I B L I O G R A P H Y

Berlin, I. "Two Concepts of Liberty," in *Four Essays on Liberty.* Oxford, England: Oxford University Press, 1969.

Nagel, T. *Mortal Questions.* Cambridge, Massachusetts: Cambridge University Press, 1979.

Nussbaum, M. C. *The Fragility of Goodness.* Cambridge, Massachusetts: Cambridge University Press, 1986.

Rawls, J. *A Theory of Justice.* Cambridge, Massachusetts: Belknap Press of Harvard University Press, 1971.

Raz, J. *The Morality of Freedom.* Oxford, England: Clarendon Press, 1986.

Sen, A. *On Ethics & Economics.* Cambridge, Massachusetts: Blackwell Publishers, Inc., 1994.

10 Public Discourse in a Human Relations Context

Implementation of the pluralistic perspective is not only a human relations issue but also a political issue because all school districts are governed at the local level by either elected or appointed officials who are commonly referred to as the board of education.[1] In addition, federal and state revenues supporting public education are appropriated by elected officials. The property tax provides the bulk of money utilized in developing and sustaining public education. This tax revenue is appropriated by direct vote of citizens. Also bond revenues, which are used to build school buildings, are authorized by direct vote of the people. The decision to ask voters for an increase in property taxes or to place before the voters a bond referendum is that of the board of education. Thus superintendents and principals are called on to expend public monies according to the dictates of Congress and state legislatures. In like manner, they are called on to expend property taxes and bond issues in accordance with the wishes of the taxpayers in each school district.

An important responsibility of the superintendent of schools is to make recommendations to the local board of education when educational expenses require an increase in property taxes or when capital improvements are necessary and are beyond the scope of the annual budget. The bonding process is placed in motion through the leadership of the superintendent of schools, with the approval of the board of education.

It is not only a common and appropriate practice but also effective human relations for superintendents and principals to engage the constituents of the school district and individual schools in public discourse before recommendations are made to the board of education. It is also common practice for boards of education to engage the public in discourse before they create policies affecting citizens in general as well as parents and students. Such issues as the budget, curriculum development, and student rights and responsibilities are often topics of discussion at public forums.

The basis for this type of discussion is the concept that legislators and school board members are public officials responsible to the people who elected them. Voters demand to be acknowledged as having ideas and opinions, which they want their representatives to know and act on. Politicians certainly know the consequences of ignoring advocacy groups and parents of students when they enact legislation or policies affecting education. Of course superintendents and principals are equally vulnerable to that same reality if they ignore people when they formulate educational recommendations or create administrative policies and procedures.

The human relations concern of people is justified because the extensive powers of government could easily create unwanted and inappropriate legislation and policies affecting education if citizens are not diligent in monitoring the actions of elected officials.

Nature of Public Discourse

Jürgen Habermas is a contemporary philosopher who viewed public discourse as a method that can be used to resolve conflicting interests and can result in more appropriate and just decisions. He stated that the pluralism of contemporary life is such that it is impossible to come to final answers about most issues. The opinions and ideas of individuals and groups are rooted in particular traditions to such an extent that general prescriptions are impossible to formulate. What is meant by the good life is so specific to particular life-worlds that immediate conflicts are sure to arise in any discourse. Thus educational issues cannot be prescriptive.[2]

However, the pluralism of many contemporary school districts does not preclude the establishment of narrower human relations guidelines because the purpose of such guidelines is to adjudicate conflicts in a fair manner. Such a guide would have universal appeal because of the many conflicts that arise about what is fair and equitable in society in general as well as in specific subsocieties such as a given school district. In this context, effective human relations becomes a willed guideline binding on everyone. Embodied within Habermas's theoretical design is a procedure for ethical argumentation, which is reasoned agreement by those who will be affected by the guideline. The central principle of Habermas's *discourse* is that the validity of a norm or guideline rests on the acceptability of the consequences of the guideline by all participants in the discourse. Thus there is a shift away from the solitary reflection of individuals to the community of subjects in dialogue and discourse.[3] The fairness of a guideline cannot exist only in the minds of those in administrative or policy-making positions but rather must be discussed openly with other people. In Habermas's model, each person must be willing and able to appreciate the perspective of others; thus there is a sense of empathy built into the process.[4]

In his book *Moral Consciousness and Communicative Action,* Habermas demonstrated the relationship between conceptual issues and empirical research. This he accomplished by discussing the relationship of discourse to social action through an examination of research in social psychology as it pertains to ethical and interpersonal development.

The communication that occurs in everyday life touches on significant issues and problems. However, there is little insight into how this communication can effectively address the complexities of life and lead to equitable solutions. Habermas believed that the overarching problem is isolation, which has been perpetrated by science, technology, and the arts. He also believed that the philosophizing taking place in contemporary society by those who have the status to demand attention tends to bring culture into the discussion as a way of arbitrating a hope that this will bring about consensus. However, Habermas stated that philosophers should assume the role of mediator instead of arbitrator because arbitration tends to give an answer whereas mediation seeks understanding through facilitation. This is an important human relations distinction because it provides a framework within which people can communicate in a nondefensive manner. In this context everyday communication can lead to influencing based reason rather than on coercion. The claims that individuals set forth in defense of their positions can transcend the present and become the basis for future discourse.

When a superintendent or principal is confronted by a group of parents complaining that the administration does not understand the importance of interscholastic basketball to the school community because there is no money in the budget to replace the gymnasium floor, the administrator can present his or her position on a number of occasions with rational argumentation. Thus the superintendent or principal begins to establish a human relations approach to discourse that is based on rational argumentation. This contrasts with the emotional argumentation put forth by many opponents.

Furthermore, through this approach the superintendent or principal is situating the board of education so that the board can make a reasoned decision about budget allocations rather than succumb to those who are the most vocal. Thus Habermas's principle of *universalization* is operationalized because the discourse that took place between the parents, the superintendent or principal, and the board of education had a basis in reason. This reasoned position of the administration was derived through discourse rather than in isolation.

Habermas systematically addressed how public discourse is actualized. He made an imperative assertion by stating that participants to any discourse must agree with his principle of Universalization. Further, this principle acts as a rule of argumentation that he referred to as the transcendental-pragmatic argument. Habermas identified three levels of presuppositions for argumentation. First is the logical-semantic level, which in itself has no human relations content. For this reason it is not the best point of departure for the transcendental-pragmatic argument. The second is the dialectical level of procedures. This allows participants to test out validity claims that have become problematic. At this level, the participants in discourse are in unrestrained competition for better argumentation. The third is the rhetorical level of processes that presupposes an unrestricted communication community as an ideal condition. Participants are free from external and internal coercion other than the force of the best argument. At this point, there is a cooperative search for truth.

Habermas also developed rules for discourse, which are not rules in the traditional sense but rather are the form within which an argument should take place. In public discourse, rules are implicit and intuitive. They are the pragmatic presuppositions of this type of speech, and it is necessary to acknowledge them only to the degree that will allow free argumentation. In contemporary society, it is also necessary to institutionalize discourse because of the social context that is limited by time and space. Thus the topics to be discussed and the contributions of participants must be organized in terms of opening, adjournment, and resumption of discussion. In order for participants to be free in their discourse, the content must not be predetermined; also participants must give at least implicit assent to the discourse rules. These conditions will ultimately lead to operationalizing the principle of Universalization. This principle states that only those guidelines that meet the approval of the participants in the practical discourse can be valid.[5]

In his book *Justification and Application: Remarks on Discourse Ethics,* Habermas further explained his theory in an interview format, which helps to pinpoint specific issues about his theory.[6] Only four questions are dealt with in this presentation. The first question asks why Habermas focused on justice in his theory. He began his answer by reinforcing his position that conviction of a rationally motivated agreement is the objective of his theory. By this he meant that discourse can be effective only if it is applied to questions that can be dealt with through impartial judgment. This implies that the process will hopefully lead to an answer equally beneficial to all stakeholders. Thus human relations is central to this process.

In the second question, Habermas dealt with an ambiguity in his theory, that is, whether the participants in a discourse can eventually agree to disagree. The answer emphasizes the procedure of discourse, which is meant to generate convictions rather than consensus. There are various kinds of discourse, such as those dealing with self-understanding, that can be very beneficial to the participants. However, these do not constitute true discourse, which is the objective of Habermas's theory. This second question also points out the confusion found in the terms used by Habermas. The most common designation of his theory is discourse ethics, which implies that discussion is a basic human responsibility.

In his answer, Habermas made a further distinction between political will formation and public discourse. *Political will formation* occurs within a given period of time. For example, legislatures have time constraints within which individual legislators try to understand the will of the people and bring about compromise with other legislators in order to complete their task within a given time frame. The procedure for political will formation should include aspects of belief formation so that a majority-rule decision is reached under true discourse conditions.

In the third question, Habermas dealt with the issue of whether de facto social norms must be neglected in order to implement true public discourse. Habermas stated that people adhere to norms in the same way that they acknowledge truth: People hold their theories as valid because of the truth of the propositions from which they derive their theories; as soon as norms or guidelines are recognized and adhered to, it is unimportant whether or not they were derived or merely de facto norms.

The final question deals with the question of rationality. Habermas's answer is most important because it brings into focus issues that must be dealt with in a rational society cognizant of its human relations responsibilities. He stated that the degree to which a society—its institutions, its political culture, its traditions, and its everyday practices—permits a noncoercive and nonauthoritarian form of living is the hallmark of rationality, which is based on discourse. This rationality is manifested in the way certain groups (minorities, marginal groups, people with disabilities, children, the elderly) are treated; in the way people manifest their attitudes toward illness, loneliness, and death; and in the way people tolerate eccentricity and deviant behavior.

DISCUSSION QUESTIONS AND STATEMENT

1. What is the central principle of public discourse?

2. Explain Jürgen Habermas's principle of Universalization in the context of human relations.

3. According to Habermas, what is the hallmark of rationality in a society, and how does it affect human relations?

4. What deters some superintendents and principals from initiating discourse and dialogue?

5. Why is discourse a necessity in establishing effective human relations?

EXERCISE **10.1**

Assessment of Public Discourse Awareness

The following is a brief assessment of your public discourse awareness, which should be helpful to you in analyzing your understanding and feelings about how public discourse influences your professional conduct. On a scale of 1 to 3 (1 = disagree, 2 = partially agree, 3 = agree), rate the degree to which your understanding and feelings conform to the statements.

Rating

_____ When I make a decision, I am aware of the fact that the decision will have a human relations consequence.

_____ I understand that public discourse can lead to the resolution of conflicts that arise among people over specific policy or procedural issues.

_____ When I create administrative policies or procedures, I utilize discourse with those who will be affected by the policies or procedures in order to ensure that the policies or procedures truly deal with a given issue in a reasonable manner.

_____ I recognize that reasoned agreement does not mean consensus but rather clarification of the issues addressed by the discourse.

_____ I understand that the key to effective discourse is the willingness of the participants to appreciate the perspectives of other people.

_____ I consider the reasonableness of the argumentation in any discourse to be the rationale for my decision making.

_____ All participants in any discourse should be free from external and internal coercion other than the force of the best argument.

_____ I understand that there must be an organized agenda for all public discourse because of the limitations of time and space in addition to the need to bring closure to discourse.

_____ I know that public discourse can be effectively applied only to issues that can be resolved through impartiality.

_____ An effective measure for judging the degree to which a school or school district practices noncoercive rational decision making is the degree to which it utilizes public discourse.

_____ In a pluralistic society such as the United States, public discourse is the surest way to safeguard public freedoms and ensure the appropriate use of public monies.

_____ **Rating** (A maximum rating of 33 indicates that a person is significantly aware of public discourse issues. A rating of 17 can be used as a median score for purposes of analysis.)

SUMMARY

Implementing the pluralistic point of view in educational leadership is not only a human relations issue but also a political issue because public school districts are state agencies, which are impacted by federal laws and agencies. Jürgen Habermas is a contemporary philosopher who viewed public discourse as the pursuit of how conflicting interests can result in appropriate judgments. Embodied with his theoretical design is a procedure for human argumentation, which is reasoned agreement by those who will be affected by the norm. The central principle of public discourse is that the validity of a norm rests on the acceptability of the consequences of the norm by all participants in the discourse. This shifts reflection away from solitary individuals to a community of subjects in dialogue. Making a decision about the fairness of a norm cannot take place only in the minds of administrators but must be played out in actual discourse with other people. In Habermas's model, each person must be willing and able to appreciate the perspectives of other people.

Public discourse is difficult to implement. Habermas perceived the overarching problem to be isolation brought about by science, technology, and the arts. He believed that the role of the philosopher in contemporary society is to mediate and facilitate a framework within which people can communicate in a nondefensive manner. Thus communication can lead to influencing based on reason rather than coercion. Furthermore the reasoned validity people elucidate in discourse tends to transcend the present context and sets the stage for future discourse.

Habermas's principle of Universalization is operationalized within the context of a discourse that eventuates in a reasoned position. Thus reasoning is the basis of all discourse, and Habermas asserted that participants must agree to this rationality if discourse is to be effective. Participants should be free from external and internal coercion other than the force of the best argument, which at that point supports the cooperative search for truth. Because of the limitations of time and space, it is necessary to institutionalize discourse; the topics to be discussed and the contributions of participants must be organized in terms of opening, adjournment, and resumption of discussion.

Discourse can be effective only if it is applied to questions that can be dealt with through impartial judgment. This implies that the process will lead to an answer that is equally beneficial to all stakeholders. This does not mean that discourse seeks to reach consensus but instead seeks to generate convictions in the participants. Habermas stated that the degree to which a society—its institutions, political culture, traditions, and everyday practices—permits a noncoercive and nonauthoritarian form of ethical living is the hallmark of rational morality, which is derived from discourse. Developing a working knowledge and understanding of pluralism, justice, and discourse ethics will certainly lead to more effective resolution of value-laden conflicts.

ENDNOTES

1. R. W. Rebore, *The Ethics of Educational Leadership* (Upper Saddle River, New Jersey: Merrill/Prentice Hall, 2001), pp. 239–256.

2. J. Habermas, *Moral Consciousness and Communicative Action* (Cambridge, Massachusetts: MIT Press, 1995), pp. vii–viii.

3. Ibid., p. vii.

4. Ibid., pp. vii–ix.

5. Ibid., pp. 18–20, 68, 86–94.

6. J. Habermas, *Justification and Application: Remarks on Discourse Ethics* (Cambridge, Massachusetts: MIT Press, 1993), pp. 150–151, 158–161, 171.

SELECTED BIBLIOGRAPHY

Habermas, J. *Legitimation Crisis.* Boston and New York: Beacon Press, 1975.

Habermas, J. *The Structural Transformation of the Public Sphere: An Inquiry into a Category of Bourgeois Society.* Cambridge, Massachusetts: MIT Press, 1989.

Habermas, J. *Moral Consciousness and Communicative Action.* Cambridge, Massachusetts: MIT Press, 1990.

Habermas, J. *Justification and Application: Remarks on Discourse Ethics.* Cambridge, Massachusetts: MIT Press, 1993.

McCarthy, T. *The Critical Theory of Jurgen Habermas.* Cambridge, Massachusetts: MIT Press, 1978.

Rehg, W. *Insight and Solidarity: A Study in the Discourse Ethics of Jurgen Habermas.* Berkeley, California: University of California Press, 1994.

PART THREE

Human Communication and Human Relations

It may sound overly dramatic to say that communication is an essential dimension of all life, but it is. In the biological sphere, all creatures communicate with others. It is true that the lowest form of biological life, insects, communicate through instinct and mechanisms that are difficult to analyze. However, higher forms of life communicate in ways that are easily recognizable. Our pets communicate with us and we with them. Primates communicate in rather sophisticated ways that often astound us humans.[1]

Human communication occurs in four major forms: cultural, written, nonverbal, and verbal. These forms are expressed in an endless variety of settings and documents such as board of education manuals, conversations, interactive videos, kiosks, the Internet, memos, movies, newspapers, speeches, staff development presentations, staff meetings, plays, teleconferencing, and written administrative procedures. Obviously communication is the most complex of human activities.

This complexity is further amplified by human psychological phenomena because communication not only is a human mechanism per se but also emanates from the totality of each person's psychological makeup. Because there is always a *sender* and a *receiver* of what is communicated, the psychological dynamics of this transmission affect the message.[2] Thus Part Three begins with a chapter on basic principles of human communication, followed by four chapters dealing with cultural, written, nonverbal, and verbal communication.

CHAPTER 11

Basic Principles of Communication in Human Relations

The message of every communication is affected by the personality of the individual who is communicating and the personality of the individual who is receiving the communication. It can be no other way because communication is a human phenomenon; as such, it is always subjective. It is never objective because even facts or events are processed by people who have their own perceptions concerning the circumstances that surround the facts or events. Communicating to a group of people does not result in the same conclusion for everyone because each person who receives the message processes it as an individual. When it comes to communication, there is no such thing as group processing.[3]

This chapter will explore human communication for the purpose of developing a series of principles that will help superintendents, principals, and other administrators understand and operationalize their communications in more effective ways. In order to understand the significance of the principles, it is necessary to have a grasp of certain aspects of human communication. These aspects situate human communication within the larger context of life and exemplify how the quality of communication is related to the quality of human existence.

Aspects of Human Communication

There are five aspects to human communication that will be discussed in this chapter.

Assumptions about the Communication's Message

The first aspect concerns *assumptions about the message*. All communication stimulates a response in people; communication is never neutral. The response, however, starts with assumptions; it is natural for people to elaborate on a message. When the superintendent of schools consults with the board of education or parents about the possibility of increasing taxes, people of goodwill usually make an initial assumption that the superintendent believes that the school district needs more money in order to operate more effectively. Others are not quite that positive and will question the need for a tax increase. This communication has involved different interpretations.[4]

A principal may raise the issue of school safety with the faculty. The faculty will probably want to know if there has been an incident or if the principal believes that a violent act is about to occur. The discussion will progress in a number of directions until both the principal and the faculty have sufficiently explored the issue and understand the reason why the principal raised the issue in the first place. It is virtually impossible to anticipate every response of each person receiving a message. Thus no amount of information will be sufficient. Dialogue and discussion will be necessary to unveil the hidden responses of people to the initial message.

People also make assumptions about a message based on their perceptions of the person who is sending the message. This is a very important dimension of human communication, especially for educational administrators. If people have perceived in past communications that a principal raises questions for the purpose of manipulating them into doing something that he wanted them to do, they will eventually learn to distrust the principal's messages. Responses such as "He doesn't really mean that" will become commonplace among the faculty. But if people perceive the principal as a person who is always very up-front about what he says and does, people will take his communications seriously. In a sense a person becomes his or her own message. The question about school safety will receive a response that is either serious or not. The faculty may believe that the principal raised the issue in order to get them to be more attentive to the procedure of having those who are guests in their classrooms sign in at the office, with no real evidence that people have been entering the school building without following that procedure. Thus the person who receives the message is its interpreter.[5]

However, both the sender and the receiver must possess some commonality in order for a communication to occur. In ordinary conversation, the commonality is readily addressed, and the communication flows without much attention to the process itself. In educational leadership, professional communication between the superintendent and other administrators or teachers is usually based on commonalities of interest, experience, and education. Thus professional communication is initiated through common touchstones of words and ideas. The concern lies in the interpretation of motives. The motives of superintendents, principals, teachers, and others concerned with education are at issue. Even if they are not articulated, the following questions are representative of the types of concerns people have when they receive a communication: Why was this message sent? What is the underlying purpose of the communication? What is the context of the message? Why is it framed that way?

In like manner, the sender of a communication might formulate his or her communication in the same way: What kind of message should I send in order to accomplish my purpose? How should I frame the message? What should its content be? How should I deliver the message?

Personal Development and Communication Skills

The second aspect of human communication covers *personal development and communication skills*. Human beings develop their humanity only within relationships with other humans. To be human means that a person will try to learn how to engage others in meaningful ways. At some time, everyone has encountered a person who has inadequate social skills, who is unable to work with others, or who cannot get a point across in a conversation or meeting. Boiled down to the most basic problem, these people lack the ability to communicate. Without communication skills, people are left in relative isolation from others and tend to be observers rather than participants in their environment.[6]

The effects of this isolation can be most problematic for educational administrators. There are some people who are unaware of the fact that they lack communication skills because their personal lives do not require extensive communication, or at least the type of communication that is required to be a successful educational administrator. This sometimes happens when a teacher becomes a principal. She may have been able to communicate with students and parents in an effective way, but she lacks the ability to communicate with colleagues from a leadership position. When this occurs, some people begin to question her abilities, and even certain personality traits are called into question.

What these people must deal with is their public selves. To a more significant degree than teachers, superintendents and principals are public figures, much the same way as local elected officials are. The major danger for a neophyte administrator who has not had the opportunity to develop a public persona is the belief that it is too late to change. An individual's personality is in a state of continual becoming.[7]

Everyone seeks stability. However, if there is one constant in educational administration, it is change. This presents the superintendent or principal with a dilemma: how to maintain a balance between stability and change. In finding an answer to this dilemma, the administrator learns flexibility. What remains constant is his or her ability to deal with change. Thus flexibility brings control into the life of an educational leader; through this control, he or she gains the fortitude to enrich the ability to communicate.[8]

When a person communicates, who he or she is as a person is the primary message; all else follows from this. The way people perceive the messenger leads to their interpretation of the message. How the messenger feels about himself or herself will lead to modification in his or her personality.

Choices must be made by administrators about the way they perceive themselves in relation to their position in terms of how they will communicate with teachers, students, parents, colleagues, and the public in general. The superintendent who sees himself as a bureaucrat rather than a leader will communicate like a bureaucrat. The principal who sees herself as a strategist rather than a pawn of the superintendent will communicate as a strategist. Obviously the contrary is also true.

Communication's Consequences

The third aspect of human communication centers around the fact of the *consequences produced by communication.*[9] This is of particular concern to educational leaders because they are frequently asked questions by teachers, students, and parents at times when they have little opportunity to think before they speak. The principal who is walking down the hall in a school may be stopped by a teacher who has a complaint about a student with a behavioral problem or who is concerned about the remarks of a parent. What the principal must consider is that the teacher may quote him to the student or the parent when in fact the principal meant his remarks to be just for the teacher. A superintendent may find herself answering questions at a Chamber of Commerce meeting about the decision of the board of education to seek an increase in the taxes of the school district. What she says may affect the support of local businesspeople for the tax increase.

Even private in-office conversations can have tremendous consequences. Allegations that the principal or superintendent said something derogatory or inappropriate could have

significant consequences on his or her position in the school district. The perceptions people develop about an individual are created through the communications of others as well
as that person's own communications.

The issue of consequences can be dealt with through the use of personal control. A
superintendent, a principal, and other administrators can develop strategies that will help
them resist certain types of negative communicative interactions and help them foster other
types that will be beneficial. Thus consequences can be strategized. People recognize that
strategies are at work in communication and expect this to be the case in professional relationships. Very seldom do people come to see a principal or superintendent just to wish him
or her a nice day; most people have an agenda when visiting an educational leader. Certainly
most of the agendas are legitimate, but some are not and need to be carefully evaluated.

A strategy commonly used by seasoned professionals is the "I'll think about it"
response. While appearing to be trite and nonresponsive, it is the appropriate course of
action in many situations. This and similar types of behavior establish boundaries that will
affect future engagements. Eventually certain types of expectations become implicit in
communication strategies.

Communication strategies can be developed for most types of situations. The
responses that a superintendent makes at a board of education meeting are perhaps the most
obvious. When a board member makes an inappropriate remark about a staff member at a
board meeting, the superintendent can have a predetermined response ready. When the
assistant superintendent for curriculum is making a report about student test scores and a
board member asks why she did not compare the scores with those of students in a neighboring school district, the superintendent might remind the board member that he did not
ask for that information, and that such a request could have been made because the board's
agenda and a copy of the report had been received by board members one week before the
meeting.

This type of response helps to clarify the relationship between the board of education
and the administrative staff. It sets boundaries and expectations that are mutual. The superintendent and her staff can try to provide requested information if they know about board members' questions before the meeting. The communication thus becomes a two-way process.
The superintendent is in control of her communication and has formulated how she will
respond in certain types of situations. Of course, if the superintendent does not follow her
strategy in all similar situations, new boundaries with different expectations are established.

Communication's Content

The fourth aspect of human communication is the importance of educational leaders' *communication content.* If people develop perceptions about the inner core of a person's character in relation to his or her communications, and if these perceptions foster trust in that
person's ability to lead, the content of communications is important.

Furthermore, the content of communications is powerful. It changes the way people
think about serious issues. Communication also changes society; for example, all revolutions begin with a person or persons setting forth their political positions through communication. The situation is the same for educational administrators. People listen to what they
have to say and read what they write.[10]

In order to fully utilize the power of communication content, an administrator should consider those ideas and topics on which he or she is most expert. The principal who has studied the relationship between reading skills, attendance, and grade point average should communicate his research to faculty members, other administrators, parents, and the general public. Publishing research in professional journals is an important vehicle for influencing the academic community. Also it will enhance a person's reputation with other educators.[11]

The research potential of any given administrator may be seriously neglected because of other professional demands. Educational administrators have a common need: time management. The demands of the superintendency or principalship can be all-consuming. However, research and publishing are also professional demands that should receive the attention of every administrator. New information generates new ideas and concepts, which in turn generate new information. Research is a process. What can be communicated is more than just the research findings; the competency of the researching administrator is also communicated, which can lead to an enhancement of his or her influence in the academic community.

The researching administrator is a strategic communicator who can point out the connection between ideas and best practices in educating children or in managing a school district. What he or she actually does is control the way other people reflect on what they do as educators. But content alone does not produce this effect; style is also important. Some of the best information and ideas are disregarded by people because the style of the communication was either unimpressive or inappropriate. The style must reinforce the content. In order to do this effectively, not each bit of information or every idea can be communicated. Choices must be made about what is essential and what is peripheral.

Communicating about the issues of student discipline, especially in an atmosphere of concern for the safety of students, faculty, and staff members because of the unprecedented number of violent incidents in schools, will require a strategy not just in content but also in style. The style, more than the content, can produce a sense of either doom or hope. Restricting communications to just security issues does not tell the whole story and does a great disservice to students. It is important to know how to detect weapons brought into school and it is important to consider zero-tolerance policies; it is also equally important to reflect on why students are committing violent acts. Recognizing those students who are depressed or isolated from other students and finding ways to help them become participating members of the school community could be just as effective in preventing violence as weapons' detectors. Thus the gestalt of the message is the primary concern of the effective communicator.

The content of information and ideas is transmitted within a context; the context is the style. Style also refers to the medium of communication. Some information and ideas are better communicated through the spoken word and others through writing; certainly nonverbal communication is always at play in personal encounters.[12]

The superintendent who wishes to convey a new board of education policy about increased teacher compensation might use multiple styles in her communications. Information about the policy is important; it could be conveyed through a written memorandum that quotes the policy and then interprets the nuances of the policy, along with giving answers to a series of anticipated questions about the policy. The superintendent could also hold informational meetings at which she or a staff member answers questions for the teachers in attendance. Public meetings with a question-and-answer period can be an effective way to prevent misinterpretation of information. The style or context should be one of comprehensive openness, and the medium could be both writing and verbal communication. The mannerisms of the superintendent or staff member at the public forum constitute the nonverbal context.

Communication's Cultural Context

The fifth aspect of human communication is the *cultural context* and its impact on communication. Identifying the culture of an environment can be a major problem for an educational leader when he does not have a connection with the culture within which he is trying to communicate. A European American principal may have a difficult time communicating with the students and parents in a predominately Hispanic community if he does not understand the Hispanic culture.[13]

The United States is the most diverse nation on earth. More than a million people yearly immigrate to the United States. Most of them are from the Americas and Asia. What they bring with them is a unique blend of cultures that includes religious beliefs significantly different from the religious beliefs of most European Americans. The United States is now a mixture that includes Christians, Jews, Muslims, Hindus, and Confucians. There are probably more Muslims than Jews living in the United States.[14]

This religious diversity is compounded by the significant number of ethnic groups that embrace each of these religious faiths. No one ethnic group is the sole adherent to any one specific religion. Religious and ethnic diversity is further complicated by human rights issues. Some people have developed discriminatory attitudes about other people because of their age, disability, gender, illness, or lifestyle. Finally, some members of the majority society tend to treat certain people in rather stereotyped ways. Thus children, the eccentric, the elderly, the innovative, and the marginalized are often treated with less dignity than they deserve as human beings.

The underlying objective is learning how to communicate with people from different ethnic, religious, and racial backgrounds in order to foster equality, respect, and solidarity. When a principal is talking to parents at an open house, she will probably describe the curriculum and cocurricular activities available to students. Further, she will probably talk about how the parents should have an ongoing dialogue with their children's teachers as well as mention the kinds of concerns that should be brought to her, the principal. However, this is just part of the message, perhaps not even the most important part of the message. The style of the principal in transmitting this message will convey her attitude about the role of parents in the education of their children. Her style will also convey her attitude about the cultural background of the parents. There are verbal expressions and nonverbal body language that will convey whether the principal believes that the European American ethnic culture is superior to that of other cultures.[15]

For example, equality and respect are conveyed long before the parents arrive at a school for its open house by the way the school is decorated. If the school building and classrooms do not display the art and unique style of decorating specific to the cultural backgrounds of the students, it will be difficult for students and parents to believe that their heritage is valued.

If the principal and teachers do not invite people who are recognized as leaders in the various ethnic communities that make up the school community into the school, students and parents will readily recognize this disparity. Artists, businesspeople, the clergy, doctors, elected officials, lawyers, and others can be of great inspiration to students, faculty, and the administration.

The message is equality and respect. This cannot be conveyed just in written and verbal communications. Along with communications exemplifying these qualities, it is important to deal with the issue of solidarity. The school is a community in which cultural diversity must be honored and respected; however, it is equally important to foster a sense of solidarity among the diverse religious, ethnic, and racial groups, not only in the school community but also in the larger communities of the state and nation. The commitment to the local culture of the school community can eventually become an injustice to the students if it is exclusive and neglects their understanding and appreciation for other cultures.

Communicative Praxis

There is a need to develop ideas and notions that can become touchstones from which communication in different cultures can be addressed. The first consideration is the engagement of people in dialogue both about how to proceed and about issues and problems endemic to such engagement. The following questions reflect possible issues or problems that could be discussed:

- Given the diversity and pluralism of society in general, what ideas and notions about communication are possible?
- How do people become aware of communication issues?
- Given the diversity and pluralism that exist among people, how can they be engaged in meaningful discourse about communication?
- How can communication within diverse and pluralistic school communities be integrated into curricular and cocurricular programs?

In relation to these types of questions, the theory of Jürgen Habermas can be utilized as a framework for how and why dialogue on communication issues should take place in school communities. Habermas is a contemporary German philosopher who viewed discourse as the method to use so that conflicting interests can result in appropriate judgments. Embodied within his theoretical design is a procedure for argumentation, which is reasoned agreement by those who will be affected by the conclusions. The central principle in his theory is that the validity of principles rests on the acceptability of their consequences by all participants in a discourse. This shifts the locus of reflection from solitary individuals to a community in dialogue. Thus, making decisions about the appropriateness of communication principles cannot take place just in the minds of selected people but must be played out in actual discourse with many different individuals. In Habermas's model, each person must be willing and able to appreciate the perspective of others.

Isolation is the overarching problem in implementing discourse; it can be overcome only through a theory of communication that involves the collective decision making of all those who will be affected by an issue. Thus the role of communication in contemporary society is to mediate and facilitate a framework within which people can dialogue in a non-defensive manner. From this perspective, communication should lead to influencing based on reason rather than coercion. Furthermore the reasoned validity that people elucidate in discourse tends to transcend the present context and sets the stage for future discourse.

Habermas's principle of universalization is operationalized within the context of a discourse that results in a reasoned position. Thus reasoning is the basis of all discourse, and participants must agree to this rationality if it is to be effective. Participants should be free from external and internal coercion other than the force of the best argument, which supports the cooperative search for truth. Because of the limitations of time and space, it is necessary to institutionalize discourse; the topics to be discussed and the contributions of participants must be organized in terms of opening, adjournment, and resumption of discussion.

Discourse can be effective only if it is applied to questions that can be dealt with through impartial judgment. This implies that the process will lead to an answer that is equally beneficial to all stakeholders. This does not mean that discourse seeks to reach consensus; rather it seeks to generate convictions in the participants. Habermas saw the degree to which a society permits a noncoercive form of living in all situations as a hallmark of its rationality.[16]

The Social Covenant and Communication

Thomas Hobbes was a British philosopher who lived from 1588 to 1679 and wrote a famous political treatise titled *Leviathan*. This work has influenced the writings of many others since its appearance in the bookstores of England in 1651. One of his fundamental ideas concerns *social contract*. His definition of social contract entailed the delivery of something by a person while leaving another to perform his or her part of the contract at a specified later time. This notion of contract obviously calls for an element of trust because one person performs his or her part of the contract before the other party.[17]

This element of trust raised the idea of contract to the level of covenant. Communication is the key to developing the element of trust because people generally will not trust someone without knowing something about who the individual is as a person. Thus the types of communication that a principal uses with parents will instill either trust or distrust in his abilities to administer the school in a safe and effective manner. For something as important as the principalship or superintendency, various types of communication will be necessary in order to produce the kind of trust that is required.

Principals and superintendents owe the school and school district communities the effective and efficient administration of educational services. Teachers and staff members owe the school and school district the exercise of their talents in the delivery of instruction and support for the academic program. Parents and citizens owe the school and school district their financial and moral support and cooperation.

Thus people are the constituents of the social covenant. Communication is the vehicle for establishing and maintaining the covenant, and public discourse is the manner in which communication can be enhanced. People want to be heard and want to debate their ideas concerning education in general, and the schools they support in particular. Communicative discourse and the social covenant are the two components necessary for implementing effective communication in public education.

There is one final note about the five aspects of human communication. The material presented was formulated for superintendents, principals, and other administrators in relation to their communications as professional educational leaders. Spontaneous and interpersonal communication that takes place between friends and people who have intimate relationships, of course, was not the focus of this material. The assumption is that such communication is inappropriate in a professional setting, but it is recognized that such communication is essential to human growth and development. People who do not know how to communicate in a spontaneous and interpersonal way will have a rather difficult time learning the more controlled type of communication required of educational leaders.

Definition of Communication

From this treatment of communication, it is possible to set forth a definition of communication: *It is a process through which information is generated that elicits a response in people concerning the message and the sender.* As a process, communication involves making connections between current and previous communications. Such connections are made by the sender by how he or she situates the message in time; the receiver naturally makes a connection to the message filtered through the psychological structures active in his or her personality. The person who is positive in his or her thinking may interpret a message in a much different manner than the person who has a negative outlook on life. Thus it is very difficult to imagine a stand-alone message. The information that is generated may be facts, concepts, ideas, or images, which constitute the content of the communication; the style is used in telling a story, relating an event, describing a behavior, or asking a question. The response is always personal because it involves the interpretation of the message and an evaluation of the sender.

Principles of Communication

The following is a list of twelve principles of communication:

1. Because communication is endemic to the human condition, the success of administrators is significantly influenced by their ability to effectively communicate.
2. The personality of educational administrators is also communicated through their messages.
3. The personality of educational administrators will influence the way they perceive and interpret messages, as will the personality of those receiving the messages.
4. Educational administrators will make independent assumptions about the messages they receive, and others will likewise make independent assumptions about the messages administrators send.
5. An educational administrator will grow and develop as an individual and as a professional through the communication process.

6. There is a consequence to every communication transmitted by an educational administrator.

7. The development of communication strategies is one of the most important dimensions of being an educational administrator.

8. It is to the professional advantage of educational administrators to remember that the content of their communications sets the tone for how others perceive their competency.

9. A significant strategy of effective communication for an educational administrator is choosing the most appropriate medium to transmit a message.

10. The culture of those receiving a message from an educational administrator is an important consideration in selecting both the content and the medium for communication.

11. Engaging people in dialogue is an important strategy for an educational administrator who is learning how to communicate effectively.

12. Public education is predicated on a social covenant between educators and members of the community, which is strengthened by ongoing two-way communication.

DISCUSSION QUESTIONS AND STATEMENT

1. What are the four forms of human communication?

2. Briefly explain the five aspects of human communications.

3. How does Habermas's theory of discourse ethics support the importance of communication in the practice of educational leadership?

4. Explain how the social covenant idea of Thomas Hobbes is endemic to communication within human communities.

SUMMARY

Communication is an essential dimension of all human life. It takes four forms: cultural, written, nonverbal, and verbal. These forms are expressed in an endless variety of settings and documents such as books, conversations, interactive videos, kiosks, the Internet, memos, movies, speeches, and plays. Communication is the most complex of human activities. The message of every communication is affected by the personality of the person communicating and the personality of the person receiving the message. Communication is always subjective.

There are five aspects to human communication. The first aspect concerns assumptions about the message. Every communication stimulates a response; it is never neutral. People make assumptions about what is communicated. No amount of information will be sufficient. Dialogue and discussion are necessary to unveil the hidden responses of people to initial messages. People also make assumptions about a message based on their perceptions of the person who is sending the message. Thus the person who receives a message is its interpreter.

Both the sender and receiver must possess some commonality in order for communication to occur. The ordinary touchstones are words and ideas. Problems in communication usually lie in its interpretation. The motives, context, and strategies used in communication are universal considerations for both the sender and the receiver.

The second aspect involves personal development and communication skills. Human beings develop their humanity only within relationships with other humans. Communication is the vehicle for establishing such relationships. For educational administrators, the ability to form meaningful professional relationships will be a key element in their success. Public school administrators are public figures; as such, they must learn how to communicate their public selves to others. It is a process that is continual because human beings are always in the state of becoming.

Because change is a constant in educational administration, learning to strike a balance between stability and change requires flexibility. Educational administrators are continually making choices on how best to communicate their messages in an ever-changing environment.

The third aspect is based on the fact that every communication produces a consequence. This is of concern because often communication, particularly verbal communication, occurs without much thought. Once something is communicated, the consequences can be tremendous if the educational administrator said something that was inappropriate. To avoid this kind of problem, educational administrators can learn to strategize their communications. An essential strategy is the development of self-control in communicating.

Communication's content is the fourth aspect of professional communication. Because people develop their perceptions about educational leaders from their communications and because these perceptions foster trust in a person's ability to lead, the content of communications is important. Furthermore the content of communication is powerful because it can change the way people think about important issues. To fully utilize the power of communication content, administrators should consider those ideas and subjects on which they are most expert. Thus, utilizing research skills will help an educational administrator continually grow professionally, which in turn will enhance the knowledge that can be amalgamated into his or her communications.

Style is also an important dimension of communication. Some of the best information and ideas are disregarded by people because the style of the communication was either unimpressive or inappropriate. The gestalt of the message is the primary concern of the effective communicator. The content of information is sent within a context; the context is the style. The medium of the communication is also a stylistic concern. Some information and ideas are better conveyed through the spoken word; others are better communicated through writing. Nonverbal communication is always present in personal encounters.

The fifth aspect deals with the significant impact culture has on effective communication. The underlying objective is learning how to communicate with people from different ethnic, religious, and racial backgrounds in order to foster equality, respect, and solidarity. The culture of the United States is multidimensional and pluralistic. Thus there is a need to engage people in dialogue about issues and problems endemic to such engagements.

The theory of Jürgen Habermas can be utilized as a framework on how and why dialogue should take place in school communities on communication issues. The central principle in Habermas's theory is that the validity of principles is based on the acceptability of their consequences by all participants in a discourse. Decision making about the appropriateness of communication cannot take place just in the minds of certain people; it must be played out in actual discourse with many individuals. Reasoning is the basis of all discourse, and participants must agree to this rationality if it is to be effective.

The theory of Habermas is complementary to the notion of the social covenant, which had its origin in the philosophy of Thomas Hobbes. The notion of covenant requires an element of trust because some people perform their part of the covenant before others. Communication is the key to developing this element of trust.

From this treatment, it is possible to formulate a definition of communication: It is a process through which information is generated that elicits a response in people concerning the message and the sender.

E N D N O T E S

1. J. D. Korsmeyer, *Evolution & Eden* (New York: Paulist Press, 1998), pp. 81–82.

2. R. B. Adler and N. Towne, *Looking Out, Looking In,* 8th edition (New York: Harcourt Brace College Publishers, 1996), pp. 56–60.

3. R. E. Palmer, *Hermeneutics* (Evanston, Illinois: Northwestern University Press, 1969), p. 9.

4. R. Norton and D. Brenders, *Communication & Consequences: Laws of Interaction* (Mahwah, New Jersey: Lawrence Erlbaum Associates Publishers, 1996), p. 3.

5. Ibid., pp. 4–8.

6. Ibid., pp. 97–103.

7. R. S. Sharf, *Theories of Psychotherapy and Counseling: Concepts and Cases* (Pacific Grove, California: Brooks/Cole Publishing Company, 1996), pp. 219–222.

8. Norton and Brenders, *Communication & Consequences,* pp. 120–122.

9. Ibid., pp. 161–164.

10. Ibid., pp. 51–52.

11. P. D. Leedy, *Practical Research: Planning and Design,* 6th edition (Upper Saddle River, New Jersey: Merrill/Prentice Hall, 1997), p. 281.

12. Norton and Brenders, *Communication & Consequences,* pp. 73–78.

13. G. M. Gazda, F. R. Asbury, B. J. Balzer, W. C. Childers, R. E. Phelps, and R. P. Walters, *Human Relations Development: A Manual for Educators,* 5th edition (Boston: Allyn & Bacon, 1995), pp. 39–41.

14. D. L. Eck, "Challenged by a New Georeligious Reality, *In Trust,* 8, no. 2 (1997): 10–12.

15. L. A. Blum, "Antiracism, Multiculturalism, and Interracial Community: Three Educational Values," in *Applied Ethics: A Multicultural Approach,* 2nd edition (Upper Saddle River, New Jersey: Prentice Hall, Inc., 1998), pp. 14–16.

16. J. Habermas, *Moral Consciousness and Communicative Action* (Cambridge, Massachusetts: MIT Press, 1995), pp. 18–20, 68.

17. T. Hobbes, *Leviathan* (Cambridge, England: Cambridge University Press, 1996), pp. 90, 100–101, 103–104, 105.

S E L E C T E D   B I B L I O G R A P H Y

Atkinson, M. *Our Masters' Voices: The Language and Body Language of Politics.* London: Methuen & Co., 1984.

Curtis, R. C., ed. *Self-Defeating Behaviors: Experimental Research, Clinical Impressions, and Practical Implications.* New York: Plenum Publishing, 1989.

Cushman, D. P., and D. D. Cahn Jr. *Communication in Interpersonal Relationships.* Albany, New York: State University of New York Press, 1985.

Daly, J. A., and J. M. Wiemann, eds. *Strategic Interpersonal Communication.* Hillsdale, New Jersey: Lawrence Erlbaum Associates Publishers, 1994.

Duck, S., ed. *Learning About Relationships.* Newbury Park, California: Sage Publications, Inc., 1993.

Giacalone, R. A., and P. Rosenfeld. *Applied Impression Management: How Image-Making Affects Managerial Decisions.* Newbury Park, California: Sage Publications, Inc., 1992.

Glover, J. *I: The Philosophy and Psychology of Personal Identity.* London: Penguin Press Books, Inc., 1988.

Knapp, M. L., G. R. Miller, and K. Fudge. "Background and Current Trends in the Study of Interpersonal Communication," in *Handbook of Interpersonal Communication,* 2nd edition. Newbury Park, California: Sage Publications, Inc., 1994.

Littlejohn, S. W. *Theories of Human Communication,* 4th edition. Belmont, California: Wadsworth Publisher, 1992.

McCroskey, J. C., and J. A. Daly. *Personality and Interpersonal Communication.* Newbury Park, California: Sage Publications, Inc., 1987.

Petronio, S., J. K. Alberts, M. L. Hecht, and J. Buley, eds. *Contemporary Perspectives on Interpersonal Communication.* Madison, Wisconsin: Brown and Benchmark Publishers, 1993.

Stewart, J. "Interpersonal Communication: Contact between Persons," in *Bridges, Not Walls: A Book about Interpersonal Communication,* 6th edition. New York: McGraw-Hill Publishers, 1995.

Wilmot, W. W. *Dyadic Communication,* 3rd edition. New York: Random House, Inc., 1987.

12 Cultural Communication and Human Relations

When people come together for the purpose of collectively initiating some action, activity, or service, they create an *organization*. In its simplest form, it may be a club operating at a specific location; in its most complex form, it may be a government operating over vast territories, with international interests and alliances. Somewhere on this continuum are schools and school districts of varying sizes operating in diverse locations.

As organizations become institutionalized, they take on a life of their own. This life exists apart from its individual members. However, organizations also are constantly changing because they are composed of people who are constantly changing by reason of their attitudes, beliefs and values, feelings, and opinions. Because of both the ongoing changes within people and the coming and going of people, a given school and school district will likely experience a change in culture either in a relatively short time or over a longer period of time. *Culture* is a quality inherent within an organization that creates an atmosphere that sets it apart from other organizations with similar purposes.

The motives and behaviors of individuals within a school or school district can affect the communication of its culture in either a positive or negative manner. This is more clearly understood in relation to the principal and superintendent of schools because the principal can have the most extensive impact on a school's culture and the superintendent can have the most extensive impact on a school district's culture through the power of office they have; they are the chief administrative leaders. As the official leader of a school, the principal is responsible for leading the teachers and staff members in creating an effective school culture; in like manner, as the official leader of a school district, the superintendent is responsible for leading the administrators, teachers, and staff members in creating an effective school district culture. Thus, in addition to written, nonverbal, and verbal communication, educational administrators continually communicate through the cultural environment of the school and school district.

Organizational Culture and Communication

The best way to explain what is meant by school and school district culture is to use a few examples. Consider the arrival of a new high school principal who has been hired with the understanding that she has the freedom and responsibility to upgrade a rather traditional curriculum that does not meet the expectations of parents and the board of education. After six months, she realizes that most of the faculty members have never been led by a female principal. Also it is painfully clear to her that faculty members are happy with the status quo and really do not want to change the content of their lessons nor their teaching methodologies. Furthermore she realizes that there is not sufficient money in the budget to accomplish an upgrade in instructional technology that she believes is important in upgrading the curriculum. As a consequence of this situation, she begins to look for another principalship outside the district.

Also consider a newly appointed superintendent of schools who has been hired by the board of education to improve the image of the school district because the taxpayers have refused to pass a tax-increase referendum on three separate occasions. After his first year as superintendent, he realizes that the board of education has an extremely negative attitude toward teachers, believing they are overpaid and nonresponsive to the wishes of parents. The teachers' union has refused to support the tax-increase referendum because the board of education does not want to use the additional revenue to increase teacher salaries, which are below the salaries of teachers in neighboring school districts. Because of low salaries, teachers have withheld after-school services and refuse to attend parent/teacher functions. The superintendent has begun to revise his resumé.

Both of these administrators should have been able to analyze the culture of the school and school district before accepting the principalship and superintendency, not only because they would have had more information on which to make an employment decision but also because knowing the culture of an organization is the first step in changing it.

Definition of Culture

There are many definitions of culture. The definition that most fits the perspective of this presentation is as follows: *School and school district cultures consist of those attitudes, beliefs and values, feelings, and opinions that are shared by a significant number of their influential members and that are communicated to others.* Of course these attitudes, beliefs and values, feelings, and opinions can be expressed in written, nonverbal, and verbal ways. However, consistency is not always the case, and some people find that what is written and what is said do not coincide with nonverbal communication.

Thus, analyzing the culture of a school or school district involves much more than just considering what people say about it; it requires systematic analysis. It is true that all such analysis involves interpretation and is a subjective activity. However, the litmus test is the utility of the insights that the analysis produces.[1] Table 12.1 sets forth the elements of cultural analysis. Column 1 identifies the components of culture that are operationalized by the expressions listed in Column 2. The methods used in analyzing school and school district cultures, which yield data that are interpreted, are set forth in Column 3.

Components of Culture

Attitudes are those mental perspectives that fashion the way a person views his or her personal circumstances. Administrators who have a positive view of their role and responsibilities are people who like being principal or superintendent. They may not like certain people or certain tasks that the principalship or superintendency requires, but basically they

TABLE 12.1   Elements of Cultural Analysis

Column 1		Column 2		Column 3	
Attitudes Beliefs and values Feelings Opinions	**Generate**	Activities Talk Behavior	**Analyzed by**	Describing Listening Reading Observing	**Leading to Interpretation**

enjoy the job. They have a positive attitude. However, attitudes can be either superficial or deeply rooted. Liking a particular job is an attitude that can change with circumstances. Deeply rooted attitudes such as racial prejudice are not so easily changed or masked. The person who does not like people from a particular ethnic group or race may go to extreme lengths to give the appearance of being nonprejudiced, but such a deeply rooted attitude may find expression in speech patterns and behaviors. An ethnically mixed faculty may be observed as being segregated by the way the faculty members group themselves in the cafeteria during lunch.[2]

Beliefs are ideas and notions about the meaning of existence, life, and death. *Values* are self-regulating principles that people use to direct their conduct and that are based on beliefs. Most beliefs have been passed down from one generation to the next and are usually embodied in religious and philosophical tenets. Thus the belief that all people are created equal gives rise to the value of multiculturalism in the curriculum or the practice of affirmative action. The belief that all children can learn gives meaning to the value of inclusive education for children with disabilities.[3]

In this presentation, *feelings* are synonymous with emotions. Virtually everyone accepts the fact that humans are not only intellectual but also feeling creatures. In fact, it is impossible to conceive of anyone who has his or her feelings in check to such a degree that they do not influence his or her speech or behavior. It is certainly undesirable for someone to be that calculating and unfeeling. People who try to be unfeeling lack spontaneity and warmth. Educational administrators would certainly not hire someone to be an administrator, teacher, or staff member who is unfeeling because schools and school districts are service centers where people are the most important component. Common feelings include anger, joy, happiness, sadness, sorrow, and love.[4]

Opinions are the conclusions people draw from personal experiences. They are not necessarily systematically reasoned conclusions, although they can be. They are predominately conclusions drawn from a broad base of experiences applied to a specific situation. Opinions about performance-based teacher evaluations may have been formulated from the experience a teacher had with an incompetent administrator who did an inadequate job of observing and analyzing the instructional strategies used by that teacher. A principal may have an opinion about student behavior predicated on her experience with student gangs.

Opinions are not always logical and are often influenced by the attitudes, beliefs and values, and feelings of an administrator, teacher, or staff member. All these components of culture are somewhat related, and the analysis of culture must take into account their interplay. All of these components generate a host of activities, talk, and behaviors.[5]

Expressions of Culture

Activities refer to the engagement of administrators, teachers, and staff members. Such engagements can be routine professional activities, unusual professional activities, or social activities. The manner in which people are engaged with each other is the important concern in analyzing a school's or school district's culture. Observing that the engagements are always formal or informal, regardless of whether they are routine or unusual professional activities, will tell the person making the analysis something significant about the school or school district. Social activities are perhaps the most important kind of engagement because it is through these activities that people tend to convey, in a more open way, their attitudes, beliefs and values, feelings, and opinions. The people who are included or excluded from social engagements is a revealing dimension of culture. Also the inclusion of others from outside the school or school district environment may reveal something significant about the culture under analysis.

Perhaps the most important activities that reveal the culture of a school or school district are those that involve the recipients of the services provided by the professional and support staffs; students, parents, and taxpayers are those recipients. A teacher who puts a great deal of effort into such activities as decorating his classroom or displaying the work of his students could be indicating his positive attitude toward students. A principal who is always in the halls to greet and talk with students is displaying her concern and appreciation for the students. The openness of the school district to community use of facilities could be an indication of the board of education's understanding that the schools ultimately belong to the taxpayers. A superintendent of schools who attends Chamber of Commerce meetings is showing his support for the business community. All these activities are signs that reveal the culture of a school or school district.[6]

Talk refers to verbal exchanges that take place between people. In terms of cultural analysis, professional discussion is different from casual talking for the same reasons that professional activities are different from social engagements. Casual talking usually reveals attitudes, beliefs and values, feelings, and opinions in a more open way than professional discussions. Teachers who are constantly criticizing members of the board of education or the superintendent of schools are creating a culture that is far different from one in which discussing issues that the board of education or superintendent needs to address takes place. Openly talking about problematic parents or students sets up an atmosphere that will lead to a quite different analysis than when teachers limit their discussion of parent or student problems to professional settings.

The manner in which administrators, teachers, and staff members talk with students, parents, and taxpayers is also a good indication of the culture of a school or school district. A teacher who views instruction as only a professional responsibility might be missing the larger picture. Actually teaching is helping children and young people develop all their capabilities to the fullest extent possible and helping them become caring and responsible adults. This perspective places a significant responsibility on teachers and others to talk with students in a caring and supportive manner that is respectful of their humanity. Of course students, parents, and taxpayers tend to talk with all employees of a school or school district; thus it is important for secretaries, custodians, cooks, bus drivers, and other support staff members to understand that the culture of the school or school district is enhanced or hindered by the manner in which they communicate with these constituents.[7]

Behavior is a way of physically reacting to a situation. A person's behavior is observable and demonstrative. Behavior includes posturing, engagement, and verbal communication, or lack thereof. Thus it is important to understand that behavior does not always require an overt reaction. Silence and inactivity are also behaviors. A teacher's reactive behavior to an intimidating situation might be aggressiveness or nonresponsiveness. Sexual harassment of a teacher by a principal occurs when the principal makes an unwelcome sexual advance toward a teacher or when he creates an environment that is sexually hostile to that teacher. The reactive behavior on the part of the teacher being harassed might be to report the incident or explain the hostile environment to the superintendent, which would be an appropriate behavior, or do nothing, which would be an inappropriate behavior. A lack of response is just as significant as an aggressive reaction in analyzing the culture of a school or school district. If the principal in this situation is an extremely aggressive person who intimidates people, the atmosphere in the school might be inactivity and silence in relation to engagement with that principal.

In this context, the behavior of administrators, teachers, and support staff members toward other employees is only part of the issue. The behavior of these people toward students, parents, and taxpayers is also a determining factor in developing and maintaining a positive school and school district culture. For example, the posturing, engagement, and verbal communication of a principal with regard to students who are experiencing conduct problems will permeate the entire school environment. If a principal supports teachers by requiring students to live up to a code of student rights and responsibilities while using positive reinforcement through her posture and speech, the culture of the school will promote conduct that is conducive to a learning community.

It should be obvious from this presentation that school and school district culture are significantly affected by the actions of individual administrators, teachers, and staff members. These individuals constitute a corporate entity. Even though one person will not significantly affect the overall culture of a school or school district, the accumulation of activities, talk, and behaviors can and does affect culture. This accumulation occurs when a number of individuals possess the same attitudes, beliefs and values, feelings, or opinions. For an effect to be felt, there is no magic number of individuals; rather it is caused by an intensity that permeates the environment. This intensity can be generated by even a small number of very vocal or very influential people. Sometimes changes in culture are subtle, and the effects are not immediately known. The main point is that everyone is an agent of a given school's or school district's culture and can make a difference in creating either a positive or negative culture.[8]

Analysis of Culture

The method described in this presentation is geared toward understanding a school's or school district's culture as it pertains to developing appropriate leadership communications. The superintendent or principal who wants to improve communications must first analyze the present culture of his or her school or school district. In fact, it is best to understand the following methodology as an ongoing approach to learning about culture. This is a systematic, qualitative approach; in a broad sense, it can be considered research. However, the purpose is the improvement of communications.

It is a phenomenological approach; the purpose is to understand the personal experience of both the sender and receiver of a communication because the administrator is involved in both ends of the communication. Four dimensions make up the phenomenological approach: describing, listening, reading, and observing. These four dimensions are not discrete processes in themselves but rather are interrelated aspects of the same approach. They overlap, but for this explanation, they are treated separately.[9]

Describing. This is the process of gathering information and organizing it into a logical format. There are five ways that information can be formatted:

1. Describing the routine events of the day in the life of the school or school district
2. Describing the routine events of the day in the life of individual administrators, teachers, staff members, or students
3. Describing the interaction of routine institutional events with the routine events in the lives of individuals
4. Describing critical events that occur in the school or school district and in the lives of individuals
5. Formulating the routine and critical events into a narrative format describing the relationships between the individuals and the school or school district

This descriptive process gives the administrator the opportunity to synthesize and internalize his or her observations. This in turn will help the principal or superintendent take ownership of the communication process and help him or her formulate strategies that will improve communications in the school or school district. Exhibit 12.1 sets forth a format that can be used to describe cultural elements.

EXHIBIT *12.1*

Description Analysis

Description of a Routine Event by the Principal

School buses arrive at approximately 7:15 A.M. at Longfellow Elementary School. The buses are met by the teachers, most of whom are conscientious in greeting the students. The atmosphere is congenial, and the process of getting the students into their classrooms appears to be orderly and safe. The assistant principal is also usually present and converses with the bus drivers when there has been a student problem on a given bus. It appears that the bus drivers have confidence in the assistant principal and appreciate her concern. Some parents drive their children to school, and the students are dropped off in an area that is designated for this purpose and that does not interfere with school bus traffic. Some parents park their cars and use this opportunity to converse with the teachers, which appears to be a good way for teachers and parents to informally discuss the progress of the students. This does not appear to interfere with the process of getting the students to their classrooms. The teachers have been coached by the administrative staff to ask the parents to come after school to discuss an issue or problem if it seems to be rather involved. Most parents accept this approach.

(continued)

Conclusion

The arrival of school buses in the morning and the process of getting children to their classrooms are safe, organized, and effective. Furthermore the teachers and the assistant principal exhibit a positive attitude toward this professional responsibility, and the engagement of the teachers, the assistant principal, and the bus drivers is positive and cooperative. Parents and teachers periodically engage in productive conversations about the students that do not hinder school bus arrivals.

Description of a Critical Event by the Superintendent of Schools

On the afternoon of March 22, 2001, a bomb threat was telephoned into the high school office. The principal, faculty, and staff members evacuated the building in an orderly manner, and the police bomb squad was contacted. The police searched the building and determined that the threat was a hoax. The students reentered the building; classes resumed without further incident. The administration, faculty, and staff members acted in a deliberately professional manner, and the students responded in an orderly manner. The response time for the evacuation was reasonable. The response time for the arrival of the police was exceptional, and the involvement of the police bomb squad was professional and cooperative. The principal sent a letter home with the students to inform parents that the incident had occurred, how it was handled, and that the procedures for responding to critical events are effective and ensure the safety of the students. The principal also sent the same message to the parents who have email and placed the message on the school's Web site.

Conclusion

The procedures that are in place for critical events are operative and effective. Furthermore the administration, faculty, and staff members handled themselves in a professional manner, which demonstrated to students the ability of the professional staff to handle critical events. The police also responded in a professional manner, which demonstrated to the school staff the ability of the police to handle critical events. The attitudes of everyone were positive and cooperative.

Listening.   This is the process of discerning the meaning behind the dialogue that takes place among administrators, teachers, staff members, students, parents, and taxpayers. The context and manner in which dialogue occurs sometimes convey a meaning that is different from the literal meaning of the spoken words. In dialogic analysis, the following three questions constitute the basis of interpretation:

1. What emotions are evoked by the dialogue?
2. What is the thought pattern set forth in the dialogue?
3. What is unique about the words used in the dialogue?

The emotions evoked by the dialogue are important indicators of the attitudes of the participants. A teacher who speaks in a manner respectful of students generally will have a positive attitude toward students. Teachers who ridicule or use inappropriate words in a dialogue with colleagues or parents certainly harbor some negative attitudes. Not only does such dialogue reinforce the negative attitudes of the speaker, but they usually evoke negative responses in the other person or persons who are participating in the dialogue. The point is that attention to what people are saying will give an indication of the cultural milieu of a school or school district. Charting the elements of dialogue will provide a snapshot of the culture. This can be done in a simple way, as exemplified in Table 12.2.

The data indicate that administrators, faculty, and students are consistently exhibiting emotions exemplified by the words "anger," "frustration," "concern," and "belligerence." This should certainly cause a principal or superintendent to think about the reasons people are exhibiting such strong emotions. The answer might be simply the circumstances that precipitated the dialogue in the first place, or it might indicate a more deeply rooted cultural dimension in the school or school district. That dimension could be a pervasive unhappiness. Finding the cause of this unhappiness is the first challenge; changing it is the second challenge.

Reading.   The documents of schools and school districts, such as mission statements, policy manuals, procedural manuals, memoranda, newsletters, job advertisements, and student newspapers, can reveal the nuances of an institution's culture. Today the concept of "document" must be expanded to include Web sites, email, and videos that a school or school district uses to communicate with its internal and external publics.

In analyzing documents the investigator is concerned with the tone of the messages. The following four questions can help to determine the tonality in school documents:

1. Do the documents of the school or school district foster a sense of excellence in the performance of administrators, teachers, staff members, and students?
2. Do the documents of the school or school district foster a sense of community in which all members are lifelong learners?
3. Do the documents of the school or school district foster the ideal of a caring community?
4. Do the documents of the school or school district foster innovation and risk taking?

TABLE 12.2   Listening Analysis

Dialogue Topic	Participants	Emotions
New science curriculum	Two science teachers	Science teacher one—anger Science teacher two—frustration
School policy on student advisement	Two twelfth-grade guidance counselors	Two counselors—concern about time on task
Student conduct	Teacher and student	Teacher—anger and frustration Student—belligerence
Parental concerns about child	Teacher and parent	Teacher—frustration Parent—anger
New zero-tolerance drug policy	Principal and assistant superintendent	Principal—concern about reactions Assistant superintendent—frustration

In this context, it is assumed that the leadership of a school or school district wants to promote excellence in performance, wants to develop the organization around the ideals of a learning and caring community, and wants to promote the risk taking and innovation that must occur in the search for best practices. Of course schools and school districts can have a variety of goals that would inform their documents. Table 12.3 sets forth a process for analyzing documents.

In Table 12.3, the documents chosen are from three different areas. The first is the policy manual of the school district, which is the product of the board of education. However, the contents of this document are usually developed based on the research and recommendations of the superintendent of schools. Of course the board of education can initiate policies on its own or modify the recommendations of the superintendent. Thus policy manuals typically contain the thinking of both the members of the board of education and the superintendent of schools.

The student newspaper is usually the product of students as well as a faculty member who acts as an advisor to the students. The students, of course, are a reflection of the student body; the faculty member usually reflects the orientation of the administration, faculty, and staff members. In fact, the reason why most advisors are chosen by the administration is because they represent the attitudes, beliefs and values, feelings, and opinions of the professional community in a school.

The teaching job advertisement is usually the product of the central office staff. Job descriptions usually are developed with input from the administration and appropriate faculty or staff members. In this case, the job description is for a teaching position, which means that a principal and probably some faculty members reviewed the description in order to ascertain if it correctly reflects the position. Job advertisements are meant to give

TABLE 12.3   Document Analysis

Type of Document	Goals	Degree of Goal Completion (completely, somewhat, not at all)
Policy manual	Excellence in performance	Somewhat
	Learning community	Completely
	Caring community	Completely
	Innovation and risk taking	Not at all
Student newspaper	Excellence in performance	Not at all
	Learning community	Completely
	Caring community	Completely
	Innovation and risk taking	Not at all
Teaching job advertisement	Excellence in performance	Completely
	Learning community	Completely
	Caring community	Completely
	Innovation and risk taking	Somewhat

potential job applicants information that will allow them to determine if they have the qualifications for the job. Of course the job description must also entice qualified applicants. To this end, the central office administrator responsible for developing the job advertisement must present some information about the school and school district that reveals the conditions under which the successful applicant will teach. However, job advertisements in many school districts are promotional vehicles because the administrators want to attract the best candidates for job openings.

In this context, the analysis is focused on how the contents of these documents promote four goals. The assumption is that the board of education—with significant input from the administration, faculty, staff members, students, and parents—formally declared these to be the four goals that all members of the school community are striving to achieve.

The analysis of the three documents clearly sets forth the desire of the board of education, administration, faculty, staff members, students, and parents to develop and maintain a learning and caring school community. The results of the excellence in performance goal are mixed. The policy manual appears to only somewhat promote this goal while the student newspaper does not promote it at all; the job advertisement significantly promotes this goal. The innovation and risk taking goal shows the greatest disparity. Both the policy manual and the student newspaper clearly do not promote this goal while the job advertisement somewhat supports it.

In analyzing these results, the conclusion might be that there is a disconnect between promoting the goal of excellence in performance and the goal of innovation and risk taking while there is complete harmony in promoting the learning and caring community goals. The culture of this school and school district is thus centered on learning and caring, but not on excellence or innovation and risk taking. The fact that excellence is promoted in the job advertisement might be only a promotional ploy given the fact that it is only somewhat promoted in the policy manual and not at all promoted in the school newspaper. Innovation and risk taking are obviously not desired characteristics for members of the school community. In this context, it might have been a politically correct ploy by the board of education when it established this as a school district goal. From a cultural perspective, this is probably a school and school district where the board of education and administration do not want to challenge the faculty, staff members, and students but rather want to maintain a positive yet status quo environment.

Observing. Observation analysis is the process of measuring the degree to which a school's or school district's culture supports a quality environment. The extent to which a principal or superintendent impacts the culture of a school or school district is better understood when culture is viewed from a set of key characteristics.[10] In order to accomplish this analysis, the observer must determine which characteristics are indicators of a quality environment. To this end, the following ten characteristics are proposed as significant indicators that can be used to determine if a school's or school district's culture is focused on supporting a quality environment:[11]

1. *Identity focus.* This is the degree to which administrators, teachers, and staff members identify with the school or school district as a whole rather than with a job or profession. If individuals closely identify with the school or school district, then there is a positive culture operating within that school or school district.

2. *Collaboration focus.* This concerns the degree to which administrators, teachers, and other staff members organize their work activities around groups rather than individuals. If the teachers in a school collaborate in developing aspects of the instructional program rather than rely on the principal to organize this responsibility, their school exemplifies this characteristic. The obvious advantage of fostering group emphasis is the empowerment experienced by the teachers; the success of the instructional program then is no longer dependent on one person (the principal) who might retire or accept a position in another school district at some future time. In like manner, continuity is established even if some teachers leave a particular school.

3. *Concern for people focus.* This reflects the degree to which administrators, teachers, and staff members take into consideration the effects of their decisions on other people. Of course this consideration applies not only to the decisions affecting staff but also to those decisions affecting students, parents, and members of the community. A high degree of concern is a hallmark of the humanity of the decision makers.

4. *Coordination focus.* This is the degree to which units in the school or school district are encouraged to operate in a coordinated or interdependent manner. A high degree of coordination and interdependence supports and strengthens the goal attainment of a school or school district.

5. *Empowerment focus.* This concerns the degree to which rules, regulations, and direct supervision are used to control the behavior of administrators, teachers, staff members, and students. Less control and increased levels of trust and empowerment lead to greater commitment and success.

6. *Risk support focus.* This involves the degree to which administrators, teachers, and staff members are encouraged to be aggressive, innovative, and risk-seeking. A high degree of encouragement could lead to higher job satisfaction, uplifting morale, and cutting-edge programming.

7. *Performance focus.* This reflects the degree to which rewards and promotions are allocated according to staff member performance rather than seniority, favoritism, or other nonperformance factors. There is a long history in education centered at the low end of this characteristic. Performance-based salary increases and performance-based promotions into administrator ranks are the modus operandi in the private business sector. This does not mean that educational leaders cannot effect a change in how their system operates. However, it will take a considerable amount of courage and resourcefulness on the part of boards of education and superintendents to bring this about.

8. *Criticism tolerance focus.* This concerns the degree to which administrators, teachers, and staff members are encouraged to openly express their criticisms. The educational leaders of some schools and school districts mistakenly believe that they can squelch criticism. Heavy-handed techniques used with staff members who publicly criticize the school or school district will eventuate in deep-seated resentment, and in many cases outright revolt. The mark of an effective school or school district is an atmosphere of openness within which everyone, including students, will be heard without reprisals. This kind of openness sends a signal to all members of the school community that people, their opinions and their criticisms, are valued and can make a difference in how the school or school district is administered. It is important for educational leaders to understand that criticism is not a sign of failure but rather is an indication that something needs to change in order for the school or school district to progress and grow. The proper and effective handling of criticism is an important leadership skill that not every leader has developed; it can certainly enhance or detract from the culture of a school or school district.

9. *Process focus.* This is the degree to which administrators, teachers, and staff members focus on outcomes rather than on the strategies and processes used to achieve those outcomes. Particularly in education, outcomes are not a good measure of progress or success. There are too many variables to control when dealing with people to accurately measure outcomes. Thus a school or school district with a positive culture will be constantly engaged in developing, implementing, evaluating, and modifying strategies and processes.

10. *Change focus.* This reflects the degree to which a school or school district monitors and responds to changes in the external environment. Technology, corporate downsizing, shifts in population, violence, health issues, and all the other phenomena that constantly bombard our institutions require a response from educational leaders in relation to what needs to change in their school and school district cultures.

Based on these characteristics, Exercise 12.1 sets forth an observation analysis survey.

DISCUSSION QUESTIONS AND STATEMENTS

1. Define culture as it is used in relation to communication.

2. Explain the paradigm that is used in this chapter to systematically analyze school and school district culture.

3. What are the four dimensions of the phenomenological approach to analyzing culture?

4. What are the characteristics that can be used to determine the quality of a school and school district's environment?

EXERCISE 12.1

Observation Analysis Assessment

On a scale of 1 to 5 (with 5 being the highest), indicate the degree to which each of the following ten characteristics applies to your school or school district.

Rating	*Characteristic*
_____	Identity focus
_____	Collaboration focus
_____	Concern for people focus

(continued)

EXERCISE **12.1**   **Continued**

_____   Coordination focus

_____   Empowerment focus

_____   Risk support focus

_____   Performance focus

_____   Criticism tolerance focus

_____   Process focus

_____   Change focus

_____   **Rating** (A maximum rating of 50 indicates that the school or school district under observation is focused on creating and maintaining a positive culture. A rating of 25 can be used as a median score for purposes of analysis.)

SUMMARY

Educational administrators continually communicate through the cultural environment of a school or school district. Knowing and understanding the culture of a school and school district are important for an educational administrator because such knowledge and insight constitute the prerequisites to modifying or changing the culture. An operative definition of culture for this chapter is as follows: School and school district cultures consist of those attitudes, beliefs and values, feelings, and opinions that are shared by a significant number of their influential members and that are communicated to others.

Analyzing the culture of a school or school district involves much more than just knowing what people say about it. It requires systematic analysis. A paradigm that can be used to analyze culture is this: Attitudes, beliefs and values, feelings, and opinions generate activities, talk, and behavior that can be analyzed by describing, listening, reading, and observing, which in turn lead to interpretation.

Attitudes are those mental perspectives that fashion the way people view their personal circumstances. Attitudes can be superficial or deeply rooted. Deeply rooted attitudes such as ethnic prejudice are not so easily changed or masked.

Beliefs are ideas or notions about the meaning of existence, life, and death. Values are the self-regulating principles people use to direct their conduct; these values are based on beliefs. Most beliefs have been passed down from one generation to the next and are embodied in religious or philosophical tenets.

Feelings are synonymous with emotions. Obviously humans are not only intellectual but also feeling creatures. It is also obvious that a person's feelings will exert some degree of influence on his or her speech and behavior. Some of the most common feelings are anger, joy, sadness, and love.

Opinions are the conclusions people draw from their experiences. Opinions are not necessarily systematically reasoned conclusions, but they can be. They are usually conclusions drawn from a broad base of experiences that are applied to specific situations. Opinions are not always logical; they are often influenced by a person's attitudes, beliefs and values, and feelings.

All these components generate a plethora of activities, talk, and behaviors. Activities are the engagement of administrators, teachers, and staff members, which can be routine or unique professional activities as well as social activities. The manner in which people engage is an important concern in analyzing a school's or school district's culture. Observing whether the engagements are always formal or informal regardless of whether they are routine or extraordinary is also a significant aspect of the analysis. In terms of analysis, social activities are perhaps the most important because they tend to reveal in a more open way the attitudes, beliefs and values, feelings, and opinions of people.

Talk refers to the verbal exchanges that occur between people. In terms of culture, professional discussion is different from talking for the same reasons that professional activities are different from social ones. The way in which administrators, teachers, and staff members talk with students, parents, and taxpayers is also a good indication of the culture of a school or school district.

Behavior denotes a way of physically reacting to a situation. Of course behavior is observable and demonstrative and includes posturing, engagement, and verbal communication, or the lack thereof.

School and school district culture are significantly affected by the actions of individual administrators, teachers, and staff members. These individuals constitute a corporate entity; even though one person will not significantly affect the overall culture of a school or school district, the accumulation of activities, talk, and behaviors can and does affect the culture.

The analysis of culture can be accomplished using a qualitative phenomenological approach. There are four dimensions to the phenomenological approach: describing, listening, reading, and observing. Describing is the process of gathering information and categorizing it into a logical format. Descriptions can be organized around the routine events in a school or school district and the routine events of its members; the interaction between the routine events and people; the critical events in a school or school district and the critical events of its members; and the interaction between the critical events and people.

Listening involves the process of discerning the meaning behind the dialogue that takes place among administrators, teachers, staff members, students, parents, and taxpayers. Such analysis includes the emotions evoked by the dialogue, the thought patterns set forth in the dialogue, and the unique words used during the dialogue.

Reading the documents of a school or school district (such as mission statements, policy manuals, memoranda, newsletters, job advertisements, and student newspapers) can reveal the nuances of an institution's culture. Of course the concept of documents must be expanded to include Web sites, email, and videos that a school or school district uses to communicate with internal and external publics. The analysis is concerned with detecting the tonality of the messages, which can be organized around certain characteristics such as excellence in performance, learning community, caring community, or innovation and risk taking.

Observation analysis is the process of measuring the degree to which a school's or school district's culture undergirds a quality environment. In order to do this analysis, the observer must determine which characteristics indicate a quality environment. For example, key characteristics might be fashioned to focus on identity, collaboration, concern for people, coordination, empowerment, risk support, performance, criticism tolerance, process, and change.

ENDNOTES

1. V. Sathe, "Implications of Corporate Culture: A Manager's Guide to Action," in *Organizational Dynamics* (New York: American Management Association Publishing, 1983), pp. 6–8.

2. R. S. Sharf, *Theories of Psychotherapy and Counseling: Concepts and Cases* (Pacific Grove, California: Brooks/Cole Publishing Company, 1996), pp. 92–93.

3. R. W. Rebore, *The Ethics of Educational Leadership* (Upper Saddle River, New Jersey: Merrill/Prentice Hall Publishing, 2001), pp. 224–226.

4. G. Corey, *Theory and Practice of Group Counseling* (Pacific Grove, California: Brooks/Cole Publishing Company, 1995), p. 124.

5. D. W. Johnson and F. P. Johnson, *Joining Together: Group Theory and Group Skills,* 6th edition. (Boston: Allyn & Bacon Publishing, 1997), pp. 167–168.

6. Sathe, "Implications of Corporate Culture," pp. 8–9.

7. Ibid.

8. S. P. Robbins, *Organizational Behavior: Concepts, Controversies, and Applications,* 6th edition (Englewood Cliffs, New Jersey: Prentice-Hall, Inc., 1993), pp. 7–9.

9. P. D. Leedy and J. E. Ormrod, *Practical Research: Planning and Design,* 7th edition (Upper Saddle River, New Jersey: Merrill/Prentice Hall, 2001), pp. 153–154.

10. Robbins, *Organizational Behavior,* p. 601.

11. Ibid., p. 602.

SELECTED BIBLIOGRAPHY

Argyle, M. *Social Skills and Work.* New York: Methuen & Co., 1981.

Beck, C. E., and E. Beck. "The Manager's Open Door and the Communication Climate." *Business Horizons,* 29 (January–February 1986): 15–19.

Bolton, R. *People Skills: How to Assert Yourself, Listen to Others, and Resolve Conflicts.* New York: Simon & Schuster, Inc., 1986.

DeVito, J. A. *Messages: Building Interpersonal Communication Skills.* New York: Harper & Row Publishers, 1990.

Fontana, D. *Social Skills at Work.* New York: Routledge, 1990.

Friend, M., and L. Cook. *Interactions: Collaboration Skills for School Professionals.* New York: Longman, 1992.

Gordon, G. G. "Industry Determinants of Organizational Culture." *Academy of Management Review,* April 1991: 396–415.

Maier, N. *Problem-Solving Discussions and Conferences: Leadership Methods and Skills.* New York: McGraw-Hill Publishers, 1963.

Martin, R. J. *A Skill and Strategies Handbook for Working with People.* Englewood Cliffs, New Jersey: Prentice-Hall, Inc., 1983.

Murphy, J. *Managing Conflict at Work.* Burr Ridge, Illinois: Business One Irwin/Mirror Press, 1994.

Sathe, V. "Implications of Corporate Culture: A Manager's Guide to Action," in *Organizational Dynamics.* New York: American Management Association, 1983.

Schein, E. H. "Organizational Culture." *American Psychologist,* February 1990: 109–119.

Schneider, B. *Organizational Climate and Culture.* San Francisco: Jossey-Bass Inc., Publishers, 1991.

Schoonover, S. C. *Managing to Relate: Interpersonal Skills at Work.* Reading, Massachusetts: Addison-Wesley, 1988.

York, A. *Managing for Success: A Human Approach.* New York: Cassell Publisher, 1995.

13 Written Communication and Human Relations

Writing is the most important sign system ever invented by humans. It is an obvious fact that humans are the only creatures on earth that have this capability. Linguists rightly point out that speech is also a sign system, but it is much different from writing because language is endemic to being human. All known societies that have ever existed had languages, although most of them were unwritten. All peoples seem to have been able to organize their societies through verbal communication. Speech is essential to self-understanding as well as a society's understanding of its culture. Culture in this context is the wisdom that is transferred from one generation to another.[1]

Writing is a technological achievement that is not essential to humans, but it has had a most profound effect on all civilizations. It is even more impactful than the invention of the computer and the Internet because writing is the most basic component of these advances. Writing emerged probably no more than twelve thousand years ago. Modern humans, Homo sapiens, have existed as a distinct species for approximately one hundred and fifty thousand years. From this perspective, writing is a relatively new invention.[2]

Contemporary society would not exist as it does without writing. Consider this:

> [T]here would be no books, no newspapers, no letters, no tax reports, no paychecks, no identity cards, no lecture notes, no street signs, no labels on commercial products, no advertisements, no medical prescriptions, no systematic education, no dictionaries or encyclopedias, no instruction manuals for radios, cars or computers, a very different kind of religion, a very different kind of law and no science in the proper sense of the word; there would be no linguistics either.[3]

Taking this quotation into the field of educational leadership, without writing there would be no board of education manuals; no American Association of School Administrators (AASA), National Association of Secondary School Principals (NASSP), or National Association of Elementary School Principals (NAESP) codes of ethics; no administrator contracts; no administrative memos and procedures; no student codes of rights and responsibilities; and no teacher evaluation forms.

Power of the Written Word

It is obvious that superintendents and principals who write well have an advantage over those who do not. The message can be clear and compelling, confused, offensive, or just misunderstood, depending on the writing ability of a given superintendent or principal. Further, it is impossible for most administrators to communicate with large numbers of people through giving speeches. All administrators, except those in the smallest schools and school districts, must rely on the written word to communicate with constituents. In terms of good human relations, written communication via school or school district newsletters and other public relations publications is an essential responsibility of educational administrators in our contemporary society. People want to know what educational leaders think about important issues, and even about rather routine matters, that occur in every school and school district. They even expect to receive written communications from these leaders in the mail. Periodically criticism is forthcoming from parents and taxpayers when they are not informed about what is going on in their schools. Most people prefer to receive written communications over attending meetings in order to be informed.

It is primarily in crisis situations that parents and taxpayers want personal contact with administrators. They know, however, that further information will be needed; they also know that written messages are a common way for administrators to communicate about very important issues. In fact, written communication is often more specific and focused than oral communication, particularly because of the distraction that occurs in all human engagements.

The power of written communication can be easily understood in relation to the use that people can make from information and knowledge in an objective form.[4] An individual must personally convey information and knowledge through speech. Once spoken, information and knowledge disappear; nothing remains. However, through writing, information and knowledge can be stored and transmitted independently of the author. Those who have information and knowledge have power.

The superintendent or principal who regularly communicates in writing with his or her staff, students, parents, and community members is empowering them with information and knowledge. Educational administrators also enhance their power because of the dynamics involved in writing. It is impossible to "wing it" in writing. The person who is writing must know the facts, organize them, and strategize on how best to convey his or her interpretation of those facts. Configuring the information and knowledge can bring new insights and perspectives that expand the writer's understanding. Thus the task of writing is a learning activity. Typically the author will acquire a deeper appreciation for the information and knowledge.

Writing, of course, extends the range of communication, and consequently the number of people who are empowered by it. In speech, the message is tied to the messenger. Through writing, spatiotemporal constraints are lifted.[5] The message can be given to people in any place, it can be read at any time of the day or night, and can be read over and over again.

The effectiveness of the administrative infrastructure of a school or school district is directly related to the quality of its written documents. Mission statements, policy documents, curricular guides, procedures manuals, and other documents give purpose and meaning to the varied activities of individuals. It is important to note that quality is not synonymous with quantity; however, there is a predilection to equate these two notions.

Maintaining accountability within a school or school district is impossible without the type of documents just listed. The importance of written documents is easily verified by the impact that the Constitution and the Bill of Rights have on our U.S. society. When conflict arises and when people question the actions of others, there is always legal recourse to those documents that set forth the parameters of the American way of life. That should also be the way it is in schools and school districts.

From this perspective, not only are written documents essential, but so are those who write the documents; they must understand the significance of what they are doing. They are helping to establish the culture of the school or school district. Culture in this context is predicated on attitudes, beliefs and values, feelings, and opinions of the entire school community, not only teachers and administrators but also students, parents, and community members.

In essence, these documents act as a form of social control because people can and should have recourse to them when they want to know what others expect from them. When conflicts arise between teachers and parents, between students and students, and between administrators and teachers, students, or parents, these documents can be a source of clarification and direction. Rules and regulations that govern schools and school districts are the established standards of conduct that people are expected to follow in their dealings with others. The written word has an authority that is respected by most people, even though they do not always adhere to the norms that written documents set forth. Keep in mind that this is referring to the letter of the law, and that the etymology of the words "author" and "authority" is the same.[6]

Privacy is a central issue in contemporary society because of the availability of written information concerning people. Those who know the nuances of computer technology and how information can be accessed through the Internet can find out detailed personal information about almost every citizen. The security of financial and medical records is seriously in question.

Function of Writing in Educational Leadership

It should be obvious from the previous discussion that the most fundamental function of writing is to support memory.[7] Today boards of education change membership more often than in the past, superintendents have an average tenure of between five and six years, and principals seldom consider their job position as a career-long appointment.[8] In addition, memories fade with the passing of time, and what was once decided may become more legend than fact. Thus the minutes from meetings should be conscientiously taken and stored. It is much easier to store these kinds of data today given the advent of the computer disk. Unfortunately some educational administrators neglect the taking of minutes at routine meetings.

A second function of writing is the refinement of a message. The medium, writing, provides a unique opportunity for the superintendent or principal. He or she can return to the message at a later time because the words and sentences have becomes objects; they are tangible and stable. They exist on their own and are depersonalized whereas the spoken word disappears immediately after it materializes.[9]

Furthermore others can treat a written piece as an object that they can use for their own benefit. Interpreting the written word allows others to add a dimension to the writing that may not have been intended by the author yet may be present in the meaning of the words and their configuration in sentences, paragraphs, or the entire document. Even though the meaning may not have been intended, it may be present and certainly can be used to bolster an argument, make a point, defend an action, or make an accusation. In this context, writing provides the vehicle for analyzing language itself.[10]

The third function of writing is to create a milieu within which interactions can occur between the author and the reader. Such an interaction can be more self-reflective because the author is not present when the message is read. Also the reader can consider the ideas of the author in asynchronous time rather than real time. Moreover, if the written document is attractively reproduced, as is possible even for a single piece of writing through desktop publishing, it can have an aesthetic quality that will enhance its message.

This is an important consideration for superintendents and principals because people will be reflecting on what these administrators have written at considerable length and in great detail. For example, people's thoughts about an administrator-author, in addition to her message, can be either positive or negative, depending on her writing ability. Right or wrong, the impression people have of a school or school district is often predicated on the written communications emanating from administrators.

Interpretation of the Written Word

All written communication is interpreted by the reader. It can be no other way because the author is not present to explain his or her message. The reader will consciously or subconsciously make assumptions about the author and about the situation that prompted the author to communicate. Most superintendents and principals will generally draw on the contributions of other educational leaders and prominent educators from present and past generations in developing their ideas about issues, problems, and trends.

When people read a document, they seek to understand not only the words, sentences, and paragraphs but also the overall meaning and purpose conveyed by the author. Of course many people also seek the help of others in understanding the meaning of a text. What they receive, however, is an interpretation of the work; in explanations of interpretations, they receive an interpretation of an interpretation. Even the author of a work who is asked for an explanation of what he or she has written will be filtering the ideas, facts, or information through his or her subsequent experiences and is, in fact, interpreting.

The art of interpretation is call *hermeneutics,* a word derived from Greek mythology. Hermes was the wing-footed messenger god who had the task of communicating what was beyond human understanding in a form that humans could grasp. It is for this reason that the early Greeks proclaimed Hermes as the originator of language and writing as a means of conveying meaning.[11]

This conceptualization of interpretation raises certain questions: "What are the boundaries of interpretation, and does it extend beyond itself? Does interpretation refer to the external world or to specific objects that exist outside of interpretation?[12] In essence, the concept of interpretation is concerned with the degree to which humans can attain absolute knowledge. Must we be content with a chain of interpretations? In a sense, the interpretation dilemma frees humanity from the desire for absolute knowledge. Obviously interpretation mitigates against predetermined meanings; it mediates the development of connections that ultimately can create unity and harmony. Thus interpretation is a methodology by which ideas and concepts of different people are renewed and utilized in subsequent situations. Consequently board of education policy manuals and administrative directives are consulted and interpreted in order to find solutions to problems and issues facing educational administrators.

It is for this reason that even zero-tolerance policies are subject to interpretation. For example, a principal who suspends a student for giving another student an aspirin because of a zero-tolerance drug policy has interpreted the policy to include the distribution of legal as well as illegal drugs. Helping another student who has a headache is laudable, but giving an aspirin to that student was inappropriate. However, the suspension or expulsion of a student over such an incident is also inappropriate. No policy is written perfectly to cover every contingency. In this limited example, the real issue is the interpretation, which leads to three subsequent questions that must be considered in every interpretation. Using the zero-tolerance policy as a guide, the first questions is: *What does the person bring to the interpretation?* William Dilthey (1833–1911) made a significant contribution to the process of interpreting the written word. He was concerned with the role that a person's psyche, and specifically a person's personal interests, has in his or her interpretations.

Of course the major concern in interpreting a given text is objectivity gained through reflection on the precise expressions used by the author and on the logical consistency of the document. It is helpful for a person to reflect on his or her personal history in interpreting a document. The principal involved in the aspirin incident may have been a person whose son or daughter is allergic to aspirin, may be the principal of a school that has a significant number of students who abuse drugs, may have a relative who is a drug user, or may be a person who has a difficult time seeing the gray area in human behavior. Whatever a person's background, it may have an effect on his or her interpretation of written communication.

The second question is: *What is the meaning of the text?* Of course it is important to understand what the author meant to convey, what the document meant to the original audience, and what the nuances of the original situation that prompted the document were.[13] For example, the drug policy might have been formulated immediately after a student had overdosed at school after receiving drugs from another student. The local police department might have asked the school board to consider initiating the policy as a means of helping control drug trafficking in the school; or a group of concerned parents might have appeared at a board meeting demanding that the board enact the drug policy because of information they received from their children about drug problems in the school.

The third question is: *What is the relevance of this document for the present situation?* Using the hypothetical example, since the enactment of the drug policy, the situation may have significantly improved in the schools of a given district. Also the local community may have been mobilized by the problem and enacted lookout patrols in the neighborhoods, using the policy to make arrests when drug trafficking is observed. Thus the problem may not be as serious as it was when the policy was enacted.

The scope of exploration within the educational administration arena is significantly expanded through the principles of interpretation. Superintendents and principals can be as creative as the circumstances will allow in finding solutions to problems and issues. They become liberated from a rigid application of norms set forth in a document in order to find solutions to problems.

The human relations dimension of written communications cannot be overemphasized. Yet it is often a little-understood phenomenon relegated to the mechanics of correct English usage and coherence of expression. It is vitally important to understand that written communications are the cornerstones on which all institutions are founded and presently operate. Schools and school districts are no exception.

DISCUSSION QUESTIONS AND STATEMENTS

1. What is the anthropological significance of writing?

2. Explain how the written word can exercise a power independent of the author.

3. Compare and contrast the power of the written word in relation to human speech.

4. What is the overall effect of school and school district documents on stakeholders?

5. Identify and explain the functions of writing.

6. What are the three questions that can be helpful in interpreting a written document?

EXERCISE **13.1**

Written Communications Assessment

Over time, educational administrators develop ideas and notions about their responsibilities. Sometimes these ideas and notions are undetected or operate just under the surface of consciousness. Almost every administrator has developed ideas about writing because it is such a pervasive responsibility and because it is so important. The following survey is meant to help you, as an administrator, analyze your ideas about writing so that you can develop a plan to become a more effective writer. On a scale of 1 to 3 (1 = disagree, 2 = partially agree, 3 = agree), rate the degree to which your ideas conform to each statement.

Rating

_____ Written communication is an important vehicle for setting forth my agenda as an administrator.

_____ The quality of my written communications will have either a positive or negative effect on readers.

_____ Written communications from administrators are important public relations tools for a school or school district.

_____ School and school district employees as well as taxpayers want to receive written communications from administrators about important and routine matters.

____ Many people prefer to receive written communications rather than attend meetings in order to be informed.

____ Written communication is an essential responsibility of an educational administrator.

____ In a school crisis situation, written communication is essential, even if there are meetings with administrators.

____ The real power of the written word lies in its spatiotemporal independence in the sense that a document can be read and reread anytime.

____ Administrative effectiveness is enhanced through the quality of school and school district policy documents.

____ Accountability is impossible to maintain in the absence of documents that set forth administrative procedures and processes.

____ Administrative documents such as faculty manuals and student codes of rights and responsibilities are necessary for the safe and orderly management of a school or school district.

____ Written documents are important tools that support the culture of a school or school district.

____ Each reader of a written communication is, in fact, an interpreter of what was written.

____ When writing, an administrator needs to remember that the message will be affected by the background and experiences of the reader.

____ It is appropriate that the meaning of a text is subject to the various interpretations of people from different time periods.

____ **Rating** (A maximum rating of 45 indicates that a person is significantly aware of the importance of writing in the practice of educational administration. A rating of 23 can be used as a median score for purposes of analysis.)

SUMMARY

Writing is perhaps the most important sign system that has ever been invented by humans. Even though speech is also a sign system, it is significantly different from writing because language is endemic to being human. The technology of writing has had a profound effect on the human condition and is a cornerstone of contemporary civilizations. Homo sapiens as a species has existed for at least one hundred and fifty thousand years; writing has existed for approximately twelve thousand years.

The written word has a power that is unique. A written message can be clear, compelling, offensive, or misunderstood, depending on the writing skills of the superintendent or principal. All administrators must rely on the written word to communicate with other administrators, teachers, students, parents, and members of the community. The power of the written word is easily seen in its relationship to speech. Immediately after a message is communicated through speech, it disappears. Written communication, however, remains and can be stored and transmitted independently of the author. A person's possession of information and knowledge has generally been considered to be a prerequisite for his or her becoming powerful.

The superintendent or principal who communicates about substantive issues with constituents is, in effect, empowering them with information and knowledge. The administrator is also furthering his or her own power because effective communication is predicated on information and knowledge enhancement. Speech is tied to the time and place of the message, but writing has no spatiotemporal constraints. The message can be received in any place and at any time of the day or night.

The effectiveness of the administration of a school or school district is directly connected to the quality of its written documents, such as policy manuals and mission statements, curricular guides, and procedural manuals. Accountability is difficult to maintain without such documents. These types of documents provide social control for administrators, teachers, students, and other members of a school and school district because people can have recourse to them when they want to know what is expected of them.

The most fundamental function of writing is to support memory. Members of the board of education, superintendents, principals, teachers, and other staff members eventually leave schools or school districts. What remains are the written documents that help to create and maintain the culture of a school or school district.

A second function of writing is the refinement of a communication. The author can return to the message at a later time in order to reflect on what the words and sentences mean. The written word becomes an object that exists on its own. The third function is to create a milieu within which engagement can occur between the author and reader. The reader can react to the author in either a positive or negative manner. This impression is sometimes extended to the school or school district.

All written communication is interpreted by the reader because the author is not present to explain his or her message. People generally seek to understand not only the words, sentences, and paragraphs of a document but also the overall meaning and purpose conveyed by the author. Even the author will filter the ideas, facts, and information of his or her prior written documents through subsequent experiences. The art of interpretation is commonly referred to as hermeneutics.

There are three questions that can be considered in interpreting a written document: What does the person bring to the interpretation? What is the meaning of the text? What is the relevance of this document for the present situation?

ENDNOTES

1. F. Coulmas, *The Writing Systems of the World* (Oxford, England: Basil Blackwell Ltd., 1989), p. 3.

2. D. Schmandt-Besserat, "The Earliest Precursors of Writing," *Scientific American,* 238 (1978): 50–59.

3. Coulmas, *The Writing Systems of the World,* p. 4.

4. Ibid., p. 6.

5. H. Jensen, *Sign, Symbol and Script* (New York: Putnam Publisher, 1969), p. 9.

6. Coulmas, *The Writing Systems of the World,* p. 13.

7. W. J. Ong, *Orality and Literacy: The Technologizing of the Word* (New York: Methuen & Co., 1982), p. 96.

8. T. E. Glass, L. Björk, and C. C. Brunner, *The Study of the American School Superintendency 2000: A Look at the Superintendent of Education in the New Millennium* (Arlington, Virginia: American Association of School Administrators, 2000), p. v.

9. Coulmas, *The Writing Systems of the World,* p. 12.

10. Ibid., p. 13.

11. R. E. Palmer, *Hermeneutics: Interpretation Theory in Schleiermacher, Dilthey, Heidegger, and Gadamer* (Evanston, Illinois: Northwestern University Press, 1985), p. 13.

12. G. L. Ormiston and A. D. Schrift, eds., *The Hermeneutic Tradition: From Ast to Ricoeur* (Albany, New York: State University of New York Press, 1990), p. 4.

13. R. W. Rebore, *The Ethics of Educational Leadership* (Boston: Allyn & Bacon, 2001), p. 12.

SELECTED BIBLIOGRAPHY

Akinnaso, F. N. "On the Difference between Spoken and Written Language." *Language and Speech,* vol. 25, no. 2 (1982): 97–125.

Albrow, K. H. *The English Writing System: Notes Towards a Description.* London: Longman Publishers, 1972.

American Psychological Association. *Publication Manual,* 4th edition. Washington, D.C.: American Psychological Association, 1994.

Bates, J. D. (1980). *Writing with Precision: How to Write So That You Cannot Possibly Be Misunderstood,* 3rd edition. Washington, D.C.: Acropolis Books, Inc., 1980.

de Beaugrande, R., and W. Dressler. *Introduction to Text Linguistics.* London: Longman, 1981.

Carver, R. P. *Writing a Publishable Research Report in Education, Psychology, and Related Disciplines.* Springfield, Illinois: Charles C. Thomas, 1984.

Coulmas, F. *The Writing Systems of the World.* Oxford, England: Basil Blackwell, Ltd., 1989.

Coulmas, F., and K. Ehlich, eds. *Writing in Focus.* New York: Mouton, 1983.

Fries, C. C. *The Structure of English.* New York: Harcourt Brace College Publishers, 1952.

Gelb, I. J. *A Study of Writing.* Chicago: University of Chicago Press, 1963.

Henson, K. T. *The Art of Writing for Publication.* Boston: Allyn & Bacon, 1995.

———. *Writing for Professional Publication: Keys to Academic and Business Success.* Boston: Allyn & Bacon, 1999.

Kissling, M., ed. *Writer's Market: Where & How to Sell What You Write.* Cincinnati, Ohio: Writers Digest Books, 1996.

Sampson, G. *Writing Systems: A Linguistic Introduction.* London: Hutchinson, 1985.

Strunk, W. Jr., and E. B. White. *The Elements of Style.* New York: Macmillan Company, 1959.

Vachek, J. *Written Language: General Problems and Problems of English.* The Hague: Mouton de Gruyter Publisher, 1973.

Zinser, W. *On Writing Well: An Informal Guide to Writing Nonfiction,* 4th edition. New York: HarperCollins Publisher, 1990.

CHAPTER

14 Nonverbal Communication and Human Relations

The term *nonverbal communication* is commonly used and has a variety of meanings. Often it is used to refer to nonvocal expressions that convey to others our feelings and attitudes. However, nonverbal communication is more than that and can include vocalizations such as sighs and laughter along with many other noises that humans routinely make in expressing themselves.

An operative definition of nonverbal communication that is descriptive of the behavior of educational administrators is *those communications transmitted by other than linguistic means.*[1] In this context, a distinction is made between linguistics and vocalization. Linguistics is the study of the nature and structure of language used in human speech and writing. Chapter 13 was concerned with written communication, and Chapter 15 deals with verbal communication.

Nonverbal communication can be divided into physical expressions, environmental expressions, and vocalizations. Physical expressions consist of appearance, facial expressions and eye contact, gestures, orientation, posture, and touching. Environmental expressions include the way people decorate and arrange their office or work area and their desk whereas vocalizations include crying, laughing, and sighing as well as tonality and quality of voice.

Premises of Nonverbal Communication

The first and most basic premise concerning nonverbal communication is that it exists. In fact, nonverbal communication is a part of every encounter with another person, and it is safe to assert that such communication is extremely important and powerful. It is so important that communication through speech could be negated because of the nonverbal communication that accompanies it. It is powerful in the sense that nonverbal communication is immediate and can indicate the true feelings and attitudes of a person. It is inappropriate for a professional administrator to exhibit hostile feelings in speech or in writing. However, it is easy and socially acceptable to exhibit these same feelings in a nonverbal manner through posture, gestures, and facial expressions. In fact, most experienced superintendents and principals pay close attention not only to what people say but also to how they say it. Analyzing nonverbal behavior will give administrators clues concerning feelings and attitudes that they will want to explore further.[2]

The second premise is that nonverbal communication is conditioned by culture. For example, Americans usually feel comfortable conversing at a distance of approximately four feet whereas people from the Middle East tend to stand very close to those with whom they are talking. People from Latin America, southern Europe, and the United States tend to stare directly at those who are speaking to them; people from Asia and northern Europe tend to gaze peripherally at people who are speaking to them. Some studies indicate that African American students usually will not make responses unless they are directly asked by a teacher. The Japanese appear to be more controlled than Americans in their outward expressions. Other researchers have found that African American women and European American women exhibit certain nonverbal expressions when they are interacting in their respective ethnic groups but tend to take on the style of other ethnicities when they are together in a mixed group.[3]

The implications for educational administrators are obvious. Not only can a superintendent or principal be misunderstood, but he or she can misunderstand others also. Furthermore, if an administrator is unaware of the importance of nonverbal communication, he will be unable to take advantage of the opportunity to enhance his oral communication. The manner in which a superintendent or principal handles oral communication could even nullify what he or she is trying to communicate. A weak handshake and a standoffish manner could give the impression that a principal is aloof and feels superior to parents. Such an impression could override the message she is trying to convey in her speech.

The third premise is that nonverbal communication is relational in the sense that it plays a big part in how people are viewed by others. Consequently nonverbal communication has a social effect. The nonverbal communication skills of superintendents and principals will allow them to determine the kind of relationship they want to establish with others. When meeting a problematic parent, a principal might choose to shake the parent's hand while smiling or just nod with a straight face and avoid physical contact. This decision sets the tone of the meeting and establishes the milieu within which the oral communication takes place. Of course the most appropriate behavior is to establish a positive relationship so that the principal and parent can work together in the best interest of the student. However, it is appropriate at times to establish a more serious atmosphere when the issues are serious. A handshake with a serious facial expression could help to impress on the parent the gravity of the situation. Rudeness is never an option for a professional person.

The relational dimension of nonverbal communication has a second function besides defining the kind of relationship administrators create with others. Administrators can convey emotions that they are unable or unwilling to convey in speech or in writing. In the example of the principal who is meeting with a parent about a serious student issue, a serious facial expression and gestures could be used to convey a sense of frustration with the conduct of the student. Gesturing with hands in an upward manner while saying "I've tried everything to convince your daughter that she must come to school" could reinforce the principal's opinion that the parent is the only person who can help the daughter deal with an attendance problem.

The final relational function of nonverbal communication is personal identity management. The way superintendents and principals dress, and their personal grooming preferences, will create an image they have of themselves and the image they want to project to others. A superintendent who never observes "casual Fridays" has a rather formal image of himself, and that is the image he wants others to have of him.[4]

Aspects of Nonverbal Communication

Nonverbal communication can be very ambiguous and often misleading to the person or persons receiving it. The superintendent who begins to pay more attention than usual to a given principal is certainly sending him a message. That message may be appreciation for a great job or concern about the level of his performance.

Some people are more adept at decoding nonverbal messages than others, and there is research to confirm why certain people are better at this process. It is important to note that there is a significant difference between observing nonverbal behavior and decoding it. Someone may be very good at noticing even slight nuances of behavior but totally misunderstand the reason for the behavior.[5] Research indicates that extroverts are good judges of this type of behavior; those people with dogmatic personalities are not. Women are probably better than men at decoding nonverbal messages. In fact, research indicates that people who experience spontaneously expressed nonverbal behavior can only guess at the emotions they convey.[6]

Confirmation is a requirement for understanding all nonverbal communication. The ideas and concerns of a person are easily understood through speech, but the reason behind nonverbal communication will remain ambiguous unless the person receiving the message asks for confirmation. This can be done only through speech or writing. Directly asking a person if something is wrong when a negative nonverbal message is received is the best solution to ambiguity. However, making the same request in writing might be easier when the person sending the nonverbal message appears to be very hostile or very aggravated.

Another aspect of nonverbal communication is its multifaceted and simultaneous nature. Messages transmitted through speech reach us one at a time because people can speak only one word at a time. A superintendent who is annoyed with the behavior of a principal will send that message through her posture, gestures, facial expressions, and even the distance she puts between herself and the principal. The words she speaks to the principal may not be representative of her nonverbal communication, but the principal will certainly get the message that something is not right.

Nonverbal communication also can be continuous. Speech has a beginning and an end. It is obvious when a verbal message has been transmitted. This is not the case with nonverbal communication. Not only will the superintendent's annoyance be conveyed through her bodily expressions; her avoidance behavior also sends a message. The superintendent may begin the avoidance by not returning the principal's telephone calls, by not looking at the principal during an administrative meeting, or by turning away from the principal and talking to another person when they are both in the same group of people.

A final aspect of nonverbal communication is its nondeliberate nature. It is true that people can strategize their nonverbal behavior. A principal might consciously smile when greeting a parent or deliberately use a firm handshake when meeting a member of the board of education. However, nonverbal messages are often unconscious expressions of a person's feelings and attitudes. A principal's slight laughter at what a teacher says might indicate that he thinks the teacher's suggestion is unrealistic even though the principal might not confirm his true feelings in the discussion.[7]

Types of Nonverbal Communication

As previously described, there are three major categories of nonverbal communication: physical expressions, environmental expressions, and vocalizations.

Physical Expressions

Physical expressions are extremely important because people, as corporeal beings, are always in expressive positions. Controlling physical expressions is extremely important for educational administrators because teachers, students, and parents are always observing what administrators are doing and how they are doing it. Some of the most common types of physical expressions are appearance, facial expressions and eye contact, gestures, orientation, posture, and touching. The following descriptions will help to clarify the meaning and purposes of these various nonverbal methods of communicating.

Appearance.   In American society, everyone sends nonverbal messages about who they are through clothing and grooming. A person can improve his appearance not only through clothing and grooming but also through bodily, environmental, and vocal expressions (covered in the following sections). In this context, grooming also means wellness. People who take care of themselves not only through grooming but also through proper diet and exercise are recognized as being healthy, which is a crucial aspect of appearance for a superintendent or principal. Research indicates that appearance can have an effect on human interactions.[8] People who present themselves well through their appearance tend to capture the respect and cooperation of others. As people always in the public eye, educational administrators can probably enhance their effectiveness if they manage their appearance.

Facial Expressions and Eye Contact.   Of course, the face and eyes are the central focal points in all human communication; yet these can be the most difficult to read in terms of nonverbal communication. The reason for this ambiguity is that the configuration of the face and the expressiveness of the eyes are constantly changing. Further, the rapidity of the change is such that a mere second can result in an entirely different configuration or expression. Finally, most emotions and attitudes are reflected in the face and eyes.

In relation to interpretation, the best that can be expected is that certain emotions are recognized as influencing specific parts of the face and eyes. For example, happiness, surprise, anger, and disgust are expressed in the lower face; anger is expressed in the brow and forehead; and happiness, sadness, fear, and surprise are usually expressed in the eyes. A principal who is conscious of how the face and eyes express emotions may be very guarded in his expressions. At times, however, it is possible to see a contradiction between a person's emotions and his or her facial and eye expressions. Sometimes people exaggerate their expression in order to fool another person; it may be possible to observe truer expressions at moments when people think that others are not observing them. It is also possible to note that the facial expressions are trying to convey one emotion while the eyes are conveying another.

Eye contact also has universally recognized meaning. When a person deliberately meets another person's glance and continues the eye contact, it usually reveals a desire for involvement; looking away or avoiding eye contact often means that the person does not want to have contact with the other person. Eye contact also can be used to indicate dominance. When a person feels subordinate or inferior to another, she may avoid eye contact. The converse is also true; if a person feels superior to another, he may stare directly into the face of the other person as a method of reinforcing his felt superiority.[9] The pupils of the eyes are a further indication of a person's feelings. There is research that suggests people's pupils become dilated when they are interested in an object.[10]

Not only can principals and superintendents become proficient in observing the facial and eye expressions of others, but they can utilize these nonverbal methods of communication themselves. The educational administrator who greets people with a warm, open face and who makes eye contact with them can begin a discussion or relationship in a positive manner, which can be most productive when people have problems or concerns. It is often important for people in public positions such as the superintendency and principalship to avoid revealing feelings and attitudes about issues until they have had an opportunity to analyze and study the issues. This is particularly true in relation to the news media. Thus, learning how to control facial expressions and eye contact is a valuable skill.

Gestures.   Gestures are divided into two categories: illustrators and fidgeting. Illustrators are those gestures that require movement of a part of the body, such as a wave of the hand, the raising of an eyebrow, or the shrug of a shoulder, in order to convey an intentional message. As an example, the shrug of a shoulder usually indicates that a person does not know something that another person is asking. Fidgeting covers a host of bodily movements that manipulate objects or parts of the body. Spinning a pen, twirling a lock of hair, and rubbing hands together are examples of fidgeting. Most fidgeting is unintentional and usually means that the person is uninterested, bored, or nervous. A superintendent who is continually rubbing his hands together or twirling an object at a board of education meeting is certainly sending a message to the board and to those in attendance. The message might be that he is tense or nervous; it might be that he really does not care about what is being discussed. In either situation, the message is not desirable. However, fidgeting can be controlled, and administrators who cease to engage in these types of gestures could save themselves from sending others negative messages.

Orientation.   Orientation is signaled by the degree to which a person faces toward or away from another person. This is accomplished by the angle at which people position their body and face. The purpose of this is to indicate the degree to which a person is interested in another person. The interest level may be caused by unfamiliarity or avoidance. For example, a principal may be talking with a group of parents at a school event and desires to complete the conversation before engaging another group of parents. Thus she may deliberately face only those parents with whom she is talking and finish that conversation before acknowledging the presence of another group.

Posture.   Posture is the manner in which people position their body. The two postures that are most evident are the relaxed and the tense positions. A relaxed person might lean back in a chair, stand in a casual position, or perhaps lean against a wall or object. A tense person is usually more rigid in posture; sitting or standing in a ramrod manner usually indicates tension. Tension, however, might be from interest rather than fear or anger. Leaning forward usually indicates interest; in order to do this, the person has to make his or her body more rigid. Sometimes the person who is in an inferior relationship to another person will slouch in a downward position. This may happen, for example, when a teacher is discussing with the principal her inability to control the behavior of the students in her classroom.[11]

Touching.   Of course it is a common human activity to touch other people. The intention of the person doing the touching is the critical aspect. Educational administrators are required to shake hands as a minimal sign of politeness. Physicians, dentists, physical therapists, and medical technicians are required to touch people in order to help them. Hairstylists need to touch people in order to cut their hair. Early childhood and elementary school teachers often touch children during the instructional process. Professional touching is routine.

Other reasons for touch are to communicate concern, friendship, or intimacy. The intention of the person doing the touching, of course, is the primary issue; sometimes it can be detected through the types and circumstances of touch. Researchers have identified a number of factors that can be used to understand a person's intention: the part of the body touched, the duration of the touching, the pressure of the touching, the person or people present during the touching, the situation prompting the touching, and the relationship between the people involved in the touching.[12]

Of course touching can have a positive or negative effect in educational settings. Research indicates that people who receive a slight touch on the arm or shoulder are more apt to comply with a request and tend to develop a more positive attitude toward the person doing the touching.[13] However, a major caution for superintendents, principals, and all educators is the possible misinterpretations of touching. Politeness and friendliness are appropriate intentions, which means that touching between adults and between students and adults should be limited to the establishment and maintenance of professional relationships.[14]

Environmental Expressions

The way people manage their environment is an extension of their physical being. Teachers who have attractively decorated classrooms provide students with an environment that is interesting and stimulating. The same is true concerning the offices of educational administrators as well as the physical appearance of a given school building or a school district's facilities. Research shows that the attractiveness of a space has a direct influence on the energy and the contentment of those who work and learn there.[15]

The environment also extends to the manner in which superintendents or principals work in and around their office. A positive environment is usually created when a principal has an open-door policy whereby teachers and parents can stop by without an appointment. A superintendent who always keeps people waiting to see her, even if they have an appointment, is sending a nonverbal message about her perceived importance. The impression is that her time is more valuable than the time of those who have appointments. An administrator who always has his office door shut, even when another person is not in the office to discuss an issue or problem, is also sending a message about his accessibility and importance.

The concept of territoriality is an important consideration in contemporary education. In the not-too-distant past, the more important the person's job, the more office space and privacy he or she enjoyed. Status was reinforced through space and privacy. This has changed in many schools and school districts. Today functionality and atmosphere are the major concerns. The issues most commonly considered are a person's ability to work effectively and efficiently in the space and the comfort level of the space.[16]

Vocalizations

In this context, it is not what is said that is important but rather how it is said. Thus such qualities as pauses, pitch, speed, tonality, and volume can be just as important as the words that are spoken. Researchers have verified the importance of such qualities in communication through experiments with content-free speech whereby the words were electronically altered in order to become unintelligible. The participants in the experiment could still detect the nonverbal messages without understanding the meaning of the words.

Research further indicates that people are more likely to be influenced by others who have similar voice patterns; for example, fast talkers respond to fast talkers. It is also easy to detect connections between emotions or attitudes and voice patterns. Fear or anger usually causes speakers to raise or lower their voice, and the rate of talking will be faster than normal. Sadness usually causes speakers to lower the pitch of their voice and to speak both in a quiet tone and at a slower pace. Those who speak in a loud tone and without hesitation are usually perceived as being more confident while those who pause a lot and speak in a lower tone are perceived as being unsure of themselves.

Other vocalizations that send nonverbal messages are crying, grunting, moaning, sighing, and laughing. Of course this is just a partial list of vocalizations. Superintendents and principals do not usually use these types of vocalizations because they are inappropriate. However, tonality, speed, and volume are qualities that can have a significant effect on speech, and consequently on the message being sent by administrators. Vocalizations are also controllable. Because administrators are constantly communicating with people, and on many occasions to groups of people, vocalizations can become a major factor in their professional success.[17]

DISCUSSION QUESTIONS AND STATEMENTS

1. Define the term nonverbal communication.

2. What is the most basic premise about nonverbal communication?

3. Explain how nonverbal communication is conditioned by culture and has a social effect.

4. What are the four aspects of nonverbal communication?

5. Why are physical expressions so important to human communication?

6. Explain how vocalization can affect communication.

7. Does environment have an effect on communication?

EXERCISE **14.1**

Nonverbal Awareness Assessment

Educational administrators are usually somewhat aware of their nonverbal communications, but often in an unsystematic way. The following survey is meant to help you, as an administrator, analyze how you communicate in a nonverbal manner in order to develop strategies you can use to communicate in more effective ways. On a scale of 1 to 3 (1 = not at all, 2 = somewhat, 3 = always), rate the degree to which you are aware that you communicate through the indicated nonverbal manner.

Rating

_____ I select my clothing in order to convey the impression I want others to have about me and my leadership abilities.

_____ I am aware that people partially form their opinions about me as a person from my appearance.

_____ I understand that people may judge my ability to perform my responsibilities as an administrator based on the wellness my appearance conveys.

_____ When it is appropriate, I try to make my facial expressions consistent with my feelings and attitudes.

_____ When it is appropriate, I try to use my facial expressions to hide my true feelings and attitudes.

_____ I use direct eye contact to establish rapport with those I meet.

_____ I try to greet people with a warm, open expression on my face.

_____ I use hand and body gestures to reinforce my verbal communications.

_____ I avoid hand and body gestures when they would distract from my verbal communications.

_____ I avoid fidgeting as much as possible in order not to distract the attention of others.

_____ I understand that fidgeting may give the impression that I am nervous or bored.

_____ I angle my body and face toward the person or persons with whom I am communicating.

_____ I utilize the position of my body and face when I am trying to avoid an interruption from another person.

_____ I try to have a posture that is relaxed but dignified when I am in the presence of other people.

_____ I am conscious that I maintain a rigid posture when I am nervous or tense.

_____ I lean toward other people when they are talking to me in order to demonstrate that I am paying attention to what they are saying.

_____ I use a light touch on the arm to convey to others that I am a friendly person.

_____ As a general rule, I avoid touching others because they might misinterpret my intention.

_____ I use a firm handshake in order to express my professional politeness.

_____ I realize that my work environment is considered by others to be an extension of who I am as a person.

_____ I organize my office and immediate work environment in such a way that I give the impression that I am an organized but relaxed person.

_____ My office and work environment have an inviting and friendly atmosphere.

(continued)

_____ I recognize that people develop a positive feeling about their work when they have an office and work environment that are attractive and pleasant.

_____ I realize that the layout of my office can contribute to my being efficient and effective.

_____ I know that how I say something is just as important as what I say.

_____ I try not to use inappropriate vocalizations such as sighing and moaning when communicating with others.

_____ I know that tonality, rate, and volume are important vocalizations that should be controlled when I verbally communicate.

_____ **Rating** (A maximum rating of 81 indicates that a person is significantly aware of the importance of nonverbal communication in the practice of educational administration. A rating of 41 can be used as a median score for purposes of analysis.)

SUMMARY

The term *nonverbal communication* is commonly used to refer to expressions that convey to others feelings and attitudes; however, it is much more than that. An operative definition that is descriptive and applicable to educational leadership is "those communications transmitted by other than linguistic means." This is an important distinction because linguistics is the study of the nature and structure of language as it is used in human speech and writing. Nonverbal communication is divided into physical expressions, environmental expressions, and vocalizations.

The most basic premise about nonverbal communication is that it exists and is part of every encounter between people. Nonverbal communication is also extremely important and powerful. It is powerful because it is immediate and can indicate the true feelings and attitudes of a person.

A second premise is that nonverbal communication is conditioned by culture. Thus nonverbal communication can be easily misunderstood from one culture to another. However, because nonverbal communication can be controlled, an educational administrator can utilize nonverbal communication to enhance oral communications. The third premise is that nonverbal communication is relational in the sense that it plays a big part in how people are viewed by others. Consequently nonverbal communication has a social effect.

There are certain aspects that educational administrators must be cognizant of in order to use nonverbal communication effectively. First, nonverbal communication can be very ambiguous and misleading to people. Thus confirmation (the second aspect) is a requirement for understanding all nonverbal communication. This can be accomplished only through speech or writing. The third aspect is that nonverbal communication is multifaceted and simultaneous in nature; fourth, nonverbal communication is continuous. Finally, nonverbal communication is often nondeliberate in nature.

Physical expressions are extremely important because people are always expressive. Some of the most common types of physical expressions are appearance, facial expressions and eye contact, gestures, orientation, posture, and touching. In American society, we send nonverbal messages about who we are through clothing and grooming. Facial expressions and eye contact are the central focal points in all human communication. Gestures are categorized as either illustrators or fidgeting. Orientation is the degree to which a person faces toward or away from another person. Posture is the manner in which people position their body. Touching is a common human activity; the intention of the person doing the touching is the crucial aspect.

Environmental expressions are extremely important because the environment that humans create is an extension of their physical being. In this context, environment refers to the work environment of educational administrators; it includes not only what their office looks like but also the manner in which they work in and around the office. Furthermore the way the educational administrator creates and utilizes the school's and school district's environments are considerations.

Vocalization refers to the fact that how something is said is just as important as what is said. Such qualities as pauses, pitch, speed, tonality, and volume can even negate the content of speech. Of course nonverbal messages are also sent by crying, grunting, moaning, sighing, and laughing. For educational administrators, tonality, rate, and volume are vocalization qualities that most affect their communications.

ENDNOTES

1. R. B. Adler and N. Towne, *Looking Out/Looking In,* 8th edition (New York: Harcourt Brace College Publishers, 1996), pp. 227–228.

2. Ibid., p. 229.

3. Ibid., pp. 230–231.

4. Ibid., p. 232.

5. M. L. Knapp and J. Hall, *Nonverbal Communication in Human Interaction,* 3rd edition (Forth Worth, Texas: Harcourt Brace Jovanovich Publishers, 1992), pp. 466–477.

6. R. Rosenthal, ed., "Gender, Gender Roles, and Nonverbal Communication Skills," in *Skill in Nonverbal Communication: Individual Differences* (Cambridge, Massachusetts: Oelgeschlager, Gunn, and Hain, 1979), pp. 32–67.

7. Adler and Towne, *Looking Out/Looking In,* pp. 240–242.

8. Knapp and Hall, *Nonverbal Communication in Human Interaction,* pp. 93–132.

9. Adler and Towne, *Looking Out/Looking In,* pp. 247, 249–50.

10. E. H. Hess and J. M. Polt, "Pupil Size as Related to Interest Value of Visual Stimuli," *Science,* 132 (1960): 349–350.

11. Adler and Towne, *Looking Out/Looking In,* pp. 242–247.

12. J. M. Wiemann and R. P. Harrison, eds., "Touch: A Bonding Gesture," in *Nonverbal Interaction* (Beverly Hills, California: Sage Publications, Inc., 1983), pp. 47–75.

13. C. R. Kleinke, "Compliance to Requests Made by Gazing and Touching Experimenters in Field Settings," *Journal of Experimental Social Psychology,* 13 (1977): 218–223.

14. Adler and Towne, *Looking Out/Looking In,* pp. 255–257.

15. A. Maslow and N. Mintz, "Effects of Aesthetic Surroundings: Initial Effects of Those Aesthetic Surroundings upon Perceiving 'Energy' and 'Well-Being' in Faces," *Journal of Psychology,* 41 (1956): 247–254.

16. Adler and Towne, *Looking Out/Looking In,* pp. 262, 264–266.

17. Ibid., pp. 252–253.

SELECTED BIBLIOGRAPHY

Burgoon, J. K. "Relational Message Interpretations of Touch." *Journal of Nonverbal Behavior,* vol. 15 (1991): 233–259.

Ekman, P., and W. V. Friesen. "Nonverbal Leadage and Clues to Deception." *Psychiatry,* vol. 32 (1969): 88–105.

———. "Handmovements," *The Journal of Communication,* vol. 22 (1972): 353–374.

Gazda, G. M., F. R. Asbury, F. J. Balzer, W. C. Childers, R. E. Phelps, and R. P. Walters. *Human Relations Development: A Manual for Educators,* 5th edition. Boston: Allyn & Bacon, 1995.

Haase, R. F., and D. T. Tepper. "Nonverbal Components of Empathetic Communication." *Journal of Counseling Psychology,* vol. 19 (1972): 417–424.

Hickson, M. L., and D. W. Stacks. *NVC: Nonverbal Communication: Studies and Applications,* 2nd edition. Dubuque, Iowa: W. C. Brown Publishers, 1989.

Katz, A. M., and V. T. Katz, eds. *Foundations of Nonverbal Communication.* Carbondale, Illinois: Southern Illinois University Press, 1983.

Knapp, M. L., and J. Hall. *Nonverbal Communication in Human Interaction,* 3rd edition. Fort Worth, Texas: Harcourt Brace Jovanovich Publishers, 1992.

Knapp, M. L., and G. R. Miller, eds. *Handbook of Interpersonal Communication.* Newbury Park, California: Sage Publications, Inc., 1994.

Leathers, D. G. *Successful Nonverbal Communication.* New York: Macmillan Publishing, 1986.

CHAPTER

15 Verbal Communication and Human Relations

Educational administrators are in the talking business. School and school district administration, of course, is a service-to-people industry that requires personal and collective engagement. Superintendents and principals are constantly engaging other administrators, teachers, staff members, students, and community leaders in discussion and dialogue. Thus verbal communication is an essential part of the job.

Verbal communication, however, can be ambiguous. Sometimes people misinterpret what administrators say, and sometimes administrators misunderstand what others say. Yet verbal communication is a unique characteristic of humans; it is a marvelous gift that enables people to penetrate more deeply into human relationships. Linguists believe that although writing is an invention of humans and has existed for approximately ten thousand years, some form of verbal communication has always been an innate characteristic of humans.[1]

Without language, humans would be much more isolated than they are. In fact, common experience demonstrates that people who are inadequate verbal communicators tend to be more isolated from others and are often misunderstood. Furthermore verbal communication skills are a necessary requirement in most jobs because even if people are manufacturing a product, they still must communicate with supervisors and other employees. For the vast majority of job positions, if applicants cannot verbally communicate with at least a minimal level of proficiency, they will probably not get the job.

Premises of Verbal Communication

Language is symbolic; this is the most basic premise.[2] Words by themselves have no meaning; it is by common agreement that humans give meanings to words. That agreement for most words is long past, and what children are taught is the outcome of centuries of experience in word usage that is specific to a certain culture. In fact, there are semantic rules governing the meaning of words. There is no doubt that the English spoken by Americans is somewhat different from the English spoken by those in England and other countries. Yet because of semantic rules, people from these countries can and do understand each other.

Human experience indicates that people can use words to mean something different than what has been the common usage. This is particularly true when people engage in slang. Words such as "boss," "crib," and "posse" have meanings, particularly among young people, that are quite different from the usual meanings. In addition to meaning a person's supervisor or the owner of a company, "boss" can mean that a person is looking healthy and nice. "Crib" has come to mean the place where a person lives, a home or apartment; "posse" is used to refer to a person's friends. Of course principals, teachers, and others who work with children and young people are quite aware of the unique meanings that students give to some words.

Being acutely aware of the subjectiveness of word meanings is important for educational administrators because of the ambiguity and possible misunderstandings that can occur in verbal communication. Superintendents and principals can make assumptions and form conclusions about issues based on word meanings that might not accurately convey what people are telling them. Consequently it is always important to clarify the meaning of statements. Even though verbal language can be imprecise, through dialogue it is quite possible to come to an exact understanding of the issues and problems that are of concern to people.

A second important premise of language is that its structure is important. The reason why speech is an effective method of communication is because it is governed by linguistic rules. *Phonological rules* set forth how words are to be pronounced. A common method for learning a foreign language is to become familiar with cognates, which are words that have similar pronunciations in both English and a foreign language. Certain words are even spelled exactly the same way. For example, the English words "abnormal," "actor," and "animal" are spelled the same way, have the same meaning, and are similarly pronounced in Spanish. *Syntactic rules,* such as where the verb should be placed in a question, establish how words should be arranged in phrases, clauses, and sentences. *Semantic rules* are concerned with the meanings of words as explained above. Finally there are *pragmatic rules* that help people interpret communications in a given context.[3]

For superintendents and principals, the pragmatic rules require special attention. Phonological, syntactic, and semantic instruction are an integral part of every person's education from elementary school through whatever level becomes the last year of formal education. However, the pragmatic rules of verbal communication are not always taught. Pragmatic rules are primarily learned through experience and are conditioned by circumstances and culture. Exhibit 15.1 shows a paradigm that can be used to analyze the pragmatic effects of speech. The sentence that is being analyzed is "That's a really nice job of teaching." For this example, the verbal message is communicated by two different principals in two different schools to two different elementary classroom teachers.

EXHIBIT **15.1**

Verbal Communication Analysis

Statement: That's a really nice job of teaching.

Principal One

Intention: To give a compliment

Relationship: Supervisor

Context: Informal remark when visiting a classroom

Personal orientation: Usual behavior

Principal Two

Intention: To indicate that the teacher has improved

Relationship: Supervisor

Context: Formal evaluation while observing a teacher's behavior in the classroom

Personal orientation: Uncommon behavior

It is obvious from the comparison of the two situations that a simple statement can have two different ramifications depending on the intention, relationship, context, and personal orientation of the person making the statement. The two people in this example are principals; thus the similarity is that they are both supervisors. Their intentions, the contexts, and their personal orientations are different. The statement is much more meaningful coming from Principal Two because he or she is carrying out a formal evaluation of a teacher who needed to improve performance, which is so indicated by the principal's intention. Further, the fact that Principal Two does not usually make such statements gives the statement more meaning. Principal One is a person who usually gives such compliments and is making the statement in an informal way. This compliment is nice but is not as significant as that of Principal Two.

Ramifications of Verbal Communication

There are three ramifications stemming from verbal communication. First, the words, phrases, clauses, and sentences that people use can have a significant effect on the way they see the circumstances and events that are going on around them. Second, verbal communication can have a significant effect on how they view themselves. Third, speech affects how they view other people. The following treatment explains how these ramifications are played out in the lives of administrators.

It is obvious to most people that a person's name is extremely important for his or her self-identity. Children are comfortable with diminutives; adolescents sometimes use nicknames to set themselves apart from others. Adults generally use more formal names when they are in job positions that require a certain amount of respect. Hyphenated last names might indicate that a family name is important to maintain. Women may retain their family name after marriage in order to establish themselves as professionals or skilled individuals apart from their husbands. It behooves superintendents and principals to be cognizant of the importance that people place on the proper use of their names. For example, it is never appropriate to use a diminutive unless the other person initiates it. Furthermore educational administrators who know the names of staff members, students, parents, and colleagues will make a favorable impression on them.[4]

In order to establish a sense of solidarity with others, people sometimes try to utilize speech patterns that are similar to those used by the ones with whom they are trying to connect. In like manner, when people want to establish a sense of distance from others, they may use speech patterns that are dissimilar. The choice of vocabulary, rate of speaking, and use of pauses are a few ways to accomplish either solidarity or distance. Superintendents and principals may promote solidarity by avoiding educational vocabulary when talking with a parent, or they may deliberately use educational jargon to impress the parent with the fact of their professional position. There is a significant difference between the relationship a principal will establish with a parent when he says, "Your child is exhibiting dysfunctional behavior that is creating a learning problem in the classroom for other students" and the relationship he might establish by saying "Mary doesn't seem to be paying attention to her teacher, which is causing other children to do the same thing."[5] In this context, the second sentence is probably more effective because the principal is conveying the same message in a more polite manner; also the principal is establishing a relationship that will probably produce more cooperation from the parent. It is seldom that superintendents or principals have to use power tactics in speech to establish the importance of what they are saying.

The degree of abstraction that an educational administrator uses in speech can have a positive or negative effect on others.[6] The more abstract a statement is, the greater opportunity for misunderstanding. However, abstraction can also be used by superintendents or principals when they are faced with saying something that might offend another person. The principal who asks a superintendent if he likes the wall graphics that were painted by one of the art teachers might say, "They're really different and unusual." In fact, the superintendent may not like the graphics but also may not want to offend either the principal or the art teacher.

When a situation requires another person to clearly understand a message, the more specific the verbal exchange is, the better. When a principal is performing in an inadequate manner, the superintendent must use specific examples to reinforce a change in behavior that the principal must make in order to improve her performance. For example:

> You have a problem completing reports on time. The budget for your school was received in the business office three weeks after the deadline; this is the second year in a row that you have missed the budget deadline. As I discussed with you last November, not following the budgeting schedule creates a problem for the business office staff because they have deadlines to meet in preparing the budget for the board of education. Furthermore your enrollment and attendance reports have been at least four days late every month last year and this year. As I also discussed with you last May, the enrollment and attendance reports are what we use to request state aid. Finally, I can't remember an administrators' meeting over the last eighteen months when you did not come in late. The other principals are also busy, but they seem to get to the meetings on time. It's important for you to understand that if these behaviors continue, I will not ask the board of education to renew your contract as a principal.

Of course this type of discussion would also be put in writing for the principal.

In this situation, the superintendent does not use general words such as "always" and "never." Rather, he is very direct in telling the principal what the problems are by specifying numbers and dates along with explaining why her behavior is a problem. Furthermore the superintendent does not make a value judgment about the motivation of the principal but rather sets forth the problems and makes clear what the consequences would be if her behavior does not change.

The superintendent is using "I" and "you" language in this discussion. While using "I" and "you" is honest and appropriate in this situation, it can also make the other person angry and defensive. Nonpersonal words can help mitigate anger and defensiveness. For example, the superintendent might have said, "Last November it was discussed that not following the budget schedule creates a problem for the business office." All personal references have been taken out of this sentence. However, it is also more ambiguous, and in this situation being direct is more important; in a less serious situation, it might be more desirable to be less personal.[7]

For the part of the discussion about the problem of turning in reports on time, a less aggressive approach would probably be more helpful. The superintendent could have said, "We need your help. The staff in the business office and I have deadlines to meet in preparing the budget and other reports for the board of education. Please help us by following the schedule."

The superintendent is also using language that is grounded in facts. The principal was late turning in her budget and other reports; she also arrived late to administrator meetings. These are not the opinions of the superintendent but rather the reality of the principal's behavior. The superintendent is not inferring anything from the principal's behavior except that it did happen and that her behavior caused problems for and was unfair to other people. The superintendent is not using language that in and of itself will cause an emotional reaction from the principal; he is not casting aspersions on the principal's character.

There appear to be significant similarities in the topics that men talk about with other men and that women talk about with other women.[8] Of course there are also differences. Much of the differences center more on style of conversation than on content. However, in schools and school districts, the professional conversations that occur are definitely similar not only in content but also in style, regardless of whether the conversation is male to male or female to female. The factors that produce these similarities are the professional job responsibilities of administrators, teachers, and staff members.

The language people use can have a dramatic effect on their view of other people and even of the world around them. The words people choose to express themselves are the vehicles for producing these perspectives. Some people are concerned about expressing ideas, thoughts, and feelings. They tend to use direct language and look for the meaning in the words, phrases, clauses, and sentences that are spoken. People who use this style of speaking tend to be more informal in their conversations. Most administrators, teachers, and staff members have this orientation.

Others are more concerned about using language as a means of establishing and maintaining relationships. They tend to use language in a contextual sense and interpret what people are saying from this same perspective. Thus they place greater emphasis on nonverbal communication, on the situation, and on the relationship of the speaker to the listeners. These people tend to be more formal in their style of speaking. Some parents, politicians, and business leaders have this orientation.

The final ramification of verbal communication is the effect that words, phrases, clauses, and sentences have on shaping and reflecting people's view of others as well as their own personal reality. People who are prejudiced toward a certain ethnic group may transmit this attitude to their children by using derogatory language. Such language begins to shape their children's attitude and can be reinforced by the continual use of appropriate language when speaking about other ethnic groups. This same phenomenon occurs in the way some people speak to their children about members of the opposite gender.

The issue for educational administrators is not just that they themselves do not use this type of inappropriate language but also that they remind other educators, students, and parents that such language is not acceptable in the school setting.[9]

DISCUSSION QUESTIONS AND STATEMENTS

1. What is the most basic premise about language?

2. Explain and contrast phonological, syntactic, and semantic rules.

3. How are pragmatic rules learned and conditioned?

4. Identify and explain the three ramifications stemming from verbal communication.

5. Explain how verbal communication can have either a positive or negative effect on others.

EXERCISE **15.1**

Verbal Awareness Assessment

Educational administrators are usually somewhat aware of their verbal communications, but often in an unsystematic way. The following survey is meant to help you, as an administrator, analyze how you communicate in a verbal manner so you can develop strategies you can use to communicate in more effective ways. On a scale of 1 to 3 (1 = never, 2 = sometimes, 3 = always), rate the degree to which you are aware that you communicate through the indicated verbal manner.

Rating

_____ I an aware of the fact that my verbal expressions give people an impression of my abilities as an educational administrator.

_____ I know that other people may not be sure about the meaning of what I am saying to them.

_____ I recognize that dialogue and discussion with other people will help me develop a deeper understanding of who they are as persons.

_____ I recognize that good verbal skills are essential in order for me to adequately perform my job as an educational administrator.

_____ I recognize that using slang might cause other people to misunderstand the meaning I am trying to convey.

_____ When I don't understand the messages other people are trying to convey to me in verbal speech, I attempt to clarify their messages through dialogue and discussion.

_____ I am aware of the fact that good verbal communication requires the proper use of phonological, syntactic, semantic, and pragmatic rules.

_____ I understand that my intention in conveying a verbal message will have an effect on how it is received.

_____ I know that my relationship with other people will have an effect on how they receive my verbal communications.

_____ I understand that the context within which I send formal and informal verbal communications will have an effect on how people receive them.

_____ I understand that my personal orientation in life will affect the interpretation people make concerning my verbal communications.

_____ When addressing other people, I am aware of the importance that using their names will have on how they receive my message.

_____ I recognize that my vocabulary, rate of speaking, and use of pauses can give people the impression that I am trying to either establish a relationship with them or distance myself from them.

_____ I understand that the degree of abstraction in my speech will lead to ambiguity in the message I am sending to people.

_____ I use abstraction as a method to avoid saying something that will offend another person.

_____ I recognize that using general words such as "always" and "never" adds to the ambiguity of my verbal communications.

_____ I understand that the best way to communicate is to describe the behavior of others in specific terms.

_____ In communicating, I recognize that my message will be better understood if I use pronouns such as "I," "you," and "we."

_____ I understand that effective communication is grounded in facts.

_____ Although there are differences in the style and content of speech used by men and women, the style and content of professional conversations and discussions are virtually the same among men and women.

_____ I understand that the words, phrases, clauses, and sentences I use in verbal communications can affect the way I perceive people and events.

_____ I understand that the words, phrases, clauses, and sentences I use in verbal communications can affect the way I establish and maintain relationships.

_____ I understand that the words, phrases, clauses, and sentences I use in verbal communications can affect my self-image.

_____ **Rating** (A maximum rating of 69 indicates that a person is significantly aware of the importance of verbal communication in the practice of educational administration. A rating of 35 can be used as a median score for purposes of analysis.)

SUMMARY

Superintendents and principals are continually engaging other administrators, teachers, staff members, students, and community leaders in conversation and discussion. Verbal communication is therefore a key part of being educational leaders. However, verbal communication can be ambiguous, and people can misinterpret what others say and be misunderstood themselves.

The most basic premise of language is that it is symbolic. Words by themselves have no meaning but are given meaning by the agreement of people. However, experience teaches us that people can and do use words to mean something different from the common usage. Thus, being aware of the subjectiveness of word meanings is vital for educational administrators; it is important to clarify the meaning of statements.

The second premise of language is that its structure is important. Phonological rules dictate how words are to be pronounced; syntactic rules establish how words should be arranged in phrases, clauses, and sentences. Semantic rules deal with the meaning of words, and pragmatic rules help people interpret communications in their context. Pragmatic rules are mostly learned through experience and are conditioned by events and culture. Thus a statement must be interpreted by analyzing the intention, relationship, context, and personal orientation of the person making the statement.

There are three ramifications stemming from verbal communications: First, verbal communications can have a significant effect on how people view circumstances and events; second, verbal communications have an effect on the way people view themselves; third, verbal communications can affect how people view others.

Therefore, the way educational administrators verbally communicate can have a positive or negative effect on other people. Particularly important are the following issues in verbal communications: the use of a person's name, the use of certain speech patterns, the degree of abstraction used in speech, the content and style of verbal communications, the effect of speech on establishing and maintaining relationships, and the effect of verbal communications on shaping and reflecting a person's view of reality.

E N D N O T E S

1. F. Coulmas, *The Writing Systems of the World* (Cambridge, Massachusetts: Basil Blackwell, Inc., 1989), p. 4.

2. R. B. Adler and N. Towne, *Looking Out/Looking In,* 8th edition (New York: Harcourt Brace College Publishers, 1996), p. 172.

3. R. P. Philipchalk and J. V. McConnell, *Understanding Human Behavior,* 8th edition (New York: Holt, Rinehart and Winston, Inc., 1994), pp. 346–350.

4. Adler and Towne, *Looking Out/Looking In,* pp. 181–182.

5. Ibid., pp. 182–183.

6. Ibid., p. 188.

7. Ibid., p. 196.

8. A. Hass and M. A. Sherman, "Reported Topics of Conversation among Same-Sex Adults," *Communication Quarterly,* 30 (1982): 332–342.

9. Adler and Towne, *Looking Out/Looking In,* pp. 214–218.

S E L E C T E D   B I B L I O G R A P H Y

Andrews, L. *Language Exploration & Awareness.* New York: Longman, 1993.

Ellis, A., and G. Beattie. *The Psychology of Language and Communication.* New York: Guilford Press, 1986.

Floley, J. M. *The Theory of Oral Composition: Theory and Methodology.* Bloomington, Indiana: Indiana University Press, 1988.

Giles, H., and J. M. Wiemann, eds. *"Miscommunication" and Problematic Talk.* Newbury Park, California: Sage Publications, Inc., 1991.

Gronbeck, B. E., T. J. Farrell, and P. A. Soukup. *Media, Consciousness, and Culture: Explorations of Walter Ong's Thought.* Newbury Park, California: Sage Publications, Inc., 1991.

Ong, W. J. *Orality & Literacy: The Technologizing of the Word.* New York: Routledge, 1988.

Rothwell, J. D. *Telling It Like It Isn't: Language Misuse and Malpractice/What We Can Do about It.* Englewood Cliffs, New Jersey: Prentice-Hall, Inc., 1982.

Sprague, J., and D. Stuart. *The Speaker's Handbook,* 4th edition. New York: Harcourt Brace College Publishers, 1996.

Vassallo, P. "How Clearly Do Your Words Communicate?" *International Society for General Semantics,* vol. 53, no. 1 (Spring 1996): 85–90.

Wood, J. T. *Gendered Lives: Communication, Gender, and Culture.* Belmont, California: Wadsworth, 1994.

EPILOGUE

Effective human relations is such an important issue in contemporary educational leadership that it has almost become a commonsense concern. Yet common sense will not in and of itself produce effective human relations. It takes a concerted, organized, and persistent attempt by administrators to deal with this issue. The challenge is ever present because effective human relations is the milieu within which education takes place. Educators are in the human relations business. We cannot practice our profession without establishing effective human relations; there is no way around it. Everything depends on it.

Some people might suggest that the root cause for ineffective human relations is the excessive materialism of contemporary life, which seems to indicate that true happiness comes from obtaining more of everything. Of course, more of everything does not bring happiness if it cannot be shared with other people. Loneliness is often the final outcome of ineffective human relations. For human beings, nothing can fill the void created when people are no longer interested in professional or personal relationships.

Stress is also a root cause for ineffective human relations, but stress can be controlled. When administrators find that the responsibilities of their position are causing undue stress, they must find a way to reduce this condition or the condition will take control and the outcome will be ineffective human relations.

Perhaps the most fundamental principle of effective human relations is to respect the dignity of each person as a human being. It is this dignity that needs no explanation or justification; it gives each person the right to be a full-fledged member of the community within which he or she lives and functions. This clearly establishes the social context of life, and the fact that everyone's lives are interconnected. Effective human relations is the requirement for living this interdependent life. The engagement of people will be effective to the degree that each person is valued by others and the degree to which people are allowed to become fully participating members of the community. It is this participation that ensures the dignity of all people, and it also promotes the common good.

Thus administrators, teachers, and staff members have a right to be empowered to practice their profession. Such empowerment is essential to them in carrying out their responsibilities. The school and school district become the place that will either promote or devalue human dignity.

INDEX

Activities, 147, 157
Adler, Alfred, 3, 6, 17
Adler, R. B., 142, 177, 186
Adlerian Psychology, 6–7
Administrator responsibility/duty, 90–104,
    93, 101
Affirmative Action And Equal
    Employment Opportunity, 117
  Federal laws about, 117
Akinnaso, F. N., 167
Alberta, J. K., 143
Albrow, K. H., 167
American Psychological Association, 167
Andrews, L., 186
Angel, E., 18
Ansbacher, H. L., 18
Ansbacher, R., 18
Antigone, 93
Antoninus, Marcus Aurelius, 96, 97, 102,
    103, 104
Anxiety, 4
Appearance, 171
Archetypes, 5–6, 16–17
  Persona, 5
  Self, 6
  Shadow, 6
Argyle, M., 158
Aristotle, 94, 95, 102, 104
Asbury, F. R., 142, 177
Assessment exercises
  Conflict Resolution Awareness, 110
  Congruency, 41
  Defensive Power Tactics, 26–27
  Duty in Human Relations, 100–101
  Empathetic Relationships, 36–38
  Empowerment, 48–49
  Empowerment Process, 47
  Ethics of Human Relations, 70–71
  Human Relations Orientation, 14–16
  Nonverbal Awareness, 175–176

  Observation Analysis, 155–156
  Overt Administrator Power Tactics,
    26
  Political Tensions, 83–84
  Positive Regard, 43–44
  Public Discourse Awareness, 125
  Servant Leadership, 27–28
  Social Justice Awareness, 118–119
  Verbal Awareness, 184–185
  Written Communication, 164–165
Atkinson, M., 142
Attitudes, 145–146

Baier, A., 112
Balzer, B. J., 142, 177
Bandura, Albert, 10, 18
Barrett-Lennard, G. T., 39
Bates, J. D., 167
Baum, H. S., 31
Beattie, G., 186
Beck, Alfred, 12, 18
Beck, C. E., 158
Beck, E., 158
Behavior, 148, 157
Behavior, extinguish of , 11
Behavioral Psychology, 10–11
Beiser, F. C., 104
Beliefs, 146
Berlin, I., 120
Bernard, M. E., 18
Bhindi, N., 31
Bibliographies, selected
  Administrator Responsibility and
    Effective Human Relations, 104
  Basic Principles of Communications in
    Human Relations, 142–143
  Conflict, Pluralism, and Human
    Relations, 112
  Cultural Communication and Human
    Relations, 158

Human Relations in an Ethical Context, 74

Nonverbal Communication and Human Relations, 177–178

Psychological Foundations of Human Relations, 18

Public Discourse in a Human Relations Context, 127

Social Justice in a Human Relations Context, 120

The Empathetic Administrator, 39

The Genuine Administrator, 51

The Use of Power and Its Impact on Human Relations, 31

Transcendental Leadership and Human Relations, 85

Verbal Communication and Human Relations, 186

Written Communication and Human Relations, 167

Bill of Rights, 118

Björk, L., 166

Blum, L. A., 142

Bolton, R., 158

Bouchard, C. E., 73, 120

Brenders, D., 142

Brunner, C. C., 166

Buley, J., 143

Burgoon, J. K., 177

Cahn, Jr., D. D., 142

Cahoone, L., 74

Carver, R. P., 167

Categorical Imperative, 90–92, 101

maxim, 91, 101

Childers, W. C., 142, 177

Childhood development, 3

Citizens, duty of, 94–96, 102

Clark, R. W., 51

Client-Centered Psychology, 9

Coercive power, 19

Cognitive-behavioral approach, 10–14, 17

Cognitive Psychology, 12

automatic thoughts, 12

cognitive schemata, 12

Collective unconscious, 5, 16

Communication, human, 129–186

aspects of, 131–137, 140–141

assumptions about, 131–132, 140

basic principles, 131–143

consequences of, 133–134, 141

content of, 134–136, 141

cultural context of, 136–137, 141

definition, 139, 142

personal development and, 132–133, 141

praxis, 137–138, 141

principles of, 139–140

Conflict and pluralism, 105–112, 111, 113

Congruency, 41, 49

Conscience, 65

Consciousness, 77–78, 93

human, 72

levels of, 5

Constitution of the United States of America, 118

Control theory, 13

Cook, L., 158

Copleston, F., 74, 103

Corey, G., 18, 50, 158

Cottingham, J., 74

Coulmas, F., 166, 167, 186

Council of Chief State School Officers, ix, xii

Countertransference, 5

Critique of Practical Reason, 90, 91

Cultural communication, 129, 140, 144–158

analysis of, 148–155

components of, 145–146

context of, 134–136

definition of, 145

expressions of, 147–148

organizational culture, 144–155

Curtis, R. C., 142

Cushman, D. P., 142

Daly, J. A., 142, 143

de Beaugrande, R., 167

de Chardin, Teilhard, 57, 67, 72, 73, 74

Declaration of Independence, 118
Depth Psychology, 77–78
Describing analysis, 149–150, 157
de Solages, Bruno, 73
De Vito, J. A., 158
Dewey, John, 90, 97, 98, 102, 103
Dilthey, William, 163
Discussion questions and statements, 14, 28,
    30, 36, 49, 70, 83, 100, 118, 124, 140,
155,164, 174, 184
Document analysis, 151–153, 157
Dressler, W., 167
Duck, S., 142
Duignan, P. 31

Eck, D. L., 85, 112, 142
Ego, 5
Ego-defense mechanism, 4, 16
Ehlich, K., 167
Ekman, P., 177
Ellenberger, H., 18
Ellis, Albert, 11, 12, 17, 186
Empathetic administrator, 32–39, 38, 39
  definition of, 32
  nature of, 32–35
  way of being, 33
Empowerment, 10, 45–49, 50, 98–99, 103,
    187
  assessment of, 48
process of, 46
Epigenesis, principle of, 62
Erikson, Erik, 62–63
Ethical and philosophical foundations,
    53–127
Ethical decisions, 65–66
  deontologism, 66
  mixed consequentialism, 65–66
  strict consequentialism, 65
Ethical principles, 69
Ethics, 55–74
  context of, 55–74
deontological approach, 56
  human consequences of, 60–61, 72
  norms, 56–59, 72
  teleological approach, 56

Evolution, 56–57
Existential Psychology, 8
Eye contact, 171–172, 177

Facial expressions, 171, 176–177
Farrell, T. J., 186
Feelings, 146
Fletcher, Joseph, 65
Floley, J. M., 186
Fontana, D., 158
Frankl, Viktor, 66, 67, 73, 74
  will to meaning, 67
Freedom, human, 57, 60, 68–69, 72, 93
Freud, Sigmund, 3, 6, 16
Freudian Psychoanalytic Psychology, 3–5
Friend, M., 158
Fries, C. C., 167
Friesen, W. V., 177
Fuchs, Josef,
Fudge, K., 142

Gazda, G. M, 142, 177
Gelb, I. J., 167
Genuine administrator, 40–51
Gestures, 172, 177
Giacolone, R. A., 31, 142
Giles, H., 186
Glass, T. E., 166
Glasser, William, 13, 18
Glover, J., 142
Gordon, G. G., 158
Gratton, C., 85
Greer, J. T., 50, 51, 103
Grisez, Germain, 66
Gronbeck, B. E., 186
Grounding for the Metaphysics of Morals,
    90, 91
Gula, R. M., 73, 74
Guyer, P., 104

Haase, R. F., 177
Habermas, J., 112, 122, 125, 126, 127,
    137, 140, 141, 142
Hall, J., 177, 178
Hamachek, D. F., 51

Harrison, R. P., 177
Harvey, D., 112
Hass, A., 186
Hecht, M. L., 143
Hegel, Georg Wilhelm Friedrich, 93, 94, 101, 102, 103, 104
Heidegger, Martin, 8
Heifetz, R., 31
Henson, K. T., 167
Hermeneutics, 162, 166
Hermes, 162
Hess, E. H., 177
Hickson, M. L., 178
Hitchock, J., 73, 85
Hobbes, Thomas, 138, 140, 142
Humanistic approach, 7–10, 17
Human relations principles, 7, 10, 13
Husserl, Edmund, 8

Immigrants, 76–77
Inculturation, 76–77
Individual Psychology, 7
Ingram, D., 74
Instincts, 5
Interstate School Leaders Licensure Consortium (ISLLC), ix, xii

Janssen, Louis, 65
Jaspers, Karl, 8
Jensen, H., 166
Johnson, D. W., 158
Johnson, F. P., 158
Johnson, O. A., 73
Jung, Carl, 3, 5, 6, 16, 18, 77, 84, 85
Jungian Psychology, 5–6
Justice, social, 105, 113–120, 119
    basic notions of, 113–115
    commutative, 113, 119
    court cases and, 114–115
    distributive, 113–115, 119
    entitlement, 113
    legal, 114, 119
    theory of, 115–118, 119
Justification and Application: Remarks on Discourse Ethics, 123–124

Kant, Immanuel, 11, 90, 91, 92, 101, 103, 104, 115
Katz, A. M., 178
Katz, V. T., 178
Kazdin, A. E., 18
Kekes, J., 112
Kierkegaard, Søen, 8
Kipnis, D., 31
Kissling, M., 167
Kleinke, C. R., 177
Knapp, M. L., 142, 177, 178
Knauer, Peter, 65

Law of continuity, 56
Law of design, 56–57
Law of nature, 58
Leathers, D. G., 178
Leedy, P. D., 142, 158
Leibnitz, Gottfried, 91
Levant, R. F., 39, 51
Leviathan, 138
Listening analysis, 150–151, 157
Littlejohn, S. W., 142
Locke, John, 115

MacIntyre, A., 104
Maier, N., 158
Martin, R. J., 158
Maslow, A., 177
May, Rollo, 8, 17
May, William E., 66
McCarthy, T., 127
McConnell, J. V., 186
McCormick, R., 31
McCroskey, J. C., 143
McKeon, R., 104
Metaphysics of Morals, 90, 91
Miller, G. R., 142, 178
Mintz, N., 177
Monitoring reports, 81–82, 86–89
Moon, D. J., 112
Moral Consciousness and Communicative Action, 122
Murphy, J., 158

Nagel, 120
Natiello, P., 39
Natural law, 58–59, 72
Nietzsche, Fredrich, 8, 11
Nonverbal communication, 129, 140,
    168–178, 176
  aspects of, 170, 176
  definition of, 168, 176
  environmental expression of , 173–174,
    176
  physical expression of, 171–173,
    176–177
  premises of, 168–169, 176
  types of, 171–174, 176
  vocalizations, 174, 176
Norton, R., 142
Nussbaum, M. C., 120

Observation analysis, 153–155, 157
O'Keefe, 73
Ong, W. T., 166, 186
Opinions, 146
Orientation, 172, 177
Ormiston, G. T., 166
Ormrod, J. E., 158
O'Sullivan, R., 104

Palmer, R. E., 142, 177
Paton, H., 104
Pavlov, Ivan, 10
Personal unconscious, 5
Persuasive power, 20, 30
Petronio, S., 143
Phelps, R. E., 142, 177
Phenomenological approach, 149,
    157
Philipchalk, R. P., 186
Philosophical analysis, 55–56
Philosophy of right, 93–94, 102
  money and, 94
  principle of, 93, 102
Phonological rules, 180, 186
Plato, 94
Pluralism, aspects of, 106–109, 111, 113,
    121, 125

Political base, 85
  definition, 82
  tensions, 82–83
Polt, J. M., 177
Positive regard, 42–44, 49
  indicators of, 42
Posture, 172–173, 177
Posture of engagement, 44
Power
  defensive tactics, 22–24, 30
  nature of, 19–21, 30
  power tactics, 21–22, 30
  relations, 19–31, 30
Pragmatic rules, 180–181, 186
Pragmatism, 97–99
Primary values, 107
Principle of proportionality, 59
Psychodynamic approach, 3–7, 16
Psychological approaches, 3–18
Psychological foundations, 1–51
Psychological types, 6
Public discourse, 121–127, 126
  nature of, 122–124, 126
  transcendental-pragmatic argument, 123
  universalization, 123, 126, 138

Ramsey, Paul, 66
Rational-Emotive Behavioral Psychology,
    11
  pleasure principle, 11–12
Rawls, John, 115, 116, 117, 118, 119, 120
Raz, J. 120
Reality Psychology, 13
  control theory, 13
Reason, human, 58, 72, 124, 126
Rebore, Ronald W., 73, 74, 85, 103, 120,
    126, 158, 166
Rée, J., 103, 120
Rehg, W., 127
Reinforcement, 10
  positive, 11
  types of, 11
Reward power, 19
Richard, L., 74
Rist, J. M., 104

Robbins, S. P., 31, 158
Rogers, Carl Ranson, 9, 17, 18, 39
Rosenfeld, P., 31, 142
Rosenholtz, S. J., 51
Rosenthal, R., 177
Ross, W. D., 104
Rothwell, J. D., 186
Rousseau, Jean-Jacques, 93, 115

Sampson, T., 167
Sartre, Jean-Paul, 8, 69, 74
Sathe, V., 157
Schein, E. H., 158
Schelling, Friedrich, 93
Schmandt-Besserat, D., 166
Schmidt, S. M., 31
Schneider, B., 158
Schools Without Failure, 13
Schoonenberg, P., 73
Schoonover, S. C., 158
Schopenhauer, Arthur, 11
Schrift, A. D., 166
Schuller, Bruno, 65
Semantic rules, 180, 186
Sen, A., 120
Servant leadership, 24–25
Sharf, R. S., 18, 39, 142, 158
Sherman, M. A., 186
Shlien, J. M., 39, 51
Short, P. M., 50, 51, 103
Simon-Ingram, J., 74
Singer, J., 85
Sirotnik, K. A., 51
Skinner, B. F., 10
Social contract theory, 115–116, 119, 138
Social covenant, 138–139, 142
Social ethics, 59–60, 72
Sophocles, 93
Soukup, P. A., 186
Spinoza, Baruch, 11
Spirit-matter, 57
Sprague, J., 186
Stacks, D. W., 178
Stance of the observer, 44
Stewart, J., 143

Stoic philosophers, 11
Stoic philosophy, 96
Stress, 187
Strunk, Jr., W., 167
Stuart, D., 186
Subsidiarity, principle of, 80–81
Suffering, human, 68, 73
    self-agency and, 68
Swaffin-Smith, C., 31
Syntactic rules, 180, 186

Talk, 147–148, 157
Tepper, D. T., 177
Touching, 173, 177
Towne, N., 142, 177, 186
Transcendental leadership, 75–85, 84, 85
    elements of, 79–83, 85
    nature of, 76–78, 85
    premise of, 78, 85
    reflection paradigm, 79–80, 85
Transference, 4
Travers, P. D., 103
Trust, 44–45
    indicators of, 45

Unconscious, 4, 77–78, 84–85
Urmson, J. O., 103, 120

Vachek, J., 167
Values, 146
    conditionality of, 108, 111
    context-independent, 109, 112
    incompatible with, 107–108, 111
    primary, 107, 111
    secondary, 107, 111
Vassallo, P., 186
Verbal communication, 129, 140,
    179–186, 185
    analysis of, 180–181
    premises of, 179–181, 185–186
    ramifications of, 181–184, 186
Virtues, 61–65, 73
    conceptualization of, 63
    fortitude, 64, 73
    justice, 64, 73

Virtues (*continued*)
    prudence, 63–64, 73
    temperance, 64–65, 73

Walters, R. P., 142, 177
Warmth, 44–45
Wheatley, M., 31
White, E. B., 167
Wiemann, J. M., 142, 177, 186
Wilkinson, I., 31
Williams, B., 112
Wilmot, W. W., 143
Wilson, G., 31
Wolpe, Joseph, 10

Wood, J. T., 186
Worldview
    classical, 57–58
    modern, 58
Written communication, 129, 140,
    159–167, 165
    function of, 161–162, 166
    interpretation of, 162–164,
    166
    power of, 160–161, 165

York, A., 158

Zinser, W., 167